Cloth Dolls
of the 1920s and 1930s
by Polly Judd

Lenci Lombardia Girl *and* Carlos
(see page 240).

Published by **Hobby House Press** **Cumberland, Maryland 21502**

Acknowledgements

Doll people are the nicest people! They are always helpful and kind. Without wonderful friends in the doll world, this book would have never been completed.

I am honored to have photographs of dolls from California, Connecticut, Colorado, Illinois, Indiana, Kentucky, Massachusetts, Michigan, Minnesota, New Jersey, New York, North Carolina, Ohio, Pennsylvania, Texas, Virginia, Wisconsin, Prince Edward Island, Canada and Paris, France.

There were many individuals who helped in special sections of this book. Jeannette Fink, Christine Lorman, Esther Schwartz, Nancy A. Smith, Countess Maree Tarnowska, Patricia A. Vallancourt and Richard Wright were very helpful with the Lenci dolls.

Margaret M. Benike, Elizabeth Martz and Betty Shriver allowed me to take pictures of unusual cloth dolls for many years, even before this book was begun.

Mary Elizabeth Poole, as always, seemed to know just what pictures were needed to complete sections.

Gigi Williams and Sherry Balloun helped with the Messina-Vat and other sections.

The Mary Merritt Doll Museum, The House of International Dolls of Prince Edward Island, Canada, Cohen Auctions and the Galerie Saint Eloi in Paris, France, have been very kind, and now readers can see some of their lovely cloth dolls.

I also wish to thank the following people who sent photographs, allowed me to photograph their dolls or helped in other ways: Phyllis Appell, Ester Borgis, Vivian Brady-Ashley, Eleaner Broden, Shirley Buchholz, Candy Brainard, Beatrice Campbell, Jean Canaday, Celina Carroll, Kathryn Davis, Diane Domroe, K. De Armond, Ruth Eby, Marie Ezzo, Marianne Gardner, Geri and Ralph Gentile, Kathy George, Joseph Golembieski, Eleanor Guderian, Nancy S. Hance, Joane C. Hise, Betty Houghtailing, Jean Kelley, Helen Krielow, Helen Magill, Margaret Mandel, Barbara Matovina, Anne Pendleton, Gloria Robinson, Nancy Roeder, Tory Scelso, Mary Tanner, Fran Tillotson, Angela Tillman, Juanita Walker, George Wiemels, Marjorie A. Yocum, Elliot Zirlin and Bill Zito.

I am grateful to my editor, Donna Felger, and the entire staff of Hobby House Press, Inc.

A special thanks to Pat Parton for her proofreading.

Dedication

This book is dedicated to Pam Judd, Pat Parton, Sandy Strater, Barbara Comienski, Lois Janner, Thelma Purvis and Wally Judd. They are always there when I need them.

ISBN: 0-87588-353-2

Table of Contents

Preface 4

The Samuel F. Pryor Collection 5

System Used for Pricing Dolls 5

How to Use This Book 6

Companies Making Cloth Dolls in the 1920s and 1930s in
    Alphabetical Order 7

Lenci Identification Guide Table of Contents 114

Doll Identification Guide Table of Contents 224

Preface

In the very first years of the 20th century a new style of design developed. The lines flowed into new architecture, paintings, sculpture and fashions. In 1925 these new ideas came together in the Paris Exhibition of Decoratve Arts; these ideas are now known as "Art Deco."

It was exciting to be a cloth doll artist in the Art Deco period. They had an early model of excellence from the previous century in the works of Margarete Steiff, and when the couturiers of Paris decided that dolls could also be for "grown-ups" (see page 7), a whole new doll world appeared.

By 1920 both children and grown-ups were playing with a new type of cloth doll which reflected a dashing, daring, disturbing world. The long, lean look of the flapper and the skyscraper was imitated in the boudoir dolls. Adults decorated with Pierrots and Harlequins and children played with clowns and Romper Babies. The boudoir flapper dolls showed their long legs with short skirts; the children's dolls had the same lanky, flapper look. The 1920s were affluent years and doll prices were high. Quality and art were the most important ingredients.

However, the high life did not last. The economic "crash" changed the people's lives and their dolls. In the 1930s the adults quietly put away their flashy playthings and many doll manufacturers cheapened their products for the children. A few manufacturers, such as Madame Lenci, still offered quality dolls but made them smaller.

Some of the people of the 1930s turned back to home sewing and the pattern companies offered interesting patterns for cloth dolls and clothing. The government tried to help the many people who were jobless; they created the Works Progress Administration (WPA). To help out-of-work artists, many individual programs were set up to make cloth dolls for schools, libraries and displays.

Gradually, at the end of the 1930s, the economy improved, but war was eminent and the decade closed with doll factories retooling for war work. From the golden 1920s to the sober 1930s, these cloth dolls reflect their time. Today they are rapidly appreciating in value. It is strange that some of the early 1920 Lencis and some of the late 1930 WPA dolls now have prices over $1000.

It has been a joy to research these wonderful cloth dolls. The search for information has taken me from the cloistered rooms of the Library of Congress in Washington, D.C., to the huge dolls shows across the United States. With the joy comes sadness because it is impossible to show in one book the thousands of dolls which were made during this period.

This is a beginning in the search to find and identify these lovely dolls. I hope that readers will write to me through Hobby House Press, Inc., and tell me of their own dolls and contribute to the knowledge of all collectors. For me, this is a dream come true because these are the dolls of my childhood.

4

The Samuel F. Pryor Collection

The National Geographic Society in their December 1959 magazine featured the now famous article by Samuel F. Pryor who was Vice President and Assistant to the President of Pan American World Airways. He traveled widely, inherited a choice collection and enjoyed the hobby of doll collecting.

He said, "As I studied them, I realized how accurately they represented man's customs and cultures on a Lilliputian scale. I began to dream of building a collection to represent every country in the world. On our rapidly shrinking planet, the interchange of travelers and ideas is wiping out many of the differences between nations." Thirty years later his ideas are really coming true.

Not all of his dolls are cloth but many are. Since so many of them were from the 1920s and 1930s, readers may enjoy reading the article. Luckily this is not difficult to find; almost every library has a complete collection of the National Geographic Magazines.

Today the Pryor collection is no longer together, but those who managed to purchase one or more of them are preserving them well and are very proud of them. Diane Domroe is one of those collectors and this author thanks her for her help.

Mr. Pryor and other doll collectors are leaving a legacy of our world through their love of dolls.

System Used for Pricing Dolls

Most of the cloth dolls in this book are now over 50 years old and have become highly collectible. There has also been a resurgence and appreciation of the art and artifacts of the Art Deco period. Not only are doll collectors interested in these dolls, but decorators and non-collectors are using these dolls as focal points in their house decorating plans. Competition for them has pushed prices high. Also the theme of the 1920s, "Dolls for Grown-ups," is part of our present philosophy and the prices of mint examples of these dolls have soared.

The range of prices given for each doll includes good-to-mint condition with all-original clothes. Tissue-mint dolls will command higher prices and dolls in poor condition will be about one third to one half of the lowest price.

As in other areas of the art world, the cloth dolls of known companies or artists will command higher prices. However, prices are climbing for English, Spanish and other foreign cloth doll makers, as well as the United States dolls of Mollye, Georgene Averill, Kamkins and Chase.

The prices of individual dolls have been gathered from dealers and customers from coast-to-coast. Auction prices have been monitored and international prices have been considered. Local prices still vary considerably.

Many doll authorities, as well as individual collectors, have begun to realize that these cloth dolls have stood the test of time well compared to dolls of other materials of the same period.

It is not at all uncommon to see unheralded, rare dolls go for remarkable prices at auction. However, dolls that are presumed to be rare have a way of appearing after a book is published showing their pictures and listing their prices. When this happens, collectors and dealers will have to adjust to a downward scale.

How to Use This Book

This book is set up in several ways depending on your knowledge of your doll. If the doll is marked, or if you know the company name, turn immediately to the doll company section and look up the company name which is in alphabetical order. You will find a list of dolls, their characteristics, dates of production if possible and a current price range. Unless otherwise noted, all dolls have original clothes.

If a doll is unmarked, turn to the Identification Guide Table of Contents (see page 224). There you will find many doll characteristics listed and pages which give information. Examples include pictures of the undressed bodies of various cloth doll manufacturers, the type of cloth used by individual manufacturers, lists of dolls made in various countries and lists of companies which made specific types of dolls.

Perhaps the section of "Look-alikes" will help if you have seen similar dolls, but your doll is just a little bit different.

There is also another Table of Contents just before the Lenci section which will offer suggestions to help you with Lenci identification.

At the end of many sections which discuss the major cloth doll companies of the 1920s and 1930s, you will find a list of their unphotographed dolls and their descriptions.

The author realizes that all the dolls of the period are not listed in this book. Even as this book goes to press, much to my delight, I have discovered new facts to help your identification. I hope you have as much pleasure searching through this book as I have had writing it.

1. Actress Marie Dressler

During this period, dolls were very much a part of the grown-up world. They were given as presents for many occasions. Here is a picture of the famous movie star Marie Dressler as she boarded the S.S. Paris on June 27, 1932. Among her bon voyage presents were two very different types of cloth dolls. One was a Lenci or Lenci look-alike. The other was a typical cloth baby doll.

SEE: *Illustration 1. Toys and Novelties,* April 1932.

Adler Favor & Novelty Co.

This company made a boudoir-type doll with floppy arms and legs.

Dolls Not Photographed

Doodle Dear: Mask face, hand-painted smiling face; spit curl on forehead; washable.

Boo: Round painted face; round eyes; small mouth; body contained a voice box; beltless organdy dress; bonnet made like a halo.

Sal: Body contained a voice box that squealed when touched; wore a dress, shoes and pointed hat.

Rube: Similar long-legged doll that squealed when touched.

Alexander Doll Company

Beatrice Behrman, more popularly known as Madame Alexander, was the daughter of a man who operated one of the first doll hospitals in the United States. She grew up with a knowledge of dolls and doll repair. During World War I when dolls were hard to get, she started to make cloth dolls. Soon friends encouraged her to create a new commercial doll company as an outlet for her artistic talent. Her first ventures were during the early and mid 1920s.

Her first cloth dolls had flat faces, but gradually this changed into three-dimensional faces as Madame Alexander perfected her art. It must be remembered that some European doll makers had already mastered the sculpturing of beautiful "art dolls" by the middle of the 1920s and competition was keen.

In many ways Madame did not compete with the French, German and Italian cloth doll makers until the mid to late 1930s. By that time she had found her niche dressing composition dolls with her wonderful sense of style and fantasy. Gradually her yearly cloth line declined, although a few cloth dolls found their way into the annual company line for several decades after World War II.

Today doll collectors are surprised to find whimsical poodles, bunnies and other cloth animals. These are dressed in cleverly designed clothes in surprising color combinations. However, today's Alexander collector is occasionally confronted with tagged Alexander cloth dolls which are not of the same quality as the Alexander composition dolls of the time.

The Alexander marketing of the cloth dolls is also surprising because they were sold through mail-order houses such as Josselyn's, in candy stores like Schrafft's, advertised in magazines and newspapers and sold wherever necessary to keep the company afloat.

During this early period, Madame developed the insight which was to lead her through her long prestigious doll-design career. She learned that mothers and grandmothers loved to buy doll storybook characters for their small children. The beloved *Little Women* line became a standard through the years. Other "book" cloth dolls included the *Dickens' Series, Alice-in-Wonderland* and *Little Red Riding Hood*. She also made cloth babies including the *Dionne Quintuplets*.

The prices of these Alexander cloth dolls have been increasing in the last few years. Cloth dolls, in general, have become highly collectible, and fortunate is the collector who had the foresight to include these early examples of Madame Alexander's art in their collection when the prices were much lower.

Little Women: 16in (41cm); pink muslin body; pressed felt mask face; mitt hands with no stitching to define fingers; circa 1930-1933.

Jo: Light brown mohair wig tied in a red ribbon at back of neck; blue plaid dress with rickrack trim at hem; organdy collar; white cotton slip with attached pantalets; black print apron over dress; black patent shoes; cloth tag in dress "Little Women//Jo//Copyright Pending//Madame Alexander N.Y."

Meg: Auburn hair braided and pinned to top of head, white organdy green flocked dress trimmed with green rickrack; white organdy ruffle at hem; green bow at waist; white cotton slip with attached pantalets; black patent shoes; tag in dress "Little Women//Meg//Copyright Pending//Madame Alexander N. Y."

Beth: Brown mohair wig with bangs and pink ribbon; red, pink and white organdy plaid dress; white organdy collar; white cotton slip with attached pantalets; black patent shoes; tag in dress "Beth//Little Women; Trademark Pending//Madame Alexander N.Y."

Amy: Blonde hair with red ribbon; floral print organdy dress in red, blue and green; red ribbon trims the hemline; white pleated organdy collar with red bow; black patent shoes; tag in dress "Amy//Little Women//Copyright//Madame Alexander N.Y."
SEE: *Illustration 2. Late Evelyn Wiemels Collection.*
PRICE: $1400-1600 + (four dolls in set)

2.

3.

9

Alice-in-Wonderland: 16in (41cm); flat polished cotton face with painted features; pink muslin body; yellow yarn hair; blue checked dress with large flowers printed on it; white organdy collar and sash; puffed sleeves; blue socks; black shoes; very early Alexander cloth doll; all original; circa 1924.
SEE: *Illustration 3. Vivien Brady-Ashley Collection.*
PRICE: $400-550

David Copperfield: 16in (41cm); pink muslin body; pressed felt mask face; no ears; blue eye shadow around eye; two-tone lips; hand-sewn overcast seam on head; no seam on body back; mitten hands with no finger detail; legs seamed in back only; royal blue felt-like cotton long pants; black jacket and hat; white cotton shirt at-

tached to pants; large cotton bow hemstitched on edges; blonde mohair wig; black patent shoes with buckle; circa 1930s.
MARKS: "David Copperfield//Madame Alexander//New York" (cloth tag on jacket); "An//Alexander//Product//Supreme//Quality//and//Design" (octagon gold tag)
SEE: *Illustration 4. (Color Section, page 34).*
PRICE: $550-600

Oliver Twist: 16in (41cm); pink muslin body; pressed felt mask face; blue eye shadow around eye; two-tone lips; no ears; hand-sewn overcast seam on head; mitten hands with no finger detail; no seam down back; legs seamed in back only; pinkish-orange felt-like cotton long pants; royal blue double-breasted jacket with white buttons; white cotton shirt attached to pants; black ribbon tie; cap matches coat; blonde mohair wig; black patent shoes with buckle; circa 1930s.
MARKS: "Oliver Twist//Madame Alexander//New York" (cloth tag on jacket)
SEE: *Illustration 4. (Color Section, page 34).*
PRICE: $550-600

Little Shaver: 10in (25cm); pink stockinette body with black velvet feet; pink muslin mask face; black side-glancing eyes; brown floss hair; dress has rose taffeta top, pink organdy skirt with rose ribbon trim; lace gloves; rose taffeta handbag; pink organdy half slip and matching panties; black net hat with pink, purple and yellow flowers; black ribbons tied at ankles; 1940s.

5.

MARKS: "Little Shaver//Madame Alexander//New York" (cloth tag in dress)
SEE: *Illustration 5.*
PRICE: $250-300 10in (25cm) doll
$350-400 16in (41cm) doll

Suzy-Q and Bobby-Q: 13in (33cm) and 15in (38cm); pink muslin body; red and white striped cotton legs; black felt feet; pink muslin mask face; *Suzy* has black yarn pigtails (also comes with yellow pigtails); blue cotton dress; gold felt jacket with blue velvet buttons and white felt collar; *Bobby* has reddish brown hair; blue cotton short pants with attached organdy top; gold felt jacket with blue velvet buttons and white felt collar; both hats missing.

Both dolls came with unusual wrist tags. *Suzy-Q's* tag was in the

6.

shape of a purse placed on her right hand. It said, "To: //From //All Rights Reserved." Bobby-Q's tag was in the shape of a school book which said, "4th grade Reader//Bobby−Q" and was attached to the right wrist.
MARKS: Both dolls "Suzy or Bobby-Q//Madame Alexander N.Y.//All Rights Reserved" (cloth tag sewn in jacket)
SEE: *Illustration 6. Beatrice Campbell Collection.*
PRICE: $550-650

Dottie Dumbunnie: 16½in (42cm); yellow velvet face and back of ears; ears lined in suede; white muslin body; black felt shoes are part of body; white organdy pantalets; stiff cretonne petticoat; green cotton dress with yellow apron sewn in as part of dress; plaid scarf; dimity print hat with yellow ribbon trim; button eyes; embroidered mouth, nostrils and whiskers; stiff basketweave fabric molded into basket; mother chicken and baby chick in basket; circa 1938.
SEE: *Illustration 7.* (rabbit on left) *Marianne Gardner Collection.*
PRICE: $650-700 (very few sample prices available)

7.

Posey Pet: 17in (43cm); muslin body; blonde plush fur; pansy eyes with black button center; velvet mouth; ears lined with pink cotton; beige felt circle hat trimmed with flowers; cotton pantalets trimmed with eyelets; cotton slip attached to dress; pinafore-style blue dress with red and white striped trim; circa late 1930s and early 1940s.

MARKS: Posey Pet//Madame Alexander//New York U.S.A," (cotton tag attached to dress)

SEE: *Illustration 7.* (bear on right) *Marianne Gardner Collection.*

PRICE: $300-400+ (very few sample prices available)

8.

Lolly Lov-le-ler: 16in (41cm); pink muslin body; very smooth pink muslin mask face; painted features; real eyelashes attached to painted eyes; open smiling mouth with four painted teeth; dimple on either side of mouth; mitt hands with stitches defining fingers; seam in front and back of legs; machine-stitched head with wrong side showing; machine-stitching down back; no ankle seam; blonde mohair wig; red, white, blue striped piqué dress with white piqué inset in front; matching coat with white collar; white piqué teddy; white oilcloth shoes with button fastening; circa late 1930s-early 1940s.

MARKS: "Lolly Lov-le-ler//Madame Alexander N.Y. U.S.A." (cloth tag on coat)

SEE: *Illustration 8.*

PRICE: $150-300 (very few sample prices available)

Bunny Belle: 13in (33cm); body constructed of yellow cotton with white polka dots; black flannel shoes are a part of body construction; pink muslin mask face; painted features including side-glancing eyes with tiny eyelashes at side of eyes; crooked line mouth with red overpaint; rosy cheeks; yellow yarn hair with two green bows at sides of head; mitten hands with no seams defining fingers; soft yellow organdy dress with matching pantalets; green felt jacket with brass buttons; tilted straw hat trimmed with green velvet ribbon and green feathers; blue-green pompons on shoes; circa 1939.

MARKS: "Madame Alexander//New York U.S.A." (cloth tag on coat)

SEE: *Illustration 9* (color section, page 33).

PRICE: $550-600

12

In the February 1939 issue of *Playthings* on the back cover, the Alexander Doll Company advertised both *Bunny Belle* and her partner, *Bunny Beau*. They said, "Here are just two of the many Easter Novelties created by Madame Alexander that will add beauty, distinction and profit to your Easter Display."

Schrafft's, a candy store, advertised the same dolls. They had an added wicker basket with Easter treats.

Dolls Not Photographed

1. Alice in Wonderland
22in (56cm)
1930
A. Pink muslin body; flat polished cotton face; painted features; yellow yarn hair; red and white checked cotton dress; three rows of bias tape on bottom of skirt; red bias tape trim on sleeves; white organdy ruffled pinafore; white socks; black patent shoes; cloth tag in dress "Alice in Wonderland//Trademark registered U.S. Patent Office//Madame Alexander N.Y."
16in (41cm)
1930
B. Pink muslin body; pressed felt mask face; yellow yarn hair tied with ribbon in back; white organdy dress with blue flocked trim; white organdy collar with blue bias trim; white organdy apron; cloth tag in dress "Original Alice in Wonderland//Trademark 304,488//Madame Alexander N.Y."

2. Amy of Little Women
16in (41cm)
circa 1930
Pink muslin body; felt mask face; blonde hair with yellow ribbon on top; white and yellow print dress; white ruffled collar; pantalets; cloth tag in dress "Little Women//Amy//Copyright Pending//Madame Alexander N.Y."

3. Babbie from Little Minister —
Katharine Hepburn
16in (41cm)
1930s
Pink muslin body; pressed felt mask face; auburn wig; red cotton skirt with flowered print top and white organdy collar; black laced belt; cloth tag "Babbie//Adapted from 'Little Minister'//Madame Alexander//New York."

4. Baby
17in (43cm)
1937
Pink stockinette body; pink felt mask face; brown eyes; blonde yarn hair; pink organdy dress with white braid; ribbon rosettes; tag "Madame Alexander//New York."

5. Bunny Beau
13in (33cm)
not including ear
circa late 1930s
Green cotton with white polka dots; black flannel feet; pink muslin mask; blue eyes; curly yellow yarn hair; green felt jacket; brass buttons; bow tie; white felt spats; hat.

6. Beth of Little Women
16in (41cm)
circa 1930
Pink muslin body; felt mask face; brown mohair with pink ribbon and bangs; pink cotton dress with roses; white organdy collar; pantalets; tag in dress "Little Women//Beth//Copyright Pending//Madame Alexander N.Y."

13

7. Bobby-Q
13in (33cm)
15in (38cm)
circa 1938
A. Pink muslin body; felt mask face; reddish hair; blue-striped legs; black umbrella; black felt jacket; white shirt; red short pants with white polka dots; cloth tag in jacket "Bobby-Q//by Madame Alexander N.Y.//All rights Reserved."
B. Pink muslin mask face; reddish curly yarn hair; large red, blue, white, black and green plaid pants and tie; green felt jacket; white shirt; straw hat; white spats; black shoes.

8. Bonny Bunny
20in (51cm) to tip of ear; 1938; premium doll for Curtis Publishing Company.
1939 sizes included 15in (38cm), 18in (46cm) and 21in (53cm)
A. Advertisement in the *Ladies' Home Journal*, April 1938, page 88, says, "...in sunshine yellow, from her velvet cap (removable ears and all) and perky organdy skirt, to the flowers in her basket. Her dancing eyes move from side to side."; short curly yellow hair; ribbons around ankles; same basic face as *Suzy-Q*.
B. Schrafft's sold same doll dressed in fluffy dress, lace pantalets and bonnet; carried wicker hamper filled with Easter eggs.

9. Bunny Boy
Same as **Bonny Bunny**
Advertisement in the *The Ladies' Home Journal*, April 1938, page 88, says, "He wears yellow shorts with smart, embroidered suspenders, while one *arm* sticks out of a *jaunty cap*. He carries a gay hamper with two yellow chicks. Moving eyes in both dolls are guaranteed not to fall out or stick."; same basic face as *Bobby-Q*.
B. Schrafft's sold same doll dressed in long pants, jacket and dapper hat; carried wicker hamper filled with Easter eggs.

10. Bunny Belle
17in (43cm)
1939-1940
A. Pink muslin body; legs of pink cotton with white polka dots; blue felt feet; pink muslin mask face; blue yarn hair; pink organdy dress trimmed with blue felt, slip, pantalets; pink felt hat and plume; pink flowers on shoulder; cloth tag "Madame Alexander//New York."
14in (36cm)
1940
B. Pink muslin mask face and body; yellow and white polka dot legs; black felt feet; yellow and pink felt ears; pink braided yarn hair; ears; blue felt skirt; attached white organdy blouse; pink felt jacket with white felt collar and blue buttons; straw hat with flowers; gray and white box in her hands; "Madame Alexander//New York U.S.A."

11. David Copperfield
16in (41cm)
1933-1934
Dickens' Character
Pink muslin body; pressed felt mask face; blonde mohair wig; black and white plaid trousers with attached black and white checked shirt; black felt jacket; black grosgrain ties; black felt hat; black patent shoes; tag in jacket "David Copperfield//Madame Alexander//New York."

12. Dionne Quintuplets
24in (61cm)
circa 1936

14

A. Pink stockinette; felt mask face; brown hair; pink organdy dress; pink taffeta coat and bonnet; gold necklace with name on it. All the *Dionnes* were dressed in pink; wrist tag is a booklet with a picture and poem about each girl. It suggests that you ask five relatives to complete the set.
12in (31cm)
B. Pink stockinette body; felt mask face; brown eyes and hair; pink organdy dress; white trim at hem; pink taffeta coat and bonnet; knitted booties; gold name pin on coat; cloth tag in clothes "Madame Alexander// New York"; wrist tag is Dionne booklet.

13. Dottie Dumbunnie
16½in (42cm)
1938
Body of white muslin; black flannel feet; black velvet hands; yellow velvet head, ears lined in suede; yellow velvet face; white whiskers; black button eyes; orange, yellow and white plaid dress with ruffle at hem; matching shawl; stiff white hat with orange bow and orange bias trim; flowers; cloth tag "Madame Alexander//New York."

14. Eva Lovelace
23in (58cm)
1934
A. Pink muslin body with boudoir-type doll legs; pressed felt mask face; blue eyes; no lashes; auburn hair; brown cotton gored skirt; beige flannel jacket; tag "Madame Alexander//New York."
24in (61cm)
B. Pink muslin body with boudoir-type doll legs; pressed felt face mask; blue eyes with long lashes; auburn hair; corded brown skirt; beige suede

jacket with green grosgrain ribbon on cuffs; turquoise printed dicky; stockings to knee; brown leatherette shoes with bow; tag "Madame Alexander// New York."

15. Jo of Little Women
16in (41cm)
circa 1933
Pink muslin body; pressed felt mask face; brown mohair wig tied with red ribbon in back; blue cotton dress trimmed with two rows of rickrack; white organdy collar; apron of blue and white organdy print; tag in dress "Little Women//Copyright//Madame Alexander N.Y."

16. Little Agnes
16in (41cm)
circa 1933-1934
Dickens' Character
Pink muslin body; pressed felt mask face; auburn braids in buns around ears; blue and white organdy dress; white ruffle on sleeves; inset of white organdy on bodice; white organdy apron with blue rickrack trim; white cotton slip with attached pantalets; black patent shoes; tag in dress "Little Agnes//Madame Alexander//New York."

17. Little Dorrit
16in (41cm)
circa 1933-1934
Dickens' Character
Pink muslin body; pressed felt mask face; blonde mohair; green, white and orange floral print dress; white bias trim; white organdy collar; matching bonnet; white cotton slip with attached pantalets; black patent shoes; tag in dress "Little Dorrit//Madame Alexander//New York."

15

18. Little Emily
16in (41cm)
circa mid 1930s
Dickens' Character
Pink muslin body; pressed felt mask face; blonde mohair wig; red dress with white flowered print; organdy ruffle on each sleeve; red bias tape trim; matching bonnet with organdy ruffle; white cotton slip with attached pantalets; black patent shoes; tag in dress "Little Emily//Madame Alexander//New York."

19. Little Nell
16in (41cm)
circa mid 1930s
Dickens' Character
Pink muslin body; felt pressed mask face; blonde mohair wig; pink flowered print cotton dress with yoke and sleeves; white organdy collar; white straw hat with flowers; white cotton slip with attached pantalets; black patent shoes; tag in dress "Little Nell//Madame Alexander//New York."

20. Little Red Riding Hood
16in (41cm)
circa 1934
Pink muslin body; felt mask face; blonde mohair wig; white organdy dress with red flocking; organdy collar; attached white apron; red felt cape with hood; tag in dress "Little Red Riding Hood//Madame Alexander N.Y."

21. Little Shaver
21in (53cm)
A. Pink stockinette body; black velvet feet; pink muslin mask face; yellow floss hair; dress has lavender bodice; pink organdy skirt, cuffs and collar; black lace gloves; hat of pink flowers with black net.
20in (51cm)
1940s
B. Pink stockinette; black velvet feet; black eyes; dress has rose taffeta bodice; yellow organdy skirt, cuffs and collar; black lace gloves; rose taffeta purse; tag "Little Shaver//Madame Alexander//New York//All Rights Reserved."
10in (25cm)
1940s
C. Pink stockinette body; black velvet feet; pink muslin mask face; black and gray eyes; yellow floss hair; dress has black taffeta bodice; pink organdy skirt, cuffs and collar; black lace gloves; black taffeta purse; pink hat with lavender flowers and black net; black satin ribbons at ankles; tag "Little Shaver//Madame Alexander//New York//All Rights Reserved."
7in (18cm)
1940s
D. Pink stockinette body; black velvet feet; pink muslin mask face; some have red yarn hair; some have yellow floss hair; blue and white cotton print dress; matching print panties; purple ankle ties and hair bow; tag "Little Shaver/Madame Alexander//New York//All Rights Reserved."

22. Lively Cherub Baby
11in (28cm)
Late 1930s
Pink felt body and face; arms bent at elbows; legs bent at knees; dark pink circles for mouth; yellow yarn eyelashes; eyes of blue felt; yellow yarn hair; light blue print organdy gown; pink rayon bed coat and cap; music box in body that plays a lullaby when wound up.

23. March Hare
Similar to *Sir Lapin O'Hare*.

24. Meg of Little Women
16in (41cm)
circa 1933
Pink muslin body; felt mask face; dark auburn hair; white organdy dress with red flocked print; deep white organdy ruffle at bottom of skirt; white organdy collar trimmed with rickrack; pantalets; tag in dress "Meg//Little Women//Copyright//Madame Alexander N.Y."

25. Oliver Twist
16in (41cm)
mid 1930s
Dickens' Character
Came in several outfits; pink muslin body; pressed felt mask face; blonde mohair; tag in jacket "Oliver Twist//Madame Alexander N.Y."
A. Light blue cotton cord pants; attached organdy shirt; lavender ribbon tie; orange flannel jacket with white buttons; navy blue cotton cap; black patent shoes.
B. Light orange cotton shirt; lavender ribbon necktie; brown suede jacket with purple buttons; brown suede cap; black patent shoes; tag sewn in jacket "Oliver Twist."

26. Pip
16in (41cm)
circa 1933-1934
Dickens' character
Pink muslin body; pressed felt mask face; blonde mohair wig; brown tweed trousers; pink rose print long sleeve shirt; brown flannel jacket; brown patent shoes; tag in shirt "Pip//Madame Alexander//New York."

27. Pitty-Pat
28in (71cm)
also came in other sizes
circa 1935
Pink stockinette body; mitt-type hand with stitched fingers; pressed muslin mask face; yellow yarn braids; blue denim overalls with rickrack trim; matching bonnet; white blouse; black shoes; tag in blouse "Pitty-Pat//Madame Alexander, N.Y. U.S.A.//All Rights Reserved."

28. Posey Pet
19in (48cm)
A. White fur hands, head and feet; purple flower petal eyes; purple and green plaid dress; purple felt hat; tag "Posey Pet//Madame Alexander//New York, U.S.A."
17in (43cm)
late 1930s and early 1940s
B. Flower print cotton body; white plush ears, hands, feet and face; black button eyes with long lashes; green organdy dress and pantalets; orchid organdy pinafore; tag "Madame Alexander//New York U.S.A."
19in (48cm)
late 1930s and early 1940s
C. White muslin body; feet, paws, head and ears, face of white fur; eyes are purple flowers with black round buttons; purple, pink and white plaid dress; white organdy apron; green cotton weskit; white cotton pantalets; lavender felt hat with hole for ears; tag "Posey Pet//Madame Alexander//New York, U.S.A."

17

29. Sir Lapin O'Hare
17in (43cm)
1938

White muslin body; black flannel feet; yellow velveteen hands, head and ears; suede-lined ears; round button eyes; gold ring for monocle; brown and white herringbone flannel jacket; stiff white hat with hole cut for ears; pipe cleaner cigarette; tag "Madame Alexander//New York."

30. So-Lite Baby
12in (31cm)
1942

Pink muslin body and mask face; yellow yarn curly hair; pink organdy dress with lace inset at hem; pink organdy bonnet; white knitted booties; square gold wrist tag "Created by Madame Alexander//New York, N.Y. U.S.A."

31. Black So-Lite Baby
12in (31cm) and 17in (43cm)

Brown felt body; face of brown pressed felt; brown eyes; black yarn wig; pink cotton dress; pink cotton bonnet with one ruffle of white net, the other of pink ribbon; pink ribbon bow on left ankle and right wrist; tag in dress "So-Lite Baby//Madame Alexander//New York."

32. Suzy-Q
13in (33cm)
circa 1938

Came with several outfits.
A. Pink muslin body; legs of red and white striped cotton; black felt feet; black yarn braids; red cotton dress with white polka dots; white organdy collar; red bow at collar; white organdy panties and slip; dark blue felt jacket with tan buttons; matching blue hat with ribbon streamers.
  15in (38cm)
B. Green felt skirt and jacket; rose trim at collar, cuffs and around skirt; white straw hat; white spats; tag in dress or jacket "Suzy-Q//by Madame Alexander, N.Y.//All Rights Reserved."
C. Pink muslin body; pressed mask face; straight red yarn hair with bangs; large blue, red, green, white and black plaid skirt; blue top; white dimity collar with green bow; pantalets; white spats; black shoes; straw hat with flowers.

33. Tiny Tim
16in (41cm)
1933-1934
Dickens' Character

Pink muslin body; pressed felt mask face; blonde mohair wig; black and white checked trousers; black felt jacket; black bow; attached white shirt; black and white checked cap; black patent shoes; tag in jacket "Tiny Tim//Madame Alexander//New York."

Alma (Torino, Italy)

The Alma Company was one of the makers of Lenci look-alikes. The quality of their bodies and costuming was excellent. An unusual characteristic of their dolls was elastic-strung heads. This is now resulting in heads that are loose and "wobbly." They usually marked their dolls with a cloth label sewn into the clothes or a mark on one foot of the doll. The company operated in the late 1920s and early 1930s.

The B. Altman Company of New York purchased dolls with some Alma characteristics and sold them in their store under their own label.

Girl with Cat and Ball Decoration on Skirt: 11in (28cm); pale flesh tone felt body and head; mohair wig; brown side-glancing eyes; socket head strung with elastic; jointed arms which move together; white felt dress and hat; medium blue felt trim; navy blue silhouette of cat playing with a ball appliqued on skirt; for general characteristics, see Identification Guide, page 225. Many of the Alma dolls seem to have a heavy head which wobbles. This is because the elastic is no longer taut.
MARKS: "Alma//Made in Italy" (left foot)
SEE: *Illustration 10.*
PRICE: $200-250

Boy and Girl: 11in (28cm); pale flesh tone felt body and head; mohair wig; brown side-glancing eyes; socket heads which are strung with elastic; girl has pink coat and hat with blue trim; boy wears a suit with wide blue pants and hat; white top; orange polka dot tie; both dolls have matching felt shoes; for general characteristics, see Identification Guide, page 225.

UNUSUAL IDENTIFICATION FEATURE: Doll strung with elastic.
SEE: *Illustration 11. Barbara Matovina Collection.*
PRICE: $200-250 each

Russian Cossack Dancer: 22in (56cm); felt head and body; one knee bent to give the illusion of a Russian dancer; socket head strung with elas-

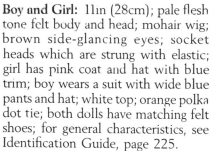

10.

19

tic; navy blue pants; white tunic with felt trim in yellow and red with brown and blue embroidery; huge brown cap with embroidered yellow and orange felt trim; cobbled painted red boots; for general characteristics, see Identification Guide, page 225; circa 1930s. The heads of Alma dolls often "wobble" because the elastic is no longer taut.

MARKS: "CREATION ALMA// MADE IN ITALY"

SEE: *Illustration 12* (Color Section, page 37).

PRICE: $500-600

11.

B. Altman & Company

This New York department store ordered dolls from some of the famous European doll companies during the 1920s and 1930s and sold them in their store. Many of these dolls were marked with a cloth label saying, "Made in (name of country) for B. Altman & Company."

The doll in this section has the body characteristics of the Alma company, but not the facial characteristics.

The Altman company is known to have imported unmarked Nora Wellings dolls from England and added their own label.

Girl with Oranges: 16½in (42cm); smooth pressed cloth mask face; soft felt arms and legs; pink cloth body; hand-painted face; unusual eyebrows with a series of tiny brush strokes; blue eyes with heavy brown eyelashes above the eye and black pupil at top of eye; large white dot at end of half-moon paint stroke under black pupil;

lips painted only one shade of dark red; no ears; black mohair wig; the neck, arms and hip joints are strung with elastic which is very unusual for a cloth doll; the seam at the back of the neck is a hand-sewn overcast stitch done in such a manner as to cause a heavy welt; the back seam is machine-sewn; the legs are only seamed in the back; the fingers are indicated only by stitching and the thumb is separate; the fingers are all "squared off" in an unusual manner; dressed in an orange rayon dress; sheer yellow blouse; red ribbon around waist; yellow organdy apron trimmed with orange braid; blue rayon head scarf; very stiff crinoline slip; black felt slippers with cardboard sole; carries a woven basket with felt oranges surrounded by green leaves; circa mid 1920s.

The registered trademarks, the trademarks and copyrights appearing in italics/bold within this chapter belong to B. Altman & Company, unless otherwise noted.

UNUSUAL IDENTIFICATION FEATURE: Entirely elastic strung.
MARKS: "Made in Italy//for//B. Altman" (ribbon label sewn on crinoline slip).
SEE: *Illustration 13.*
PRICE: $150-200

Lady with Fan: 17in (43cm); for general characteristics, see Identification Guide, page 225; beautiful period costume with lovely material; well sewn; pink taffeta overdress with deeper pink and white flowers; organdy collar and cuffs trimmed with lace; five organdy ruffles trimmed with lace on underdress; crinoline underskirt; felt roses; silk fan; black tricorn hat with veil; blonde mohair wig; late 1920s and early 1930s.

UNUSUAL IDENTIFICATION FEATURE: Strung with elastic.
MARKS: None
SEE: *Illustration 14.* (Color Section, page 39).
PRICE: $350-400

Name of Company Unknown: This doll is being placed in the Altman section because it has some of the major characteristics of the Altman and Alma dolls.

Mussolini's Fascist Boy: 11in (28cm); pressed felt mask face with seam only in back of head; no ears; head shaped over papier-mâché made of newsprint which can be seen at top of head; felt-stuffed arms; cloth body and felt legs glued over a hollow papier-mâché body; mitt hands with separate thumb and stitching indicating fingers; nicely painted face; gray eyes; two-tone lips; eyelashes and eye liner above eye; blonde mohair wig; body is entirely

13.

strung with joints at neck, shoulders and hips; black shirt; gray wool pants and socks; black felt shoes; for dolls with similar construction, see *Illustrations 13* and *14*; middle 1930s.

This authentically-dressed doll with the "M" for Mussolini was brought to the United States by a family who often toured Italy before World War II. Each time they returned, they brought back Lenci or Lenci-type dolls and preserved them carefully. This doll is in excellent condition. The patch on the hat represents the Eagle which was a symbol of power.

UNUSUAL IDENTIFICATION FEATURE: Entirely elastic strung.
MARKS: None
SEE: *Illustration 15* (Color Section, page *218*).
PRICE: $200-250

21

Louis Amberg & Son

Amfelt Art Dolls: Various sizes; 14 styles; jointed at neck, shoulders and hips; washable faces; pretty clothes with hats or bonnets; designed by European artists; shoes were single-strap slippers; 1928.

Amberg imported these dolls from Paris to compete with Lenci.

SEE: *Illustration 16. Playthings,* April 1928.

The registered trademarks, the trademarks and copyrights appearing in italics/bold within this chapter belong to Louis Amberg & Son.

Amberg's Amfelt Art Dolls

16.

American Art Dolls

This company was controlled by Strobel & Wilken (see page 200). The dolls were cloth character dolls dressed as children, babies and children in nationality costumes. They were made in America and were in competition with the Käthe Kruse dolls. They made a line of *Susie's Sister* dolls in 1915 along with a *Tootsie* line. In 1917 there was a line of 35 different dolls dressed in nationality costumes. As late as 1931 Strobel & Wilken were advertising 11in (28cm) cloth dolls in nationality costume. However, they sold them under the American Art Dolls name.

The registered trademarks, the trademarks and copyrights appearing in italics/bold within this chapter belong to American Art Dolls.

American Needlecraft, Inc.

Orphan Annie and Sandy: Colorful fabric dolls by exclusive license with Famous Artist Syndicate; stuffed with kapok; hand-decorated with ravel-proof fabric; also developed *Smitty* and *Herby;* all were well-known characters of radio, movies and newspapers; dolls retailed for $.50 and $1.00 at that time; 1933.

SEE: *Illustration 17. Toys and Novelties,* September 1933.

By exclusive license with Famous Artists Syndicate, Orphan Annie, Sandy, Smitty and Herby, America's favorite cartoon characters, have been developed in colorful fabric dolls by American Needlecrafts, Inc., 389 Fifth Ave., New York. This company made an outstanding success last year with their Be Ba Bo line and they have achieved an amazingly lifelike quality in creating this cartoon group. The dolls are stuffed with prime Kapok and are hand decorated with ravelproof fabric. They retail for fifty cents and one dollar.

Orphan Annie, Sandy, Smitty and Herby are so well known through radio, newspapers and movies that they offer an unusual opportunity for quick sales.

17.

American Stuffed Novelty Company

This company used the trade name *Life-Like* for a line of cloth dolls about 1923 and continued on into the 1930s. In the 1920s they produced art and boudoir dolls with clothes by Morris Politzer. The dolls had pressed cloth faces and bodies covered with sateen. Their wigs were made of mohair or silk. Some of their boudoir-type dolls were as large as 31in (79cm). In 1931 they added composition dolls.

Trilby (center two dolls in top row): 11in (28cm), 16in (41cm) and 19in (48cm); eyes painted in great detail; mohair wigs; pink cotton bodies; Lenci look-alikes; 1925.

Pierrot (doll in lower right corner): 20in (51cm); variety of styles and colors; 1925. They also made *Pierrot's* sister, *Pierrette*.

Flapper (doll in upper right hand corner): Thin boudoir doll with bushy hair; sold undressed for home sewing; 1925.

Rabbit Doll (doll in left corner); Easter promotion; 1925.

SEE: *Illustration 18. Playthings,* January 1925.

SENSATIONAL NOVELTY DOLLS
TO RETAIL AT POPULAR PRICES
FEATURING
TRILBY   PIERROT and PIERRETTE

18.

19.

20.

Boudoir Dolls: Group of slender, long-legged popular dolls of the period. Often these dolls were purchased undressed. They were packed in their boxes with their arms wrapped around their knees.
SEE: *Illustration 19. Playthings,* January 1927.

Aunt Jemima: 15in (38cm), 18in (46cm), and 27in (69cm); assorted print dresses; large white apron over dresses; Mary Jane shoes.

This doll was one of the "The Lifelike Line." According to *Playthings,* the line included mama, baby dolls and art dolls of a very fine type.
SEE: *Illustration 20. Playthings,* March 1930.

Dolls Not Shown in Photograph

1. Yama Doll: 26in (66cm); boudoir-type; pressed face; mohair or silk wig; removable clown costume; designed by Morris Politzer; dark top; light pants; 1926.

2. Follies Girl: 26in (66cm), *Collegiate Flapper* and *Silk Flapper;* all had pressed mask faces and were costumed by Morris Politzer; 1926-1927.

24

American Toy & Novelty Corp.

This company made soft, inexpensive cloth toys for the mass market. They specialized in stockinette, plush and other soft materials. Their large cloth doll, *Priscilla*, was one of their most popular numbers in 1929. She had a flat face (no molded mask); side-glancing eyes; large vertical mouth; checked dress; long legs; late 1920s-early 1930s.

In 1930 The Plotnick Company took over the American Toy and Novelty Corporation and made a stockinette doll called *Kutie*.

SEE: *Illustration 21. Playthings*, October 1929.

The registered trademarks, the trademarks and copyrights appearing in italics/bold within this chapter belong to American Toy & Novelty Corp.

"Priscilla" Doll a Big Seller
The American Toy & Novelty Corp.'s factory is working full blast taking care of the many large orders that have been placed on their new "Priscilla" Doll, illustrated herewith. Walter Oppenheimer, president of the company, says that it is one of the most popular numbers they have ever brought out, and at $1.00 retail is meeting the demand of buyers looking for a large doll at a popular price.

21.

Anita Novelty Company
(See also European Doll Manufacturing Co.)

The "Anita Line" pioneered making boudoir dolls and novelties. In 1929 they became part of the European Doll Manufacturing Company. According to a February 1931 advertisement in *Playthings*, they made flapper dolls, pillows and novelties. They called their flapper dolls *French Head* dolls. Often the dolls were sold undressed and lay in their boxes in twisted condition waiting to be dressed by the buyer (see *Illustration 19*). Some of them had a cigarette in their mouth in imitation of the "It" girl, Clara Bow.

Many of the boudoir dolls found today may be attributed to Anita.

The registered trademarks, the trademarks and copyrights appearing in italics/bold within this chapter belong to Anita Novelty Company.

Averill Mfg. Corp., Georgene Novelties, Inc., Mme. Hendren, Georgene Averill, Brophy Doll Company

Georgine Averill was one of the most prolific designers of dolls from 1913 until the 1950s. She worked in cloth, compostion, bisque and other materials. She and her husband used several combinations of her names for their different companies which distributed her dolls. These included Georgene Novelties, Mme. Hendren and Georgene Averill. The name Brophy Doll Company was used in Canada.

Some of her well-known cloth dolls included *Minnehaha;* Grace Drayton's *Dolly Dingle; Chocolate Drop;* ethnic and regional dressed dolls; *Raggedy Ann* and *Andy;* Maud Tousey Fangel's *Snooks, Sweets* and *Peggy Ann;* storybook characters, *Little Lulu; Nancy* and *Sluggo* and many others.

Georgene quickly adapted her dolls to headlines. The Tutankhamen novelties were examples. She also followed the newest games and cartoons. As late as 1953 she made a wonderful cloth *Becassine*, a popular French cartoon figure popularized in the periodical *La Semaine De Suzette.*

During various periods in her career, Georgene Averill was connected with other companies. George Borgfeldt & Co. announced in *Playthings* in January 1923 that he had made arrangements with her for the exclusive sale of her famous *Wonder Dolls*

— walking, talking and dancing.

It is interesting to note that under the name of Mme. Hendren, one of her first mama dolls was a doll named *Val-Encia*. Although the doll was made of composition, her face was flocked to resemble felt and she was dressed in the "Lenci" manner. At the same time Madame Lenci was pressing her felt in the mold so hard that it resembled composition (see *Illustration 177*).

An interested collector could make a large, unique collection of just Averill cloth dolls and novelties.

Egyptian Dolls Based on the Discovery of Tutankhamen's Tomb:

1. **U-Shab-ti** is dressed in a costume from the days of King Tut. It has a cloth body and limbs and a composition face.

2. **Tut's Pup** said on the label, "They crossed the desert to get me."

3. **Pharaoh Doll** is stuffed with soft cotton. Nursery rhymes which appeal to children are printed on the mummy-like casing of the doll.

The discovery of King Tutankhamen's tomb in November 1922, was an exciting event world-wide. The doll manufacturers created many dif-

ferent dolls and toys to captilize on the craze. Costumers also offered Egyptian costumes and wigs for children.
SEE: *Illustration 22. Playthings,* April 1923.

Maud Tousey Fangel was born in 1881 in Medford, Massachusetts. She studied art at a time when this was not a fashionable career for young ladies. By 1908 she was painting illustrations in lovely pastel colors for *Harper's Bazaar* and other publications.

She married, had a son, Lloyd, and used him as a model. Soon she won fame for her children's drawings. Her paintings of the Dionne Quintuplets who were born in 1934 became very famous. She also drew a first set of *Quintuplet* paper dolls.

In the middle 1930s her pretty dolls made by the Averill Mfg. Corp. sold for $.59. Today they are eagerly sought by collectors and command high prices.

Maud Tousey Fangel Snooks and Sweets: 12in (31cm) to 16in (41cm); printed faces; stuffed bodies; movable arms and legs; 1936.

An article in the May 1936 issue of *Toys and Novelties* says, "*Snooks* and *Sweets* are new creations in novelty dolls. These dolls are accurate reproductions from the works of the celebrated artist Maud Tousey Fangel, whose drawings have appeared as cover designs on many important magazines of wide circulation. (Her work is in demand by national advertisers.) These dolls are soft and cuddly, distinctly the baby type, washable and waterproof. Anyone familiar with the work of Maud Tousey Fangel knows the lovable expressions and natural

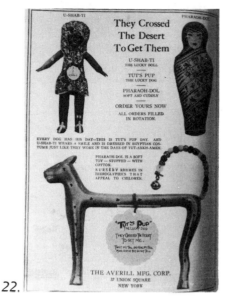

22.

baby charm she puts into her creations. It is this irresistible appeal which the manufacturers have captured and reproduced with such convincing accuracy. The dolls are copied from pastel drawings preserving all the color value of the originals. The Maud Tousey Fangel dolls are made in two faces and in four sizes. The brunette is *Snooks* and the blonde is *Sweets.*"
SEE: *Illustration 23 Snooks. Toys and Novelties,* May 1936.
SEE: *Illustration 24 Sweets. Toys and Novelties,* July 1937.
PRICE: $500-550 each
$700-750 large size

Doll Not Photographed

1. Peggy Ann: 14in (36cm); long legs; mitt hands with no stitching for fingers; body made from yellow print which served as part of the costume; yellow crisp cotton skirt and bonnet.
MARKS: "Art in Cloth Dolls//Peggy

23.

Ann//by Maud Tousey Fangel//An
Original//Georgene//Novelty" (tag)

Uncle Wiggily: 21in (53cm); body
and face of cotton broadcloth; painted
face and ears; black felt hat; white
cotton shirt; maroon tie; gold felt vest;
pink cotton broadcloth pants with lavender and white checked cuffs; pink
flannel coat; mid 1930s.
MARKS: "Georgene Averill" (tag)
SEE: *Illustration 25* (Color Section,
page *40).* *Kay DeArmond Collection.*
PRICE: $375-425
The Uncle Wriggly game board is behind the doll.

New Group
SOFT BABY DOLLS

Created Exclusively for Us by
MAUD TOUSEY FANGEL
America's Foremost Baby Painter

GEORGENE NOVELTIES, INC.
48 East 21st Street   New York, N. Y.

24.

**Two-faced Raggedy Ann and
Andy:** 12in (31cm); painted face;
black button eyes; black outline
around nose which is distinctive to
early dolls; *Andy* has a red and blue
plaid shirt with solid blue pants; *Ann*
has a blue and red print dress with
white apron; all original; one side of
head has a "smiling" face; the other
side of the head has a "sleeping" face;
late 1930s.
MARKS: "Raggedy Ann & Andy
Dolls//Copyright 1918, 1920//Geor-
gene Novelties, Inc." (tag sewn into
side of body)
SEE: *Illustration 26. Candy Brainard
Collection.*
PRICE: $150-200 each (very few
sample prices available)

26.

Bridal Party Bride: 13½in (34cm); hard pressed mask face; real eyelashes attached over eyes; tiny lines for each eyebrow; for further general characteristics, see Identification Guide, page 226; taffeta bridal gown which is buttoned down the front with rhinestone buttons; lace headpiece; long net veil; yellow curly yarn hair; rhinestone earrings.

Bridesmaids (2): 13in (34cm); hard pressed mask face; real eyelashes attached over eyes; tiny lines for each eyebrow; for further general characteristics, see Identification Guide, page 226; lavender rayon dress with lavender headpiece; yellow curly yarn hair; second bridesmaid wearing matching peach costume.

Ringbearer: 11in (28cm); hard pressed mask face; brown painted eyelashes over right corners of each eye; tiny lines for each eyebrow; for further characteristics, see Identification Guide, page 226; white cotton shirt trimmed with lace; blue taffeta pants with silver trim; matching taffeta pillow with ring attached; short yellow curly yarn hair.

Flower Girl: 11in (28cm); hard pressed mask face; brown painted eyelashes over right corners of each eye; tiny lines for each eyebrow; for further characteristics, see Identification Guide, page 226; blue satin dress with deep ruffle at hemline; blue ribbon headpiece; long yellow curly hair; pink crepe paper basket filled with roses.

Because this bridal party was used as a centerpiece for a shower in the late 1930s, there is no groom. It was lovingly stored away and is still in excellent condition.

MARKS: None
SEE: *Illustration 27.* (Color Section, page 35).
PRICE: $350-400 for entire set

Miss America: 14in (36cm); Statue of Liberty costume; red, white and blue skirt; white cotton blouse; silver cardboard crown which looks like the top of the Statue of Liberty; yellow kinky yarn hair; real eyelashes; red, white and blue sash and headband; metal flag stick with little ball on top; for general characteristics, see Identification Guide, page 226; late 1930s.

This doll was a patriotic symbol of the period just before World War II.
UNUSUAL IDENTIFICATION FEATURE: Kinky yarn hair and real eyelashes.
MARKS: "Georgene's//Nu-Art Doll//A Product of//Georgene Averill Novelties, Inc.//Made in U.S.A.//Miss America" (tag)
SEE: *Illustration 29* (Color Section, page 36).
PRICE: $125-150+

Mary Had a Little Lamb: 13in (33cm); blue-flowered pinafore; white blouse, apron and pantalets; orange felt hat; blue felt lamb on apron; school slate with sponge; real eyelashes; for general characteristics, see Identification Guide, page 226; late 1930s and early 1940s.
UNUSUAL IDENTIFICATION FEATURE: Kinky yarn hair.
MARKS: None
SEE: *Illustration 30.*
PRICE: $75-100+

Patrica: 21in (53cm); for general characteristics, see Identifiction Guide, page 226; real eyelashes; resembles *Shirley Temple*; printed bloomers that match the yellow trim

30.

31.

on the sleeves and dress; bright red dress; deep yellow bow in hair; beautiful curly blonde wig; 1930s.
MARKS: "Art in Cloth Dolls//An Original 'Georgene Novelty'//Patrica" (tag); "37044" (back of tag)
SEE: *Illustration 31. Helen Magill Collection.*
PRICE: $350-400

Russia: 13in (33cm); dressed in yellow taffeta skirt with green felt trim; white blouse; black felt bolero trimmed in orange; high Russian boots; high Russian headdress trimmed in felt; red U.S.S.R. flag with metal flag holder topped with tiny metal ball; black yarn pigtails; real eyelashes set in the cloth mask face; late 1920s — early 1940s.
MARKS: "Georgene's//Nu-Art Doll//Russia//A Product of Georgene Novelties, Inc.//Made in U.S.A." (tag)
SEE: *Illustration 32* (doll on left). The doll on the right is a Mollye.
PRICE: $80-90+

Becassine: 13½in (34cm); sateen-type cotton cloth mask; muslin body; red checked slip and bag; green flannel dress with black velvet trim; salmon flannel vest; white cotton top; starched white flannel cap; blue striped socks and black shoes which are part of the body; 1953.
MARKS: "Becassine//...from Paris// Amie Des Enfant//Children's Favorite//Copr. 1953 Editions Gauter-Languereau//Georgene Novelties, Inc." (tag)
SEE: *Illustration 33.*
PRICE: $75-100+

32.

33.

The Bing Corporation (Germany)

The Bing Corporation was a large German company with headquarters in Nürnberg. It had offices in various countries to handle orders. In the 1920s there were 31 subsidiaries including many of the bisque and composition makers.

They competed with the various cloth companies. One of their popular lines of dolls resembled the Käthe Kruse dolls. Another line resembled the Lenci dolls.

Dutch Boy and Girl: 10in (25cm); painted mask face; Käthe Kruse look-alike; mitt hands with fingers indicated by stitching, thumb separate; cloth body; girl dressed in black felt skirt; flowered blue and white blouse with blue and white striped sleeves; blue denim apron with checked blue and white cotton top; pink and white painted felt Dutch hat; boy dressed in dark blue felt pants and high hat; dark

34.

pink felt shirt; both wear felt Dutch shoes.

SEE: *Illustration 34.*

PRICE: $300-500 each (hard-to-find doll; very few samples)

The registered trademarks, the trademarks and copyrights appearing in italics/bold within this chapter belong to The Bing Corporation.

Welsch Specialty Dolls: Lenci look-alike dolls dressed in felt clothes. Some of the dolls had cloth heads. Others had composition heads. **SEE:** *Illustration 35. Playthings*, January 1927.

35.

Chas. Bloom, Inc.

Doll Not Photographed

Boudoir Flapper Doll: One type was 28½in (73cm); mohair wig; unusual long, widely-spaced eyelashes above and below eyes; beauty spot under painted eyes; vertical-type mouth; circa 1925.

MARKS: "Patented June 2, 1925// No. 1540384//Chas.Bloom, Inc., New York" (body)

Blossom Doll Company

The Blossom Company made all-fabric dolls that were well made and beautifully dressed. They featured long real eyelashes on some of their dolls. Their mask faces were hand-painted silk. The girl dolls had special shoes with very high wooden heels.

They made many different types of long-legged boudoir-type dolls such as Harlequin men and women and a wedding party with the bride, groom, best man, bridesmaids, junior bridesmaids, flower girl, ring bearer and minister.

Boudoir Doll: 30in (76cm); silk-stiffened mask face hand-painted with delicate coloring; real eyelashes on eyes; blue eye shadow under eye; thin brown line over eye; bow mouth; curly blonde mohair wig; jointed at

Continued on page 41.

Alexander *Bunny Belle*
(see page 12).

Alexander *David Copperfield* and *Oliver Twist* (see page 10).

Bruckner *Topsy Turvy* (see page 44).

34

Averill Wedding Party (see page 29).

Averill *Miss America* (see page 29).

Chad Valley *Long John Silver* (see page 47).

Alma *Russian Cossack Dancer* (see page 20).

Dean's A1 girl (see page 58).

Dean's *Alice in Wonderland Set* (see page 61).
Countess Maree Tarnowska Collection.

Lady with fan (see page 21).

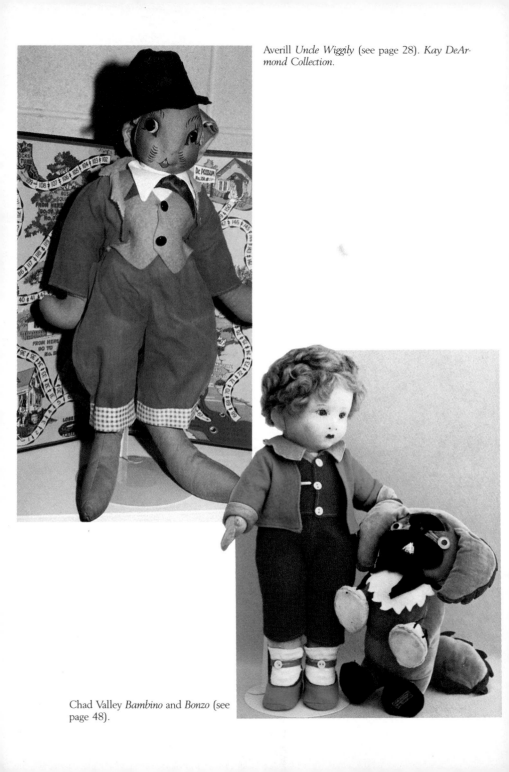

Averill *Uncle Wiggily* (see page 28). *Kay DeArmond Collection.*

Chad Valley *Bambino* and *Bonzo* (see page 48).

Blossom Doll Company
Continued from page 32.

neck, shoulders and hips; hand-sewn seam at back of head; no ears; no seam down the back; darts on back of lower body to allow doll to sit; arms and legs sewn on by machine; silk stockings; high-heeled shoes with buckles; white organdy slip and pants combination; large print dress of various shades of peach; "floppy" hat made of same material; hemstitched faille sash and trim on hat; ruffles at neckline; pearl necklace; late 1920s-1930s. Clothes are all original except the lace gloves.
MARKS: None on doll
SEE: *Illustration 36. Phyllis Appell Collection.*
PRICE: $150-200

36.

Blum-Lustig Toy Co., Inc.

French Dolls in the Flapper Mode: Designed by Madame Emilia Milobendzka of Paris for the Pompeian Art Works Department of Blum-Listig Toy Co., Inc.; 1927.

SEE: *Illustration 37. Playthings,* January 1927.

FRENCH DOLLS

in the latest

Flapper Mode

EXCLUSIVE IN DESIGN
NOVEL IN COLOR SCHEME
UNIQUE IN ATTIRE
SURPRISING IN PRICE

These many numbers are the exclusive creations of Madame Emilia Milobendzka, late of Paris, designed expressly for the

POMPEIAN ART WORKS DEPT.

of

BLUM-LUSTIG TOY CO., Inc.

11 East 17th St.   New York City

37.

Boudoir Dolls (Also Called Bed Dolls and Pillow Dolls)

Art-type dolls became popular in the late 19th and beginning of the 20th century. Often they were dressed in the latest fashion. By 1910 women's fashions had slimmed down from the huge skirts and rounded look of the Victorian period, and the long, lean look of the flapper era emerged.

Although the boudoir dolls were first called "French Dolls," these dolls with the very long legs began to appear in England and Germany about the same time. Paul Poirot, a well-known French couturier, made dolls to accompany his original designs in 1912. Hilda Cowhan in England painted pictures of girls and ladies with exaggerated legs. In Germany a few of the artists of the Munich Art

Dolls Group also experimented with these new art dolls. Soon doll artists in other countries followed the trend.

The adult world seemed to be ready for these imaginative, frivolous dolls and they had the money in the 1920s to indulge their fancy.

These dolls evolved into five types 1. Commedia della arte characters 2. Parisienne fashion dolls 3. Flappers 4. Historical costume dolls 5. Portrait dolls of famous personalities including Hollywood stars. However, the collector will find other types upon occasion.

They were used to decorate beds, rooms and cars, carry on the streets, store pajamas and other boudoir items and occasionally to play with.

Readers can find examples of these dolls throughout this book. For a list of companies which made cloth boudoir-type dolls during the 1920s and 1930s, see Identification Guide, page 250.

Blonde Girl in Purple Dress: 27in (69cm); well-made doll with silk French-type sculptured mask face; blonde mohair wig; side-glancing, slitted eyes; heavy black lines around eyes; eyelashes; eyebrows; no eye shadow; pointed chin; heart-shaped mouth; lavender marquisette dress; matching cotton print bolero; trim at bottom of skirt and on garden hat; composition hands; late 1920s. This doll resembles a slitted-eye Lenci boudoir-type doll with the "dreamy" look. It was purchased at the May

38.

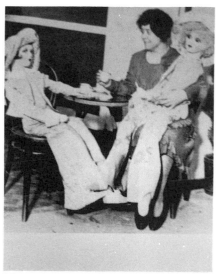

39.

40.

Company in Cleveland, Ohio, undressed and then dressed to match a bedroom color scheme. It is attributed to Blossom.

MARKS: "7B//6230W" (cardboard tag stapled to body)
SEE: *Illustration 38*.
PRICE: $85-125

Mannequin Boudoir Dolls: Life-size novelty dolls; according to *Toys and Novelties*, July 1932, one of these dolls was going to be presented to Princess

Elizabeth of the British Royal Family.

SEE: *Illustration 39*. *Toys and Novelties*, July 1932.

English Boudoir Dolls: Display of dolls in a London store window in January 1930. The Norah Wellings *Islander* doll can be seen in the middle of the long-legged art dolls.

SEE: *Illustration 40*. *Playthings*, January 1930.

Bruckner's Sons

In 1901 Albert Bruckner invented a process of stamping out a mask for cloth dolls. He established a factory and made dolls. For the most part he sold these dolls to other marketing companies including Horsman.

In 1923 *Toys and Novelties* reported that he was selling to the general trade. He then advertised under his own name. That year he added a new doll called *Dollypop* with an oil-painted face and a squeeze-type voice mechanism.

Through the 1920s and into the 1930s the company made such cloth dolls as *Tubby-tot, Tubby, Dollypop*,

The registered trademarks, the trademarks and copyrights appearing in italics/bold within this chapter belong to Bruckner's Sons.

Pancake Baby and their *Topsy-Turvy* doll which they changed to *Two-N-One*.

Their cloth dolls included some made of terry cloth and their *Tubby-tot* was made of rubberized cloth with removable rubberized suit and hat.

Topsy-Turvy White and Black: 12in (31cm); two sculptured, painted mask faces, one white and the other black; white doll dressed in red checked cotton dress and bonnet; white cotton apron and collar on dress; painted hair; black doll has same red checked skirt; black checked apron with cross-stitching; red blouse with braid trim; black mohair wig; red ribbons in hair; face has painted open mouth with red lips and white teeth (uppers and lowers); red bandana on head; 1905 to mid 1920s.
MARKS: "Bruckner Doll//Made in U.S.A." (tag in dress).
SEE: *Illustration 41* (Color Section, page 34).
PRICE: $350-400

Cartoon Dolls

There were many cloth dolls made to represent the popular cartoon characters of the time. These dolls ranged from well-made dolls from such companies as Dean's Rag Book Co. to printed cloth cutout dolls which could be purchased by the yard and made at home. A large collection of dolls could be built on just this one type of doll.

Little Orphan Annie: 18in (46cm); painted mask face; mitten hands with no sewn fingers; overcast seam down back of neck and body; side seams on legs; red and white dress; dolls usually tagged with "Saturday Evening Post"; circa early 1930s.
MARKS: "Orphan Annie" (printed on dress)
SEE: *Illustration 42. Candy Brainard Collection.*
PRICE: $135-165

Popeye the Sailor Man: 17in (43cm); square jaw; extra piece for sewn-on nose; one eye winking and one is open; sewn-on ears; anchor tattoo on muscular arms; black middy shirt with red collar trimmed with black; corncob pipe; white sailor pants; composition

42.

feet; pictured in 1933 Butler Bros. Catalog.

This is a rare cloth Effanbee advertising doll.

MARKS: "SPINACH//that// MAKES POPEYE STRONG//POP-EYE//AN EFF AN BEE DOLL" (paper tag).

SEE: *Illustration 43. Candy Brainard Collection.*

PRICE: $150-200

Cayuga Products Co., Inc.

Girl in Checked Dress: 13in (33cm); soft hand-tinted dolls; came in six colors; made of percale; 1923.
SEE: *Illustration 44. Playthings*, September 1923.

43.

44.

Century Doll Co.

The Century Doll Company was founded in New York in 1909. They started by using Kestner bisque heads on many of their dolls. In 1921 Grace Corry Rockwell designed a line of *Fiji-Wiji* black cloth dolls for them. Most of the other dolls made by this company were composition and bisque, mama dolls and dolls which wore Jantzen bathing suits.

The registered trademarks, the trademarks and copyrights appearing in italics/bold within this chapter belong to Century Doll Co.

Grace Corry's "Fiji-Wiji" Dolls Are Launched

45.

Fiji-Wiji: Black cloth dolls with bobbing heads; stuffed with cotton; chubby brown bodies; shock of unruly hair; fringed shirts; designed by Grace Corry Rockwell who designed dolls for several companies including Borgfeldt, Averill and Schoen & Yondorf (Sayco) from 1920-1929.

The family of *Fiji-Wiji* included girls, boys, clowns and other characters.

SEE: *Illustration 45. Playthings,* January 1921.

Chad Valley Co. Ltd.

The Chad Valley Doll Company understood the fantasies of childhood, and their dolls captured the trends, styles and the charm of their era.

In the small village of Harborne, Staffordshire, Joseph and Alfred Johnson established a factory where they made children's toys. In 1920 they produced their first dolls made of stockinette. These featured hand-woven wigs which could be brushed and combed. There were 12 of these boy and girl dolls. They also made less expensive stockinette dolls without the wigs. Their line included such popular characters as *Pierrot* and *Pierrette* and a chef and nurse. These dolls had painted eyes.

In 1923 a different line of 13in (33cm) dolls of pink stockinette material was introduced. These dolls had round blue glass eyes and curly mohair wigs. They were dressed in brightly colored velvet with plush fur and mother-of-pearl buttons. Many of the dolls had winter sports clothes.

46.

Early Stockinette Doll: 13in (33cm); pink stockinette body; glass eyes; pink velvet coat and hat trimmed with white plush; velvet slippers; 1923.

These dolls are rare today because they are so fragile. This one is in mint condition.

MARKS: "Hygienic Toys//Made in England By//Chad Valley Co. Ltd." This mark was used on most of the dolls of the 1920s and 1930s.

SEE: *Illustration 46.*

PRICE: $200-275

Chad Valley not only made stockinette dolls in their regular line, they also made stockinette character dolls.

Long John Silver: 11½in (29cm); stockinette body; bright blue glass eyes; painted face; mitt hands with stitching indicating fingers; costume is part of the felt body; red knicker-type pants and shoes; long orange vest; blue overcoat with brass buttons; hand-carved sword in right hand; intricately carved crutch under arm; circa 1926.

There is a green felt parrot on the pirate's shoulder (back of doll). It is interesting to note that the second leg is not cut off but is costumed and tucked up into the body. This also came in a 20in (51cm) size.

The pin on his chest is a doubloon souvenir made for the Philadelphia sesquicentennial celebration in 1926. It has both the Liberty Bell and the Skull and Crossbones on it.

MARKS: "Hygienic Toys//Made in England//Chad Valley Co. Ltd." (cloth tag sewn on coat)

SEE: *Illustration 47* (Color Section, page 36).

PRICE: $700-900 (very rare doll).

In 1924 Chad Valley changed the material for the dolls' heads. Textiles or felt, stiffened with shellac or starch, were used to make the dolls that were less destructible. Glass eyes were still inserted from the inside. With this innovation, many of the beautiful dolls could be saved for future generations.

Most doll bodies, but not all, were made of velvet in the 1920s and 1930s (see Identification Guide, pages 226-227). In the late 1930s and after the war in the late 1940s some bodies were made of felt or cloth.

In 1927 Chad Valley introduced their *Bambina* dolls. There were four sizes from 14½in (37cm) to 18½in (47cm). The dolls had glass eyes and a mohair wig sewn in circular strips. The body and limbs were made of velvet. The elbows and knees were shaped with small thread knots. The wrists were pulled in by pink thread to shape the arms. This extra sewing ceased by 1929-1930.

Most of these dolls had a metal and celluloid button fastened onto some part of the body or clothing. The two colors reported are blue and greenish yellow.

The Mabel Lucie Attwell dolls appeared in the company catalogs from 1927 on. They advertised: "Personally designed by Miss Mabel Lucie Attwell, these delightful hand-painted felt and velvet dolls faithfully reproduced the inimitable features of her well-known drawings of children." There were 16 dolls in the line including girls with fashionable dresses and cloche hats, boys in "Buster Brown" suits, girls in pram suits with leggings and a black boy with dungarees.

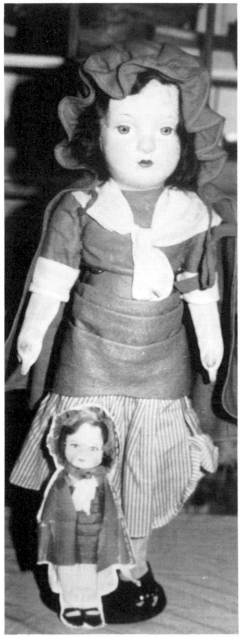

Early Bambina Doll: 14½in (37cm); felt head; velvet body; glass eyes; curly mohair wig; double thickness of felt for ear; shaped elbows and knees; pink thread tied around wrist; orange "Buster Brown" suit; green waistcoat; matching ankle-strap shoes; striped white-on-white socks.
MARKS: "Hygienic Toys//Made in England by//Chad Valley Co. Ltd." (cloth label sewn on left foot). "Chad Valley//'BAMBINA'//Redg. & Pat." (cloth label sewn on right foot). "Chad Valley//British//Hygienic// Toys" (greenish yellow celluloid and yellow button fastened to body just above left leg).
SEE: *Illustration 48* (Color Section, page 40).
PRICE: $450-550

Bonzo: 6in (15cm) high and 8in (20cm) long; light orange velvet body; deeper orange felt trim on ears and tail; white velvet front paws; black velvet back paws; black velvet face; yellow and black glass eyes; 1920.

Chad Valley often made stuffed toys of subjects already popularized in books, film cartoons and newspaper strips. Bonzo was one of the first. He was the bull terrier pup drawn by G. Studdy for the *Daily Sketch*. Chad Valley hired a dwarf dressed as Bonzo to entertain King George V and Queen Mary at the 1920 British Industries Fair.
MARKS: "Hygienic Toys//Made in England by//Chad Valley Co. Ltd."
SEE: *Illustration 48* (Color Section, page 40).
PRICE: $75-85 +

Little Red Riding Hood: 19½in (49cm); all-velvet face and body; painted eyes; mitt hands; typical Eng-

49.

48

lish Red Riding Hood costume; red
cape; long green blouse; striped green
skirt; white tie, collar and cuffs; black
slippers; circa mid 1920s.
MARKS: None
SEE: *Illustration 49. Marjorie Yocum
Collection.*
PRICE: $500-600 up

Little Red Riding Hood: 6in (15cm);
stuffed, oilcloth-type material; exact
same face and costume as the larger
doll; circa mid 1920s.
MARKS: "Ireland" (tag)
SEE: *Illustration 49. Marjorie Yocum
Collection.*
PRICE: $35-50
COMPANY: UNKNOWN

50.

Her Royal Highness, the Duchess
Of York, approved the first doll by
Chad Valley of Princess Elizabeth as a
small child in 1930. This doll is now
rare.

Princess Elizabeth: 17in (43cm);
pressed molded felt face; all-velvet
body; glass eyes; mass of blonde curls;
party dress with ruffles on skirt, neck
and sleeves; pearl necklace; button
slippers; socks; 1930.
SEE: *Illustration 50. Elizabeth Martz
Collection.*
PRICE: $850-1000

The Chad Valley military *Foot
Guard* dolls were very popular. There
are five regiments of *Foot Guards*, the
Grenadiers, the Coldstream Guards,
the Welsh, Irish and Scots Guards.
When on ceremonial duty, they all
wear the scarlet tunic, blue trousers
and bearskin caps. It is easy to identify
the different regiments by looking
closely at the spacing of their tunic

51.

buttons. The oldest regiment, the Grenadier Guards, have single-spaced buttons; the buttons of the Coldstream Guards are in groups of two; the Scots, Irish and Welsh Guards are in groups of three, four and five buttons respectively.

Foot Guard, Grenadier, from Special Characters Series: 18in (46cm); stiffened felt mask face; glass eyes; no ears; cloth body; velvet arms and legs; for more general characteristics, see Identification Guide, page 226. Circa 1935-1938.
MARKS: "Hygienic Toys//Made in England By//Chad Valley Co. Ltd." (cloth tag sewn to bottom of feet)
SEE: *Illustration 51.*
PRICE: $500-650

In 1938 Chad Valley was granted a Royal Warrant. A label stating this appeared on dolls on the sole of one foot. The traditional label was sewn on the sole of the other foot.

Girl in Checked Dress: 16in (41cm); pressed felt face; cloth body; curly brown wig; gray checked skirt and gray bodice; felt shoes; 1938 and later.
MARKS: "Chad Valley Hygenic Toys//Seal of Purity" (on one side of dark blue and gold vertical tag); "The certificate of the Royal Institute of Public Health and Hygiene has been awarded in respect of Chad Valley Toys. The Chad Valley Co., Ltd. by appointment Toymakers to Her Majesty the Queen" (on the back of the tag)
SEE: *Illustration 52. Mary Elizabeth Poole Collection.*
PRICE: $400-500

In 1938 the Chad Valley catalog announced that *Princess Elizabeth* and *Princess Margaret Rose* dolls had been approved by their Majesties, the King and Queen, and the *Prince Edward* doll had been approved by HRH, the Duke of Kent. These dolls had specially sculptured faces with curly hand-woven wigs. They were dressed in the same styles as the royal children.

Margaret Rose: 16in (41cm); portrait doll; pink coat and tam; 1938.
MARKS: They did not have the usual tag because the company thought their faces were recognizable. However, they came with a special blue label.
SEE: *Illustration 53. Cohen Auctions.*
SEE: *Illustration 54. Cohen Auctions.*
PRICE: $1400-1600 up

52.

Dopey: 7in (18cm) painted felt mask face; seams at side of head; body made of flesh-colored cotton on top and orange-colored cotton that serves as pants on the bottom; orange felt hat; black felt shoes; 1938. The original box shows an Alpine scene with "Chad Valley" printed above it. The entire set included *Snow White* and the *Seven Dwarfs*.
MARKS: "Hygienic Toys//Made in England//Chad Valley Co. Ltd." (tag sewn on chest)
SEE: *Illustration 55.*
PRICE: $135-175

Black Boy: From a series of six black dolls; 12in (31cm); black velvet face and body; side-glancing brown glass eyes; wide smiling mouth with painted teeth; curly black plush wig; dressed in brown tweed knicker-type pants and large cap; red suspenders; brown tweed cap; doll weighted so he sits and dangles his legs. 1930.
MARKS: "Hygienic Toys//Made in England By//Chad Valley Co. Ltd." (label sewn on right foot); "Chad Valley//Hygienic//Toys//Made in//England//The//Seal of//Purity" (vertical blue and gold tag)
Another doll in the series was *Carolina* who wore a grass skirt, beads, bracelets and headband. *Rahaj* wore an East Indian outfit with a turban, full trousers and earrings. *Nabob* wore full trousers and a huge cap of printed material and a wide collar. There were six dolls in the series. They were also made in a 14in (36cm) size.
SEE: *Illustration 56. Nancy Hance Collection.*
PRICE: $450-550. This is a rare doll. Very few prices are available.

53.

54.

55.

56.

Little Bo Peep and Little Boy Blue from the Nursery Rhyme Character Series of 1935: 15in (38cm); felt face; cloth body; overcast hand-sewn seam in head; machine-sewn seam in back; blonde mohair wig; rounded mitt hands with stitching indicating fingers and separate thumb; traditional nursery rhyme costume with dress top and pannier made of pink printed cotton; blue cotton underskirt; white socks; pink felt shoes with mother-of-pearl buttons; matching bonnet; metal crook in right hand; papier-mâché sheep covered with white wool in left hand; *Little Boy Blue* wears blue felt pants, shoes and hat; white shirt with mother-of-pearl buttons; wooden horn; 1935.

A similar *Little Bo Peep* and *Little Boy Blue* were made after World War II.

MARKS: "Chad Valley//Hygienic Toys//Made in England//The Seal of Purity" (long vertical dark blue and gold tag sewn on back of dolls)

SEE: *Illustration 57* (Color Section, page 165).

PRICE: $400-500 each

Dolls Not Photographed
1. **1920, 13in (33cm):** Twelve stockinette girls and boys; hand-woven wigs which could be brushed and combed; removable clothes; usually marked with round Chad Valley metal button 1/2in (1cm) with "Chad Valley//British//Hygienic Toys" marked on it; dolls included *Zoe; Lady Betty* with long curled wig and picture hat; *Welsh Girl; Pierrot* and *Pierrette.*
2. **1920-1929, 12in (31cm) — 13in (33cm):** Stockinette dolls with patented wrist watch; some had woven wigs that could be combed; in various years the series included, *Jack, Jill, Peter,*

Pretty Prue, Iris Drolley, Joan and others.

3. **1920-1929+ Jack O'Jingles Novelty Art Doll:** Pointed cap with pompons; collar with points; belt; pompons hung from short skirt; *Jester*-type doll.
   A. 1920, 9½in (24cm): Stockinette-faced; all had same appearance.
   B. 1924, 15in (38cm): Stockinette dressed in red, blue, green and gold; Aerolite doll.
   C. 1927-1929, 15in (38cm) *Caresse* series: Velveteen.

4. **1920-1921 Stockinette Dolls:** Woven wig.
   A. *Marjorie* 9in (23cm).
   B. *Miss Muffet* 9in (23cm).
   C. *Nora* 9in (23cm).

5. **1923-1926 Aerolite** (trademark): Dolls with kapok-stuffed cloth; clothes printed on cloth; flat faces.
   A. 1923, 11in (28cm): *Pixie, Soma, Red Cloud, Peggy, Beaver, Jean, Peter Pan* and *Dan.*
   B. 1924 *Mephistopheles Novelty Art Doll:* 10½in (27cm); Aerolite (kapok-stuffed cloth); devil dressed in bright red. Other dolls included *Tinkle Belle, Pretty Jane, Jack, Jolly, Olga, La Petite Caresse, Jack, Jill, Baby Doll, Betty, Caresse, Ching-a-Ling* and *Red Cloud* (American Indian).
   C. 1926 continued line of *Aerolite* dolls.

6. **1923 La Petite Caresse:** Four sizes, 14½in (37cm) to 18in (46cm); stockinette; pudgy girl dolls dressed in felt clothes decorated with felt flowers: some had mama voice boxes.

7. **1923 Peter Pan:** Flat-type face; printed clothes.

8. **1924 Jack Novelty Art Doll:** Dressed in white knickers and stocking hat.

9. **1920s Carnival Dolls:** Boudoir dolls; *Pierrot* (men dressed in bright colored outfits with caps and flared pants); girl dolls who wore dresses with short skirts and pointed hats; small black curls; all dolls had painted-on cheeks.

10. **1926 Peter Pan:** 22in (56cm); molded face; green and brown felt suit.

11. **1927-1928 Tango Tar Baby:** 21in (53cm); long legs which could be made to walk and dance; striped long trousers and hat; short double-breasted jacket.

12. **1928-1931+ Carina Series:** In six sizes, 14in (36cm) to 30in (76cm); velvet dolls; jointed at neck, shoulders and hips; clothes also made in velvet.

13. **1929 Golliwog:** In four sizes, 10½in (26cm) to 17in (43cm); round eyes; large mouth; plush fur wig; blue, red and yellow suit.

14. **1930 Automobile Association Royal Scout Mascot:** Boy with fierce look and bulging eyes; small black mustache; felt uniform; arm has permanent salute position.

15. **1930 Royal Automobile Club Royal Scout Mascot:** Nicer expression; wore uniform open at the neck; shirt.

16. **1931 Carina Velvet Dolls:** In six sizes, 14in (36cm) to 30in (76cm); jointed at neck, shoulders and hips; clothes also in velvet.

17. **1933 Carina Series:** Inexpensive

version with calico limbs; dressed in various materials; cloche hat or wide-brimmed bonnet.

18. **1933-1934 Special Character Dolls Series:** 19in (48cm); velvet arms and legs; fabric heads; costumes correctly detailed; included *Policeman, Highlander, Nurse, Grenadier, Colleen, Scots Girl* and others. There were various tartans used for the *Highlander.*
MARKS: "Chad Valley Seal of Purity" (tag tied to wrist)

19. **1935 Sofa Dolls:** 21in (53cm); dressed in the elegant fashion of the period; beautiful faces; small rosebud mouths; slitted eyes.

20. **1935 Nursery Rhyme Character Dolls:** Approximately 14in (36cm) to 15in (38cm); *Mary* (carried a little lamb); *Jack Horner* (carried his pie); *Mary-Mary* (carried flowers); *Miss Muffet* (spider in her lap).
MARKS: "Chad Valley Seal of Purity" (tag tied to wrist)

21. **1935 Novelty Dolls:** 8in (20cm) and 13½in (34cm); types of dolls included *Sailors* and *Soldiers* which had a wide grin and stockinette face over a hard mask; gnomes and pixies.

22. **1939 Reduction in Quantity of Dolls:** Matched pairs were made.

Chase Stockinette Doll

A SIZE TO FIT EACH PURSE

THE BEST DOLL THAT IS MADE

The Chase Stockinet Doll

A glorified Rag Doll. A High Grade Doll made of the best materials and with the best workmanship. A doll that children love the best of all dolls.

58.   M. J. CHASE   :   :   :   :   Pawtucket, Rhode Island

The Chase company made dolls for almost a century. Their early cloth dolls were made with stockinette stretched over a mask face. This stockinette was treated and then painted with oils. Later pink sateen was used for the bodies.

In the 1920s they made character dolls, educational dolls and bathtub dolls from 12in (31cm) to 39in (99cm). In 1923 they offered a line of dolls in six different heights. These dolls had the pink sateen body which was waterproofed and painted.

The character dolls included *Alice in Wonderful, Duchess, Frog, Footman,*

The registered trademarks, the trademarks and copyrights appearing in italics/bold within this chapter belong to Chase Company.

59.

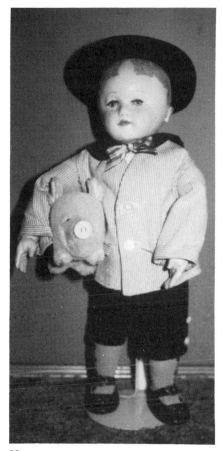

60.

George Washington, Mad Hatter, Mammy Nurse, Pickaninnies and *Tweedledum and Tweedledee.*
Soft cloth dolls included *Bessy Brooks, Silly Sally* and *Tommy Snooks.*
For general characteristics, see Identification Guide, page 227.
SEE: *Illustration 58. Playthings,* April 1923.
PRICE: Depends on height, condition and type of doll. Black dolls are three to four times the price of white dolls. Molded, bobbed hair dolls are higher than dolls with regular hair. Character dolls and other special dolls range from $1000 to $6000+.
Baby: 18½in (47cm) washable oil-painted baby doll; for general characteristics, see Identification Guide, page 227.
MARKS: "The Chase Stockinet Doll//Made of STOCKINET CLOTH//stuffed with cotton//Made by Hand//Painted by Hand//Made by

Especially trained WORKERS" (polished paper tag sewn into the body)
SEE: *Illustration 59. Ruth Eby Collection.*
PRICE: $500-2000 (depending on height, condition and type of doll)
Chase Boy: 16in (41cm); for general characteristics, see Identification Guide, page 227; dressed in a blue striped jacket, blue hat and pants.
SEE: *Illustration 60. Betty Shriver Collection.*
PRICE: $900-1100 (depending on height, condition and type of doll)

S. Cohen & Son

Flapper Doll and Japanese Doll: 21in (53cm); soft stuffed; equipped with voices.

SEE: *Illustration 61. Playthings,* September 1924.

61.

Community Craft

Scottish Girl: 18in (46cm); cloth mask face and body; Mollye-type yarn hair; no stitching in hand for fingers; red and white Scottish plaid skirt and tam; white blouse with puffed sleeves; 1930s.

MARKS: "Community Craft" (box)
SEE: *Illustration 62. Ann Pendleton Collection.*
PRICE: $55-85

62.

Consuela Originals (Italy)

Provincial Girl: 7½in (19cm); Eros characteristics (see Identification Guide, page 229); red rayon jumper dress; blue and white ribbon trim around bottom of skirt; white blouse; white rayon pleated headpiece with red ribbon trim; white nylon apron with red ribbon trim; brown mohair wig with pigtails; red felt boots with cardboard soles; 1950s.

This doll was probably made by Eros and sold to the Consuela Company for dressing.

56

MARKS: "Consuelo Originals// Hand Made in Italy" (ribbon tag sewn to back of dress)

SEE: *Illustration 80* (page 72); first doll on left. This doll is pictured in the Eros section.
PRICE: $20-15

Crowley, Milna & Co. (Austria)

Flapper Lady: Approximately 30in (76cm); silk face beautifully painted; needlesculptured features; dark eye shadow; rosy cheeks; all-felt mature body; open mouth with painted teeth; wig; earrings; pink felt dress with pointed hemline trimmed with lavender felt; "stovepipe-type" lavender felt hat with black ribbons; lavender flat felt shoes.

Flapper Girl: 22½in (57cm); silk face beautifully painted; needlesculpture for features; dark eye shadow; rosy cheeks; all-felt body; open mouth with painted teeth; wig; velvet body; all-felt black and orange costume; low felt slippers.
MARK: "Made in Austria" (sewn under skirt for both dolls) "Made in Vienna//for//Crowley, Milna & Co.//Made in Austria" (tag on girl)
SEE: *Illustration 63* (Color Section, page 224). *Joe Golembieski Collection.*
PRICE: $175-225 30in (76cm) doll $125-150 22½in (57cm) doll

Dean's Rag Book Co. Ltd. (England)

Dean's Rag Book Co. was established in 1903, and they have made many cloth books, toys and dolls ever since. Their first dolls were cutout dolls printed on cloth. By 1912 they were printing a life-size baby which was 24in (62cm) tall when completed and could wear baby clothes.

Soon they turned to making completed dolls which they advertised as hygienically stuffed and finished, indestructible and washable. The English Institute of Hygiene soon certified their dolls and the Dean dolls had their new certification printed on their bodies (see *Illustration 65.*).

Always innovative, Dean's Rag

Book Co. introduced story dolls from nursery rhymes, fairy tales and Shakespeare's tales. They made lady dolls dressed in Victorian costumes.

During World War I they made patriotic dolls including soldiers, sailors, *John Bull*, a wounded soldier, *Charlie Chaplin* and other personality dolls.

By 1920 they had introduced the first molded, pressed three-dimensional shaped dolls called *Tru-to-Life* rag dolls. They also continued to make their *Cut-Out Knockabout Dolls.* Dur-

The registered trademarks, the trademarks and copyrights appearing in italics/bold within this chapter belong to Dean's Rag Book Co. Ltd.

57

ing the 1920s and 1930s they introduced new dolls each year and continued to produce their best sellers.

For a list of dolls produced from 1920 to 1939, see pages 62-68.

A1 Girl: 22½in (57cm); for general characteristics, see Identification Guide, page 228; blonde mohair wig; white and blue print dress; pink collar; white pantalets; pink hat (not original); white socks; pink felt shoes; carries a bunch of flowers; Lenci lookalike; 1924-1925.
MARKS: "Hygienic A1 Toys//picture of a bulldog and a terrier having a tug-of-war over a Dean's book//Made in England//Deans Rag Book Co. Ltd." (oval on bottom of right foot)
SEE: *Illustration 64* (Color Section, page 38).
PRICE: $350-400

Dean's Trademark: Patented when the A1 line of toys was introduced; showed a terrier and English bulldog having a tug-of-war with an indestructible Dean's Rag book. The A1 line was made by British Novelty Works, a Dean's subsidiary. They were made from 1923-1927. Each doll had a black and silver pendant attached to it.
MARKS: "Hygienic A1 Toys//Made in England//Deans Rag Book Co. Ltd" (printed on sole of right foot)
SEE: *Illustration 65.*

Joan and Peter: 14in (36cm); molded, painted faces; Dean's eyes (see *Illustration 66*), heavy eyelashes around entire eye; open mouth with painted teeth; *Joan* has brown plaits; *Peter* has blonde fuzzy hair; mitt hands with stitching indicating fingers; *Joan* has felt dress with picot edging; *Peter* has black felt jacket; cotton checked trousers; white shirt with starched collar; Dean's knit striped white socks; dolls introduced in 1928 and made into the 1930s.

The doll dances while dangling from a gold elastic cord.
MARKS: "Dean's Dancing Dolls// Head Design//No.735890//illegible// DRGM Pat. Pending U.S.A." (oval stamp on bottom of both feet of both dolls)
SEE: *Illustration 66.*
PRICE: $450-500 pair

65.

58

Frilly on a Trike: 14in (36cm); oil painted cloth mask face; special Dean's eyes; velvet arms and legs; rose velvet dress and shoes which are part of body; rose velvet cloche; grosgrain trimming; ribbed stockings which are common on Dean's Rag Book dolls; well-made metal tricycle pulled by cord; flapper-style clothing; late 1920s.

In 1929 Dean's made a *Trike Boy.* This was a plush-headed rabbit riding the same bicycle as *Frilly.*
MARKS: None on doll
SEE: *Illustration 67* (Back Cover).
PRICE: $400-600

Flapper in Velvet Coat and Hat: 14in (36cm); pink cloth body; silkish pressed *Tru-to-Life* mask; painted face; Dean's eyes (see *Illustration 66,* girl on right); seam in back of leg only; back seam (see *Illustration 299*); lavender velvet coat with plush lavender fur; lavender velvet cloche made as part of head; velvet two-tone lavender shoes with mother-of-pearl buttons are part of leg construction; mitt hands with no stitching for fingers; circa 1923-1924. The *Mother Goose Nursery Rhymes* book used the designs of John Massall. The book has been washed many times; the cover is faded but the inside pictures are bright.

66.

68.

69.

MARKS: "Made in England//By// Dean's//Ragbook//Co.Ltd." (circular stamp on body of doll)
SEE: *Illustration 68.*
PRICE: $20-30 (book)
$100-150 (doll)

Princess Dolls: Large doll approximately 36in (91cm); small doll approximately 12in (31cm); flapper-type; cloth body; pressed mask face; long, slender legs; dressed in pin velvet with fur trim on hat, collar and bottom of coat, fur muff; circa 1926. The dolls came in seven sizes from 10in (25cm) to 36in (91cm); ten different colors; trimmed with white bear plush.
These dolls are similar to the Chad Valley dolls (see *Illustration 46*).
SEE: *Illustration 69. Mary Merritt Musuem.*
PRICE: $150-800 depending on size

Alice in Wonderland Set:
Mad Hatter: 15in (38cm); expressive painted mask face; cloth body; blonde wig; brushed velvet brown top hat; light blue felt waistcoat; orange felt vest with orange buttons; flowered scarf; blue and orange checked pants; black shoes; 1931.
March Hare: 21in (53cm) including ears; brown velvet body; green belt waistcoat; yellow vest; blue and white striped shirt; gray, blue and orange striped pants; flowered shoes (same material as *Mad Hatter's* scarf); 1931.
Alice: 24in (61cm); blue velvet dress with white organdy collar; organdy ruffled apron; white stockings; dark blue felt slippers; blonde wig; ribbon on hair tied on the side; 1931.
White Rabbit: 19in (48cm) including ears; whitish-gray plush body; brown checked waistcoat; red felt vest with

yellow buttons; blue and tan plaid shirt; 1931.
Not Photographed
Dormouse.
MARKS: *Mad Hatter:* "Made in England by Deans Ragbook//Coats" (stamp on foot)
March Hare: "Made in England by Deans Ragbook//Coats" (stamp on foot)
Alice: No stamps or other marks
White Rabbit: No stamps or other marks
SEE: *Illustration 70* (Color Section, page *38*). *Countess Maree Tarnowska Collection.*

PRICE: Rare set of dolls; very few sample prices available.

Lillibet (Elizabeth): 16in (41cm); oil painted cloth face; special Dean's eyes (see *Illustration 66);* cloth body; blonde mohair wig; seam at back of legs; no ankle seam; blue felt coat and hat with white picot lace trim; white socks; blue felt shoes; came with toy dog; 1935-1938.
This doll was purchased in Bermuda.
MARKS: "Made in England//by// Dean's Rag Book Co. Ltd.//London" (label sewn to foot)
SEE: *Illustration 71. Lois Janner Collection.*
PRICE: $500-900+ (rare doll; very few sample prices available)

Cot Cat: Fur head and cuffs; body made from maroon and white striped velvet; bells used for buttons on coat; cord on head for "bouncing"; 1920s.

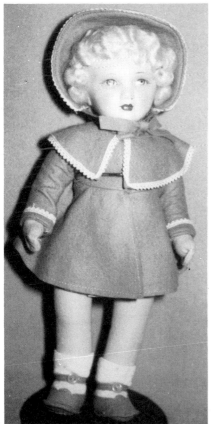

71.

72.

73.

MARKS: "Dean's Al Dolls & Toys//Hygienic//Guaranteed//Made in England//Cot Cat" (tag)
SEE: *Illustration 72. Kathy George Collection.*
PRICE: $200-250

Mickey Mouse: 8in (20cm); velvet body; brown velvet pants; 1939. These are reported to have been dressed for the 1939 World's Fair. *Minnie Mouse* was made at the same time.
MARKS: None on doll
SEE: *Illustration 73. Kathy George Collection.*
PRICE: $200-250

Dolls Made by Deans's Rag Book Co. from 1920 to 1939

1920 *Charlie Chaplin:* Reproduced in 1982 for export only.
Jumper Doll: 12in (31cm); flat-faced cloth doll; one of *Knockabout* series #D 253; doll wore skirt, pullover top and tam.
Curly Locks: 14in (36cm); made in the cut-out version and

also the *Tru-to-Life* version; other dolls included *Baby Puck, Betty Blue, Big Baby, Bow Bells, Dolly Dips* and *Florrie the Flapper.*
Cosy Kids: Felt or plush; Tru-Shu feet; wore double-breasted coat, cloche or bonnet, leggings or single-strap slippers, socks.
Hilda Cowham was a well-known English illustrator of children's books. She specialized in children with long legs. Dean's produced a line of dolls based on her designs.
Hilda Cowham Kiddies: Had long legs; made in small size and life-size; *Motherly Molly; Spiffkin's the Sport; Dainty Daphne; Florrie the Flapper; Miss Folly; Saucy Sally; Scuttie the Scout; Mademoiselle; Cheeky Charlie; Nurse Norah Demure Dora; Jolly Jack.*
Hilda Cowham Rag Dolls: Patterned after her paintings; *Captivating Cora* with a print rosebud dress; *Darling Dora* with a white dress with red dots, *Tantalizing Thora* wore a felt costume and tam; *Natty Nora* had a dotted blouse and checked skirt; *Laughing Laura* wore a flowered print dress; *Flaxen Flora* had an embroidered dress. These dolls had wigs with bands or bows, patent shoes, mercerized cotton stockings. Some dolls had downcast painted eyes which gave them a coy look.
Goo Goo Series.
Pauline Guilbert Dolls.
Nursery Rhyme Series: 9in (23cm); flat face; *Mother Goose;*

Bo Peep; Blue Bell; Mary, Mary; Red Riding Hood.

1921 Gilbert the Filbert: Named after a Music Hall song; wore monocle.

Wooly Wooly: Trade name of a Golliwog.

1923 Evripoze: Stockinette body with cotton stuffing around an armature which allowed the child to pose the doll; 14in (36cm) and other heights; pressed head and shoulder plate of stiff fabric; painted eyes; mohair wig; neck jointed so head turns; jointed also at shoulders and hips; composition lower arms; wooden lower legs; one of A1 Tru-to-Life line.

These first A1 dolls were called the dolls with a disc because the arms and legs were fastened to the body with discs imprinted with "Dean's A1." They came in 13 different costumes. Each costume was color-coordinated with the doll's hair.

MARKS: Dean trademark and "Hygienically stuffed//Deans A1 Doll//Made in England" (sole of right foot); "Deans A1 Doll//Made in England//Tru-to-life Patented//British No. 25151, USA Apl 9/18.Depose, France" (sole of left foot) Cherub Jenny and Cherub Johnny: 10½in (27cm), 13in (33cm) and 16in (41cm); Tru-to-Life cloth baby dolls.

A1 Sunbonnet Babies: Dressed in checked rompers and bonnets. Betty Blue, Big Baby Doll, Curly Locks and Kuddlemee: 10½in (27cm), 13in (33cm) and 15in (38cm); baby dolls stuffed with down.

Dean's Dancing Darkies: Series of black dolls which included Uncle Remus and Ta-Ta dolls.

Mother Goose Series: Cut out cloth dolls.

Pinafore Dolls: 9¼in (24cm); wore apron over costume.

1924 Dean's registered a British trademark with a picture of a bulldog's head with the initials "B.N.W." This was after they had purchased British Novelty Works, Ltd.

A1 Line: Included Dora, Maisie, Wendy and Trixie in the Tru-to-Life series.

Trixie: 12in (31cm); pleated crepe muslin print dress; ribbon sash; patent black shoes.

1924 Posie Line: Included Poppy,
and Rose, Daisy, Marigold and Blue-
1925 bell, Violet, Lily, Peony, Primula, Syringa, Marguerite and May. The costumes followed the early 1920s English garden fashions of the period. They came in 13in (33cm), 17in (43cm) and 20in (51cm) sizes. These dolls had molded felt faces and were Lenci look-alikes.

Poppy: Knee-length dress with flower on chest; jacket; cloche hat; flower in right hand.

Rose: Knee-length dress; skirt made of layers in semi-circles; carried flower in hand.

Marigold: Knee-length skirt trimmed with shamrock design; neckline had bands of colored material; hat with brim.

Marguerite: Dressed like white

petals of daisy with hand-kerchief points at hemline.
Wendy (A1 True-to-Life Doll): 12in (31cm); printed clothes and hat.
Cherub Toddler Series: Included *Jess, Jose, Jenny, Jim, Joe, Johnny, Benny* and *Bonny.* They were filled with soft down and were 16in (41cm). They came with Evripoze joints.
Buddy and Biddy: 11in. (28cm); similar to *Cherub* dolls.
Bertie and Buddie: 13in (33cm); similar to *Cherub* dolls.

1926 Velvet-faced dolls introduced to compete with Chad Valley and Norah Wellings.
A1 Buster Brown: Cartoon character; bobbed flax wig; painted face with teeth showing; Buster Brown suit and tam.
Dickie Blob.
Inkwell Fairy: Character from a story on a popular record for children.
Dinkie Dolls: 12in (31cm); came in four models; fashionable lady (boudoir) dolls.
Playtime Dolls.
Posy Dolls.
Princess Dolls: Dressed in velvet with white bear plush trim and muff; six different colors; seven sizes from 10in (25cm) to 36in (91cm); similar to a Chad Valley doll (see *Illustration 46*).
Elegant Dolls: Fashionable lady (boudoir dolls).
Floral Dolls.

1927 **Frilly Dolls and Smart Set Dolls:** 12 models; 21in (53cm); flapper dress and fancy hat; costumes made in velvet, plush, imitation fur and leather; some dolls wore knickerbocker trousers and a jacket.

1928 **Smart Set Dolls:** Continuation of 1927 line. One carried a cigarette.
Series of dolls with marcel waved mohair wigs.
Posy Buds: Dressed in felt outfits.
Dean's Dancing Dolls: 14½in (37cm); very popular; boy and girl pairs which came in dancing position and bobbed up and down on a golden string. They could be made to imitate current dance crazes. These were considered *Mascot* dolls. These were widely imitated and caused legal problems.
Joan and Peter Dancing Dolls: Molded, painted faces; mohair wigs; *Joan* had blonde hair with two plaits, felt dress with picot edging, white socks, black shoes; *Peter* had a fuzzy wig, checked trousers, dark jacket, white shirt (see *Illustration 66).*
Bunty and Bobby:
Novelties: Dolls' head characters were used for gift boxes; popular characters included a *Jockey, Minstrel, Sultan* and *Pierrot;* dolls were made into complete boxes especially to contain a small, expensive present; popular figures included *Billy Buttons* and *Jolly Tar.*
Pierrette: Flat face; made of art silk.
Grumpy.
Long Cloth Baby Dolls: Reissue of baby dolls in long gowns.
Luvly Dolls.
Sunshine Dolls.
Daisy Dolls.

Erbie Brown.

Travel Tots.

Wabbly Wally, Willow Pattern Dolls.

1929 *Charlie Chaplin:* 13in (33cm); mask face; wool yarn hair; blue eyes; closed mouth; floppy feet (new in 1929); black felt coat with tails; black and white checked trousers; red felt vest.

Dainty Dolls.

Hetty: Marked "1 Am Hetty// The//Help Yourself Girl."

1930 **Husheen Dolls:** 7½in (19cm), 9in (23cm) and 10in (25cm); mask faces; the rest of the dolls made of silkeen plush except for soles of feet.

Princess Dolls.

Sunshine Dolls: Dressed in bright print picture dress with matching hat.

Sylvie Dolls.

Ta-Ta Dolls.

Modern Doll. Came in nine sizes; wore velvet clothes trimmed with silk.

Mickey Mouse: 6in (15cm), 8in (20cm), 9in (23cm); 12in (31cm), 14in (36cm), 16in (41cm), 18in (46cm) and 21in (53cm); Dean's held the registered design No. 750611 produced with the consent of Walt Disney-Mickey Mouse Ltd. (see *Illustration 73).*

Minnie Mouse: See sizes and design number for *Mickey Mouse.*

1930 Other cartoon characters produced during this period included *Felix the Cat.*

1931 *Alice in Wonderland:* 19in (48cm) and 27in (69cm); waist-length hair; blue dress;

white pinafore; stockings; black ankle-strap shoes.

March Hare: 13in (33cm) and 25in (64cm); long ears; frock coat; striped trousers.

White Rabbit: 13in (33cm) and 25in (64cm); plush body; checked coat.

Mad Hatter: 15in (38cm) and 25in (64cm); top hat; dark coat; checked trousers.

Dormouse: 12½in (32cm); animal figure.

Bosco and Honey: 8in (20cm), 9in (23cm), 12in (31cm), 14in (36cm) and 17in (43cm); boy and monkey from *Looney Tunes.*

1920s *Coogan Kid (Evripoze):* Two sizes.

1932 *Gem:* Girl with different jeweled necklaces.

Flo: Black girl with green hat; large earrings; pleated skirt.

1933 *Peter and Patsy:* Curl on middle of forehead; dressed in romper suits.

1935 *Nightdress Cases:* They were used by adults and young girls, a popular item in 1935.

Yvonne: Silver-blonde marcelled wig; tight-fitting bodice with V-neckline and puff sleeves; flounced skirt; costumes made in pink and sky blue, black and scarlet, rose and maroon; hand-painted face.

Marina: Victorian-style costume; ruffled skirt; poke bonnet; costumes made in black, flame, rose or marine green.

Olga: Winter costume of velvet and white fur muff, shawl collar, cloche hat; blonde curls; choker necklace; made in black,

turquoise, reseda, salmon, cornflower blue and flame; painted face with slight pout.
Blinkums: Doggie nightdress case; glass eyes; zipper fastener.
Dinkums: Matching handkerchief sachet; glass eyes; zipper fastener.

1936 *Sam:* Stanley Holloway's monologue character; soldier with large head and mustache; rotund body; slender bowed legs.
Becky: 17in (43cm); dressed in checked organdy; trimmed bonnet; came in pink, blue and red; came with hoop and stick.
Madeline: 17in (43cm); net and taffeta party dress; large bow in hair; came in yellow, white, pink and sky blue.
Cherry: 17in (43cm); white summer dress with circular skirt; several underskirts; large circles on skirt; poke bonnet.
Colette: 14in (36cm), 16in (41cm), 19in (48cm), 21in (53cm) and 30in (76cm); wore a velvet coat with white plush collar; pull-on hat; costume came in blue, yellow and red.
Sheila: 15in (38cm), 17in (43cm) and 19in (48cm); blonde wig; party dress of silk taffeta; wide-brimmed bonnet; came in blue, yellow, green, scarlet, rose and white.
Pickaninny: Elf-like boy; body made of polka-dotted material.
Sylvia: 17in (43cm); brunette wig; large garden hat; organdy dress trimmed with embroidery.
Popeye: 9in (23cm), 14in (36cm), 16in (41cm), 20in (51cm) and 36in (91cm); made of velvet; tattoo on arm; pipe; *Evripoze:* jointed; famous cartoon character.
Henry: Popular cartoon character.

1938 *Lillibet:* 17in (43cm); curly wig; wore A-line coat; wide-brimmed hat; molded felt face; jointed at neck, arms and legs; childhood name of Elizabeth II (see *Illustration 71*).
Pickaninny: Plump, elf-like doll.
Cami Doll: Wore cami-knicker outfit.
Eskimo: Plush outfit with fur trimming.
Mariette: 30in (76cm); Gainsborough lady-styled dress.
Carole: 30in (76cm); Gainsborough lady-styled dress.
Victoria: 30in (76cm); Victorian-styled dress.
Becky: 17in (43cm); Victorian child.
Stormy Weather: Dressed in Mackintosh, sou'wester hat, Wellington boots.
Judith: Dressed as bridesmaid.
Robin: 17in (43cm); boy doll.
Policeman: 20in (51cm).
Girl Guide: 20in (51cm).
Boy Scout: 20in (51cm).
Welsh Girl: 17in (43cm).
Highland Lassie: 17in (43cm).

1938 *Playmate Series:* Each doll held a toy under one arm; they were often sold in the 1930s nightclubs.
Bridget: 40in (102cm); curly hair; flowered dress; held a spotted rabbit.
Sonia: 40in (102cm); pigtails; Russian tunic; held a black dog.
Corona: 40in (102cm); winter

coat with muff; held a white dog.

Sailor Girl: 40in (102cm); sailor dress and beret; held a sailor doll.

Beryl: 42in (107cm); jodhpurs and riding hat; did not carry a toy.

Jennifer: 42in (107cm); curly hair; held a black dog.

Susan: 40in (102cm); curly hair; wore a beret; held a sailor doll.

Sally: 40in (102cm); curly hair; big bow in hair; held a teddy bear.

Pamela: 40in (102cm); blonde pigtails; polka dot dress and wide brimmed hat; held a black rag doll.

Margaret: 40in (102cm); blonde pigtails; pleated skirt, jumper, plaid scarf; tam; held a Scottie dog.

Will Hay: 16in (41cm); an *Evripoze:* personality film star doll; wore a headmaster's gown, cane and book, (his costume is from English films).

1939 *Lupino Lane:* 9½in (24cm), 12in (31cm) and 28in (71cm); music hall personality doll; dressed in checked suit and bowler hat; tiny moustache; remembered for *Lambeth Walk;* a special 12in (31cm) version featured Dean's dancing dolls and were called *Nipper* and *Nippy.*

Peter Pan: 17in (43cm); molded felt face; velvet body; wore suit of gold velvet.

Wendy: 17in (43cm); molded felt face; velvet body; wore a white nightdress.

Sailor Boy: 42in (107cm); dark blue sailor costume.

Highland Lassie: 42in (107cm) and 24in (61cm); Scottish tartan costume.

Merrie: 42in (107cm); blonde wig; velvet and cloth dress with gored skirt; beret and scarf; held a toy dog.

Valerie, Tessa, Dawn, David, Phyllis, Jack and *Saucy Sue:* 18in (46cm); felt faces.

Angeline, Nell and *Nita:* Approximately 18in (46cm); beautiful wigs; period costumes.

Kitty: 24in (61cm); smooth hair; checked suit; beret; held toy animal.

Arline, Muriel and *Rosemary:* 18in (46cm); pretty party frocks; curly hair which looked like Shirley Temple.

Village Blacksmith: 9in (23cm); velvet body.

Ben Bolt Sailor Doll: 16in (41cm); velvet body.

Cheeks the Marine: 14½in (36cm); velvet body.

Dean's Rag Book Dolls Made for Many Years

1. **Pierrot and Pierrette:** Made from 1914 through 1938. The most popular dolls were made in the middle 1920s.
2. Animal figures.
3. Advertising dolls such as *Jimmy Whiteshine* (polishing company), *Miss Sue* (Sue Flake's Beef Suet), *Betty Oxo* (Oxo Beef Cube Company).
4. Dolls designed by Hilda Cowhan from 1915-1930.
5. **Mickey Mouse:** Made throughout the 1930s. By 1930 they were made

in nine sizes up to 42in (107cm).
6. **Night Dress Cases:** Examples include *Gypsy, Mickey* and *Minnie* *Mouse, Popeye, Donald Duck, Cowboy, Dutch Boy,* bears, ducks and dogs.

S. E. Delavan

74. **S. E. Delavan, 24 W. Washington St., Chicago, Ill.**

Sophie E. Delavan was a wig maker in Chicago, Illinois. She was in business during World War I and into the 1920s. She introduced a new line of rag dolls at the New York Toy Fair in 1921.

Buds and Buddies, Rag Dolls of All Nations: The advertisement shows girl dolls, clown, Mammy doll, *Red Riding Hood,* boy doll with bare feet and a nurse doll. According to the advertisement, "...novel features, very shapely and beautifully dressed. Each doll has a wondrous printed story in each little pocket." The dolls were designed by Katherine Rauser and Queen G. Thomas.
SEE: *Illustration 74. Playthings,* January 1921.

Katherine A. Rauser was a Delavan designer of doll clothing from 1904 into the 1920s. In 1913 *Toys and Novelties* said, "Mrs. Rauser is probably the leading manufacturer of fine doll outfits, dresses, underwear, aprons, hats, novelties in America. She vies with Worth or Paquin in the creation of dolls' clothes and outfits." Throughout the 1920s she continued designing and making clothes for many types of dolls including a boudoir doll named *Vanity Van* in 1928. This doll was dressed in black or colored satin; had separate pockets for face powder, mirror, lipstick, purse and handkerchief.

Denmark Company
(Name Unknown)

Danish Soldier: 9in (23cm); velvet mask and head; oil-painted face and brown hair; bright blue side-glancing eyes; open mouth with four painted teeth; applied ears with no extra stitching; red felt Danish soldier's tunic with brass buttons; black velvet pants; mitt hands; zigzag stitching on back of head and body; black leather pouch; wooden feet which allow doll to stand alone; swivel head; Norah Wellings look-alike.
MARKS: "Made in Denmark" (left armband)
SEE: *Illustration 75.*
PRICE: $50-70

75.

E.N.A.P.L.

Vatican Guard: 10in (25cm); one-piece felt, molded, pressed face and head mask; hand-painted face; glossy eyes with white dot on the upper left side and light blue dot on lower left side of eye; heart-shaped one color red lips with fine line at each side of center; eyelashes are unusually large above and below the eye; felt zigzag wig similar to Fiore wig (see *Illustration 89*); hand-sewn overcast seam in back of head; jointed at neck; metal pin joints at shoulders and hips; square mitt hands with thumb separate; stitching defines the fingers; felt Vatican Guard costume with the stripes indicated by strips of felt; black felt slippers; 1930-1950.

76.

The registered trademarks, the trademarks and copyrights appearing in italics/bold within this chapter belong to E.N.A.P.L.

MARKS: None; Sicily doll made by same company has paper tag which says "Sale Campion_i //E.N.A.P.L// Approvate del//(round stamp) Comitato Nax Perle Trad...//Firenze."

UNUSUAL IDENTIFICATION FEATURE: Glossy eyes and spider-like eyelashes.
SEE: *Illustration 76.*
PRICE: $60-80

Effanbee Doll Corporation (Fleischaker & Baum)

Buttons, the Effanbee Monk: 22in (56cm), 27in (69cm) and 31in (79cm); felt face; brown mohair, plush neck, head and backs of hands; well-stuffed body; long felt tail; bellhop uniform; red flannel jacket; cap with chin strap; braid trim; black trousers; red oilcloth boots; gilt buttons; loud crying voice; 1923.
SEE: *Illustration 77. Playthings*, February 1923.

The registered trademarks, the trademarks and copyrights appearing in italics/bold within this chapter belong to Fleischaker & Baum.

77.

Louis Eisen

Some of the most interesting art dolls from this period were imported from France by Louis Eisen. His advertisement in *Playthings*, June 1927, said, "The French artistry and dainty charm of these exclusive dolls will lend a sparkling touch to your doll Display.."

Apache (center doll): Doll was dressed as a Paris ruffian in checked pants and cap; black jacket; red scarf around neck; 1926-1928.

Jeanette (doll on right): Little girl dressed in coat, cloche, single strap shoes; Lenci look-alike; 1927.

Gascon (doll on left): Boudoir doll with smock top; striped pants and cap; sabots (wooden shoes worn by Gascony peasants); 1927-1928.

Dolls Not In Advertisement But In Company Line

GASCON   APACHE   JEANETTE

78.

The registered trademarks, the trademarks and copyrights appearing in italics/bold within this chapter belong to Louis Eisen.

Argentine: Boudoir doll with Argentinian costume in vivid colors; 1928.
Aviator or Aviatrix: Boudoir doll with either felt or khaki costume; 1928.
Black and White Doll: Boudoir doll dressed as black dancer; 1928.

Boudoir Doll Dressed as Sportswoman: 1927-1928.
Colonial Belle: Boudoir doll; wore a white wig; colonial costume; 1928.
Russian Boy: 1928.
SEE: *Illustration 78. Playthings*, June 1927.

Eros
(Florence, Italy)

The Eros company has been making dolls for many years. Many of the dolls from this company were made in imitation of the Lenci company. Most of them are provincial-costumed dolls, but a few have unusual costumes relating to storybooks or Italian legends. Four years ago the author picked up new Eros dolls on a trip to Italy.

Some of the original Eros dolls are all-cloth and command higher prices than the more recent dolls which have some plastic or hard plastic parts. This company as well as Lenci, Magis and others have been making novelties and dolls throughout the period after World War II. Some of the Lenci look-alikes are not as old as the original Lenci dolls made in the 1920s and 1930s.

Most of the Eros dolls were either small 7½-8in (19-20cm) or the larger 11in (28cm) dolls. Eros dolls have decorated purses, pillows and other novelties.

Even today mothers and grandmothers in Italy prefer their children have the "old" felt dolls. The author has heard them asking for them in Italian toy stores. In most of the larger Italian towns, there is at least one store which caters to the sale of cloth dolls, including the new Lencis.

For information on the Eros general characteristics, see Identification Guide, page 229.

Girl in Red and White: 11in (28cm); for general characteristics, see Identification Guide, page 229; white organdy skirt trimmed in red felt; red felt short jacket with white organdy trim; red felt bonnet with lining of white organdy trimmed with red felt; white felt shoes with cardboard soles; late 1930s-1960s.
MARKS: "Original//Eros//Florence" (on small round gold tag which can be seen in illustration)
SEE: *Illustration 79.*
PRICE: $70-85 depending on costume

Skier: 7½in (19cm); for general characteristics, see Identification Guide, page 229; felt ski outfit; royal blue pants; light blue jacket lined with royal blue felt; belt with brass buckles; white felt gloves; beige felt ski boots; blonde hair with pigtails; wooden ski poles; 1950s. The doll on the left is a Consuela doll (see page 56).
MARKS: None on doll

The registered trademarks, the trademarks and copyrights appearing in italics/bold within this chapter belong to Eros.

71

SEE: *Illustration 80* (center doll).
PRICE: $35-45

Group of Dolls: For general characteristics, see Identification Guide, page 229.

Venetian Gondolier: 7½in (19cm); blue cotton pants; white sailor shirt with middy collar; black tie; red cummerbund; felt shoes with cardboard soles glued on; straw hat; long wooden pole; late 1930s-1960s.
MARKS: "Original//Eros//Florence" (round gold tag); "Made in Italy" (second round gold tag); "Made in Italy" (printed on bottom of shoe)
SEE: *Illustration 80* (doll on right).
PRICE: $35-45

79.

80.

Etta, Incorporated

Miss Etta Kid started an unusual doll company with all women workers. The firm made cloth art and boudoir dolls.
1927: Boudoir dolls dressed as *Pierrot* and *Pierrette* and clowns; girl dolls, boy dolls, baby dolls including a 16in (41cm) baby with a silky molded cloth face; some dolls had mama voices or criers.
1928: Baby dolls, big and little girl dolls with either bobbed hair or long curls.

The registered trademarks, the trademarks and copyrights appearing in italics/bold within this chapter belong to Etta, Incorporated.

Etta
Incorporated

29 West 36th St.
New York City

GOOD NEWS!
ETTA DOLLS AT
LOWER PRICES

Old and New Buyer friends are welcome
in our showroom to view the
1930 Doll Styles.
Kiddie Fashions for the
South — for the North.
Easter Bonnets and Easter Bunnies
at popular prices.

81.

had human hair wigs and hair eyelashes.

1930: Many new designs added to original line including babies, cowboys, pirates, men and women pairs; girls with long curls or bobbed hair; boudoir dolls; dolls with fancy costumes.

Advertisement: Dolls from the 1930 line.
SEE: *Illustration 81. Playthings,* February 1930.

Advertisement: Etta advertised, "For the first time in the history of America the attempt to rival European Creations of Boudoir Dolls, art novelties,

Pillows has been successful. Etta, Inc., claims this distinction by offering a varied and increasing line of extraordinarily attractive Boudoir Dolls, Novelties D'Art, Pillows and Bags of the Vogue, Animals and Toys of Topical Interest."
SEE: *Illustration 82. Playthings,* January 1927.

Dolls Not Photographed
Baby: 16in (41cm); pressed silk-like, brightly painted face; mohair wig; curved baby arms and legs; white organdy dress and matching outfit; late 1920s.
UNUSUAL IDENTIFICATION FEATURE: Very bright blue eyes.

82.

European Doll Mfg. Co., Inc. (see Anita Novelty Co.)

European Doll Mfg. Co., Inc. New Handy Bag
Messrs. Senior and Junior Forster of the European Doll Mfg. Co., Inc., have just brought out what bids fair to be a real hit in their new "Handy Bags" to sell for 25c to 50c. These bags are decorated with a French Composition Doll Head of striking beauty, and are made of cretonne in assorted colors. They are designed for beach and boudoir use.

83.

This company was actually an American company which used this name as a sales gimmick. They started their business about 1911 and were still going in the 1930s. The Anita line of dolls became part of their company about 1929. They made a full line of composition and mama dolls in addition to many different types of cloth dolls. After the merger with Anita, they added many of the art dolls and novelties which were so popular during that period. They often used "EDMA" to identify their dolls.

Handy Bag: Made of cretonne in assorted colors; used especially for pajamas and for the beach, but often used for any type of appropriate storage during the 1920s and 1930s.

In this case, the head was composition, but such bags were also made with cloth heads.

SEE: *Illustration 83. Playthings*, March 1928.

J. K. Farnell & Company (Alpha) (England)

This company was founded in 1871. At first they made soft toys of natural skins and materials. By the 1920s they were using felt, velvet, plush, stockinette and other cloth materials. Along with animals, they made cartoon figures and dolls with typical English names such as *Little Britain*. By 1924 they were making cloth dolls dressed in the romper outfits of the period.

This company registered a patent in 1935 for *Alpha Cherub* dolls and *Joy Day* dolls. These dolls are often confused with the dolls of Norah Wellings or Chad Valley. Like the dolls of both of the other companies, they were marked with a cloth label sewn firmly to the doll's foot. It said, "Farnell's Alpha Toys//Made in England." However, these labels sometimes came off or were taken off the dolls.

They made chubby dolls with felt faces that had smiling mouths and side-glancing eyes and stockinette bodies. These bodies had seams at the front, back and sides of each leg. Usually the wigs were a curly mohair sewn in a circular motion onto the head. One such doll was 10½in (27cm) tall.

Another chubby-type doll had a velvet face and body. The velvet was sometimes dark brown to represent the *Islander* dolls beloved in the British Empire.

In the late 1930s one of their most important lines was the portrait dolls of King Edward VIII and King George VI. They did make and market a handsome coronation doll of King Edward VIII but when he abdicated, they quickly withdrew this doll from the market. Today these dolls are rare and expensive. Farnell immediately redesigned the doll as a souvenir of the coronation of King George VI. Other *George VI* portrait dolls were dressed in one of several different ceremonial outfits.

Because cloth novelty and tourist dolls were so popular, they made these types of dolls to compete with the Norah Wellings products. It is difficult to tell their sailor dolls sold aboard ships unless they are marked because the Norah Wellings products were similar. Their child dolls are also very similar to the Norah Wellings dolls.

Large Spanish Boy: 23in (58cm); felt mask face; white satin shirt; black velvet pants; black velvet bolero trimmed in gold braid; red moire sash; velvet Spanish hat; 1930s.
UNUSUAL IDENTIFICATION FEATURE: Applied ears.
MARKS: "Farnell's Alpha Toys" (tag)
SEE: *Illustration 84. Ester Schwartz Collection.*
PRICE: $600-700

Girl: Approximately 16in (41cm); painted felt face; velvet arms and legs; pink cotton body; human hair wig; brown and white organdy dress; combination teddy and slip; 1930s.

84.

MARKS: "Farnell's//Alpha Toys// Made in England" (tag)
SEE: *Illustration 85. Elizabeth Martz Collection.*
PRICE: $300-375

Scottish Man: 8in (20cm); velvet face and black coat and Scottish hat; wool plaid bell-bottom pants; coat and pants are part of body construction; painted face with one eye winking; character face; open mouth with painted teeth; painted hair; applied ears made from a single piece of felt; 1930s.
UNUSUAL IDENTIFICATION FEATURE: Applied ears.
MARKS: "Farnell/Alma Toy Co.// Made in England" (tag on left foot)
SEE: *Illustration 86.*
PRICE: $25-35

Sailor: 15in (38cm); felt character face; side-glancing eyes; open mouth with painted teeth; applied ears with double seam; navy blue velvet uniform which is part of body construc-

85.

tion; jacket trimmed with white braid; white sailor cap with "HMS Queen Mary" on band; late 1930s.

Many English and Italian doll companies made sailors which were sold aboard ships. These usually had the ship's name on the cap.
UNUSUAL IDENTIFICATION FEATURE: Applied ears with double seam.
MARKS: "Farnell//Alpha Toy Co.// Made in England" (tag on left foot); "HMS//Queen//Mary//Mascot// Made in England//By//J.K. Farnell & Co. Ltd// Acton, London//W3" (paper wrist tag)

SEE: *Illustration 87. Jean Canaday Collection.*
PRICE: $400-450

George VI: 13in (33cm); portrait; pressed felt painted mask face; ear made of single piece of felt; cotton stockinette arms and legs; jointed at neck, shoulders and hips; square push-and-pull seam on back of head; dressed in full Highland dress with kilt, bearskin, sporran (pouch), and Order of the Thistle; jacket trimmed with piping and gold braid; brass buttons; leather shoes with buckle; 1937-1939.
MARKS: "H.M.//THE KING// Made in England//by//J.K. Farnell & Co. Ltd//Acton, London//W3" (tag)
SEE: *Illustration 88.*
PRICE: $400-600 up

87.

86.

88.

Fiore
(Italy)

For many years doll collectors have wondered about the charming Lenci look-alikes with the printed cotton ribbon which said, "Made in Italy" attached to the soles of their felt shoes. Often these dolls were imported by the major mail order companies such as Kimport and Krug.

Janet Johl in her book, *Your Dolls and Mine*, reported that they were made by Fiore. After a long search, the author finally found a tagged pair. Although not of the same quality as Lenci, they are well made, attractive dolls that seem to have survived the years well. However, often the printing on the cloth ribbon on the shoes has faded or the ribbon itself has disap-

peared. This has made identification difficult. For general characteristics, see Identification Guide, page 230.

Boy and Girl from Napoli: 8¼in (21cm); for general characteristics, see Identification Guide, page 230; girl dressed in black felt dress with red felt trim at hem; white blouse; blue bow in front; felt scarf on head; thread hair is plaited but over ears; black felt shoes with stitching around sole; boy is dressed in black felt pants with red felt buttons; red felt vest with black buttons; white shirt; red bow tie; black felt Naples cap with red tassel; zigzag felt hair; 1930s.

MARKS: "Fiore" (five-pointed star

89.

tag); "Made in Italy" (cloth ribbon sewn to sole of shoe); "Napoli" (tag on boy)
SEE: *Illustration 89.*
PRICE: $75-100 pair

Italian Boy, Girl Carrying Basket with Chicken: 8¼in (21cm); for general characteristics, see Identification Guide, page 230; girl has rust, blue and maroon rayon striped skirt and head scarf; yellow blouse; maroon rayon apron; brown felt shoes with stitching around the sole; boy has black felt pants; red cummerbund; scarf of same material as girl's skirt; brown felt shoes and hat with stitching around outer edges; provincial tag missing.

90.

MARKS: None on doll
SEE: *Illustration 90.*
PRICE: $75-100 pair

Gerber Baby Products Company

Gerber Baby Girl and Boy: One of the first advertising dolls of the Gerber Baby Products Company. Only three baby food labels and ten cents were needed to obtain each one of these baby dolls which were printed on cloth and stuffed. The girl has pink clothes, a pink dog in her left hand and a can of Gerber Baby Food in her right hand. The boy wears blue pajamas, carries a toy duck in his left hand and a can of Gerber Baby Food in his right hand. This offer was withdrawn at the end of 1936 and today these dolls are very rare. The dolls illustrated here are in excellent condition.
SEE: *Illustration 91. Kathryn Davis Collection.*
PRICE: Rare doll; very few price samples available.

The registered trademarks, the trademarks and copyrights appearing in italics/bold within this chapter belong to Gerber Products Company.

91.

Poupées Gerb's (France)

Gerb's, a French company, was located in Paris from 1927 into the 1930s. They made dolls and exported many of them.

Scottish Girl: Felt mask face; painted face; eyes have blue eye liner around entire eye; very large black pupils in eyes; curved highlight under pupil; two-tone lips; white silk wig; dressed in kilt costume; plaid skirt; red felt jacket; red Scottish hat; white Scottish boots; Lenci look-alike; late 1920s-early 1930s. This photograph was taken in the Galerie Saint-Eloi of the Louvre Des Antiquaires.
IDENTIFICATION FEATURE: Very large pupils in eyes.
MARKS: "Poupées Gerb's//29 Rue Gauthey Paris//Made in France" (cloth tag sewn on skirt)
SEE: *Illustration 92. Galerie Saint-Eloi, Louvre Des Antiquaires.*
PRICE: $400-450

Girl in Pink Coat: 13in (33cm); felt mask face with no side seams; brown painted eyes with gray eye liner around eyes; very large pupils; white highlight dots on right side of each

92.

93.

eye; curved lighter brown highlight on left side of eye; two-tone lips with gloss over paint on lower lip; no ears; blonde mohair wig put on in strips; all-felt body and limbs; jointed arms operate together; jointed at shoulders; push-and-pull (zigzag) seam in back of head; machine-stitched on back of body; hand-sewn closing seams on upper arms and legs; mitt hands with separate thumb and fingers indicated with stitching; legs have only one seam in back; darts at knee level on outside of legs; stuffed body and limbs; cotton teddy trimmed with lace; white felt untrimmed dress; pink felt coat with attached cape trimmed with white felt; matching hat; pink button shoes; white silk socks. This doll was purchased in the United States. It is attributed to Poupées Gerb's.

IDENTIFICATION FEATURE: Unusually large eye pupils.
MARKS: None on doll
SEE: *Illustration 93.*
PRICE: $250-450 depending on size and condition of doll

Gre-Poir, Inc.
(France and United States)

The company made two types of fabric dolls, felt and cloth, during the late 1920s and early 1930s. Both are pert and pretty dolls and are very collectible today. Many of them are dressed in organdy with pretty trimming, most often felt. They have two shoe styles:

1. Side button felt slippers (with elastic thread).
2. Leatherette shoes with ties or side buttons (with elastic thread).

The short socks have three colored stripes.

There were at least three different wig styles. The poodle wig (see *Illustration 94*) is very curly. The softly waved "marcelled" wig was a little longer (see *Illustration 95*) and a straighter style with bangs (see *Illustration 96*).

The Gre-Poir dolls are rare but once in a while a new model shows up in the doll market. Recently, pictures of a little cowboy have been seen.

For further general characteristics, see Identification Guide, page 230.

Cowboy: 18in (46cm); for general characteristics, see Identification Guide, page 230; blonde "Buster Brown" wig; gray felt pants and cowboy hat; white, brown and gray checked shirt; red kerchief at neck; sheepskin chaps; leather belt; black button shoes with elastic.
MARKS: None
SEE: *Illustration 94* (Color Section, page 224).
PRICE: $600-700

Cloth Doll in Organdy Dress: 17in (43cm); for general characteristics, see Identification Guide, page 230; reddish-brown "poodle" wig; dressed in all original clothes; silk teddy; green organdy dress with five ruffles on skirt; draped collar; unusual hat with two tiers of ruffles protruding over actual

95.

97.

hat; both dress and hat trimmed with blue, gold and pink felt flowers; leatherette tie slippers; socks with three lines of color.
MARKS: None on doll
SEE: *Illustration 94* (Color Section, page 224).
PRICE: $450-600+

Girl with Felt Face and Limbs: 17in (43cm); for general characteristics, see Identification Guide, page 228; brown wig; organdy dress with tiny stripe of blue and yellow trim; blue felt hat trimmed with felt flowers; felt slipper shoes with elastic thread closing; late 1920s-early 1930s.
MARKS: None on doll or dress
SEE: *Illustration 95. Betty Houghtailing Collection.*
PRICE: $600-700

Girl with Cloth Face and Limbs: 17in (43cm); for general characteristics, see Identification Guide, page 228; dressed in organdy dress with felt bodice; ruffles at bottom of dress; organdy hat with felt trim; felt bows on skirt; late 1920s-early 1930s.
MARKS: None on doll or dress
SEE: *Illustration 96.* (Page 232). *Diane Domroe Collection.*
PRICE: $600-700

Doll Not Photographed
Balsam Baby: Cloth doll; molded, painted mask face; partial wig; jointed at neck, shoulders and hips; mitt hands with separate thumb and fingers indicated by stitching; circa 1930s.
MARKS: "Pat. Pending Trade Mark Reg.//Balsam Baby//Healthful Cuddling Doll//Easily cleaned with//art gum//Gre-Poir, Inc." (tag)

82

Gund Manufacturing Company

Santa Claus Music Box: 16in (41cm); cloth mask face; red corduroy Santa Claus suit used as body and hat; black corduroy boots; fur trim; jingle bells for buttons; painted face with eyes similar to Mollye's cloth dolls; metal winder for music box in back of body; plays "Jingle Bells;" late 1930s. **MARKS:** "Gund Mfg. Co.//J. Swedlin, Inc. succ." (tag sewn into side of body) **SEE:** *Illustration 97.* **PRICE:** $100-150

Harwin & Co.

Harwin manufactured Steiff look-alike felt dolls from 1915 to 1921, during World War I. They were not required to honor the German patents while England and Germany were at war.

Among the dolls they made were British, Scottish and French soldiers and sailors, clowns, *Brownies*, family dolls, cooks, *John Bull, Pierrot, Aborig-ines, Arabs, Sheiks, Boy Scouts, South Sea Islanders, Topsy, Bo Peep, Red Cross Nurse, Father Christmas, Fumsup, Indians, Rosebud, Snow Boy, Tinkles, Wobbles, Zulu Chief,* educational dolls and many others.

The registered trademarks, the trademarks and copyrights appearing in italics/bold within this chapter belong to Harwin & Co.

Hauser Company (Hausser) (Austria and Germany)

In 1922 the Emil Pfeiffer Co. sold a hard material for doll making to the Hauser Company who later used it for dolls under the name of the Hausser Company.

In the mid 1920s there was a series of reorganizations of a company that made dolls in Vienna. It was operated for short periods by such owners as Hubert, Hans and Fritz Pfeiffer; Otto Hausser; and finally Emil Pfeiffer & Sons. Emil Pfeiffer also had connections in Köppelsdorf-Sonneberg in Germany. The company is known to have made doll parts in both Germany and Austria.

About 1923 Emil Pfeiffer made a doll called *Hubsy* which had either a felt or composition head. This doll had tiny dots for eyebrows and short, oddly-shaped legs. By 1927 the company was making a Lenci-type felt doll. The doll in *Illustration 98* is similar to *Hubsy,* and it does have "Hauser" printed on the shoe. This doll is only attributed to Hauser until more dolls are located.

The registered trademarks, the trademarks and copyrights appearing in italics/bold within this chapter belong to Hauser Company.

Hauser (Vienna, Austria)

Girl: 15in (38cm); ribbed (similar to stockinette), beautifully painted face with eye shadow; dressed in blue felt dress; yellow felt blouse; white felt skirt trimmed with pink and blue felt appliqued flowers; matching white hat; circa late 1920s.

This is a very pretty art doll.

MARKS: "MSAL//Hauser//Wien" (stamped on bottom of shoe inside a triangle)

SEE: *Illustration 98. Elizabeth Martz Collection.*

PRICE: $300-350

The registered trademarks, the trademarks and copyrights appearing in italics/bold within this chapter belong to Hauser Company.

98.

Hausman & Zatulove

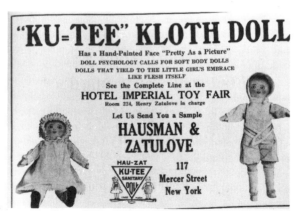

"KU=TEE" KLOTH DOLL

Has a Hand-Painted Face "Pretty As a Picture"

DOLL PSYCHOLOGY CALLS FOR SOFT BODY DOLLS
DOLLS THAT YIELD TO THE LITTLE GIRL'S EMBRACE
LIKE FLESH ITSELF

See the Complete Line at the

HOTEL IMPERIAL TOY FAIR

Room 224, Henry Zatulove in charge

Let Us Send You a Sample

HAUSMAN & ZATULOVE

HAU-ZAT
KU-TEE
SANITARY
DOLL

117 Mercer Street New York

99.

"Ku-tee" Kloth Doll: A line of dolls with hand-painted faces and soft doll bodies. Their advertisement said, "Doll psychology calls for soft body dolls//dolls that yield to the little girl's embrace like flesh itself." The company logo showed a triangle with "Hau-Zat//Ku-Tee//Sanitary//Doll" and a doll on each side of the triangle.

SEE: *Illustration 99. Playthings,* January 1920.

The registered trademarks, the trademarks and copyrights appearing in italics/bold within this chapter belong to Hausman & Zatulove.

84

Hecht, Else (Munich, Germany)

Regional Couple from Germany: Man 11in (28cm); woman 10½in (27cm); all-felt, wool hair on lady; felt hair on man; bead eyes; man has black felt provincial suit and red shirt; woman has black felt skirt with red, orange and black felt trim; felt vest, white cotton blouse; red felt pillbox (provincial) hat; oilcloth-type shoes on man; felt slippers on woman; cloth baby with yarn hair; circa 1920s.

These dolls are from the Pryor collection (see page 5). Else Hecht made many sizes and types of dolls including a tea cozy and an egg warmer. They were made in the workshop of Else Hecht in Germany between 1920 and 1930. She was one of the artists working with the Munich Art Doll Group. Others included Brunhilde Einenkel, Elise Israel, Betty Krieger, Dora Petzold, Lotte Pritzel and Strasser.

100.

MARKS: "Hecht Puppe" (tag)
SEE: *Illustration 100. Diane Domroe Collection.*
PRICE: $175 pair

The registered trademarks, the trademarks and copyrights appearing in italics/bold within this chapter belong to Else Hecht.

Holzer & Cie (S. Paulo, Brazil)

Holzer & Cie competed in Brazil with the Perotti Doll Company. They made similar dolls in many sizes. However, no connection between the two companies has been uncovered. They made tourist dolls as well as large play dolls. Some of their dolls were sold to mail order doll companies in the United States, including Kimport.

The faces and limbs of the dolls have a dark flesh color and their costumes are very colorful. They usually are tagged with the company name or just "Made in Brazil."

Girl with Guitar: Approximately 27in (69cm); dark skin; pink felt Spanish dress with blue, red, white, black and yellow felt trim; Spanish pillbox hat with attached scarf; playing a guitar; jointed at neck, shoulders and hips; painted fingernails with black line above red paint; circa late 1920s-early 1930s.
MARKS: "Fabrica de bonecas 'Mariposa'//Holzer & Cia -S.Paulo//R.S.

The registered trademarks, the trademarks and copyrights appearing in italics/bold within this chapter belong to Holzer & Cie.

85

Ephigenia 379-Ind. Bra" (paper tag glued to clothing)
SEE: *Illustration 101. Mary Merritt Museum.*
PRICE: $400-500

101.

102.

Boy and Girl from Bahai, Brazil: 9in (23cm); felt head and limbs; cloth body; girl dressed in orange felt skirt and shawl which are decorated in multi-colored felt pieces and felt rickrack; dotted red blouse and apron; boy dressed in orange felt pants and green felt hat; dark cotton plaid shirt; red rayon scarf; both have clogs with cardboard soles; 1938-1940s.
MARKS: "Made in Brazil" printed on bottom of shoe; "Kimport//Dolls// Independence, Mo.//This doll was made in//Brazil" (cloth tag sewn to clothing)
SEE: *Illustration 102.*
PRICE: $50-60 pair

E.I. Horsman & Aetna Doll Company

In 1919 the Aetna Company merged with the Horsman Company to form the E.I. Horsman & Aetna Doll Co.

Manikin Dolls (French Models): This picture was the cover of the March 1920 *Playthings*. There is very little information available about these dolls. They appear to be cloth. Their long legs are an indication of the French boudoir vogue; 1920.
SEE: *Illustration 103. Playthings*, March 1920.

Dolly Jingles: Approximately 20in (51cm); oilcloth, either smooth or mottled; several different color com-binations including blue and pink, blue and yellow, and brown and blue; tinkly bells fastened to her costume; 1923.
SEE: *Illustration 104. Playthings*, November 1923.

\ new doll creation of t: I. Horsman Co. that has very favorably received called "Dolly Jingles." gains her name from se: tinkly little bells fastened her costume. The latte: made of oilcloth, either sm. or mottled, and is colore: several different combinat: Some of them are pink, blue, blue and yellow, br: and blue, etc. "Dolly Jing: is about 20 inches high.

104.

ANIKIN DOLLS
FRENCH MODELS
FINE QUALITY SILKS
TNA DOLL CO.

103.

Ideal Toy and Novelty Company

105.

is printed on the costume. Dolls in the set include:

N1 *Little Miss Muffet*
N2 *Little Bo Peep*
N3 *Mary Had a Little Lamb*
N4 *Mistress Mary — Quite Contrary*
N5 *Queen of Hearts*
N6 *Daffy Down Dilly*
N8 *Little Boy Blue*
N9 *Tom Tom, the Piper's Son*

Queen of Hearts: Dressed in organdy dress decorated with red hearts. **MARKS:** "The Queen of Hearts" (printed near the bottom of the skirt) **SEE:** *Illustration 105. Margaret Benike Collection.* **PRICE:** $500-650

Scarecrow: 16in (41cm); pink sateen mask face; raised triangular eyebrows; raised button-type eyes; sculptured nose; yellow yarn hair; arms and legs sewn to white cloth body; back seam on head is machine-sewn; back seam on body is hand-sewn; black flannel coat with patches; black felt hat and shoes; pink flannel pants with patches; brown flannel mitt hands with separate thumb; 1939. The Ideal *Judy Garland* doll and the *Scarecrow* were

In June 1939 Ideal published a catalog of their line for the year. Ideal was an innovator in the doll field and they were making many fine dolls throughout the 1930s. Although they are best known for their composition dolls, their cloth dolls are very collectible.

Storybook Dolls: 16in (41cm); stuffed with kapok; mask face; washable hands; turning head; worsted straight hair with bangs; picture book dressed in the traditional storybook costumes. The name of each character

The registered trademarks, the trademarks and copyrights appearing in italics/bold within this chapter belong to Ideal Toy and Novelty Company.

Continued on page 97.

Lenci Oriental Man (see page 127).

Lenci Miniature Flower Boy (see page 122).

Lenci Rope Jumper
(see page 129).

Lenci *Fetish* (see page 121). *Ester Borgis Collection.*

Lenci Mascotte men (see pages 120, 123 and 124).

Lenci *Fad-ette Cigarette Girl* (see page 143).

93

Lenci #110 girl in red with smooth face (see page 136).

Lenci pocketbook (see page 122).

94

Lenci Girl with Pompadour Costume (see page 130).

Lenci #149 early girl in green (see page 131-132).

Lenci Oriental Lady (see page 197). *Jeannette Fink Collection.*

made when the *Wizard of Oz* was released in 1939.
MARKS: None
SEE: *Illustration 106. Lois Janner Collection.*
PRIZE: $250-300

In the 1930s punchboard games were the vogue in candy and other novelty stores. In 1938 when she was a child, Jean Kelley of Belvidere, New Jersey, won the complete set of *Snow White and the Seven Dwarfs* when she punched out the winning number. All of her dolls still retain their beautiful color and original clothing and *Dopey* is still near his beloved *Snow White*.

Seven Dwarfs: For general characteristics of the dwarfs, see *Illustration 108*. Dwarfs from left to right are *Sneezy, Happy, Grumpy, Dopey, Sleepy, Doc* and *Bashful*.

Snow White: Dress has a white skirt with cartoon characters printed on it; blue bodice and cutout puffed sleeves.
Jean Kelley reports that her set did not come with the toy lanterns and picks.
MARKS: None on dwarfs; "Snow White" and drawings of the dwarfs on the skirt of Snow White.
SEE: *Illustration 107. Jean Kelley Collection.*
PRICE: Complete set $1500-2500 + depending on condition of dolls, labels, boxes, and so forth.

Disney Dwarfs: 12in (31cm); overall body slim and petite; pressed oilcloth-type mask face; painted face; machine-stitched closing on back of

106.

head; side seams on head; body flesh-colored cotton with overcast hand-stitching on back seam; legs part of body; shoes are black felt sewn to body; cardboard in soles so doll can stand; coats of suede-like material; twill cotton pants; arms are oilcloth-like material; gauntlet hands with only four fingers; 1937.

Each of the dwarfs came with a lantern and pick for use in the mines. This is clearly shown on the tag. However, there is evidence that some sets of dwarfs did not have these tools originally.

107.

108.

Doc: Tan coat; light brown pants; gold hat; lamp and metal pick are attached to his belt; glasses painted on face; springs in legs; "Doc" painted in blue on hat with widely spaced capital letters.

When dwarf is pressed down, the springs produce a whistle and the dwarf jumps up and down.

IDENTIFICATION FEATURE: Springs in the legs.

MARKS: "Snow White//and the// Seven Dwarfs//c1937//W.D.ENT." (one side of tag); "Authentic//Walt Disney's//Snow White//-and the Seven Dwarfs//Made in U.S.A. by// Ideal Novelty and Toy Co." (other side of tag)

Another tag on a dwarf is reputed to say "..one of Walt Disney's whistling Dwarfs. Dance us up and down. We whistle while we work.."

SEE: *Illustration 108.*

PRICE: $200-250 each

Dopey: Gold coat; dark blue pants; lavender hat; large felt ears; "Dopey" painted in blue on hat with widely spaced capital letters.

98

Irwin & Company, Inc.

Novelty Stuffed Toys: A line of cloth stuffed dolls and animals; 1930. **SEE:** *Illustration 109. Playthings,* January 1930.

PLAYTHINGS   January, 1930

NOVELTIES IN STUFFED TOYS

Our line of Novelty Stuffed Animals and Dolls offered for the first time in 1929 met with such an enthusiastic reception that we have enlarged the line for 1930, adding many new numbers for your inspection. These Stuffed Novelties measure up in every way to the well known IRWIN standards of originality and quality. They are well made, colorful, different and BIG VALUES at 50c and up retail.

We Are Now Located in Our New, Convenient Showrooms at

27-33 WEST 20th STREET
BETWEEN 5TH AND 6TH AVENUES
NEW YORK CITY

Visit our new showrooms and see the wide range, uniqueness, clever costumes, and profit possibilities of our line of Stuffed Novelties.

IRWIN & COMPANY, Inc.

Also Makers of Infant Dresser Sets, Celluloid Toys, Rattles, Airships, Etc., including Numerous New Features

109.

Josselyn

This mail-order company carried a line of cloth dolls. They sometimes came in pairs. They had mask faces and some have been attributed to Mollye.

John & Priscilla: 12in (31cm); painted hair; pictured in *House & Gardens,* December 1937. The advertisement said, "A couple to warm the heart of any child. They are exquisitely made in blue and white Pilgrim costumes;" attributed to Blossom.

George and Martha Washington: 12in (31cm); dressed in satin, brocades and lace; white wool wigs; circa 1937-1938; attributed to Mollye.

Seth and Amanda: 12in (31cm); Civil War dolls; mask face with side-glancing eyes; boy dressed in Civil War schoolboy-style costume with ankle-length pants, short jacket and cap; the girl was dressed in a flowered print school dress with a high bonnet; advertised in *House Beautiful,* December 1939; attributed to Mollye.

110.

Uncle Sam and Columbia: 12in (31cm); (see *Illustration 110* for a picture and description). Columbia wore a star-sprinkled white dress; striped hat; yellow yarn hair; attributed to Mollye.

Also available in the 12in (31cm) size were *Captain Smith* and *Pocahontas* and a *Gay 90s* couple. **PRICE:** $65-85 each

Uncle Sam: 12in (31cm); pink mask face; muslin body; hand-sewn seam in back of head; seam on both sides of body; no seam up the back; no defined fingers; painted face; delicate Mollye-type eyelashes; Mollye-type mouth; white yarn hair and beard; dressed to represent Uncle Sam; red striped pants; cuffs on sleeve; tie; blue jacket and sash; white shirt; trimmed with silver paper stars; blue top hat; black leather shoes; all original; 1939-1940.

A photograph of this doll was in the Josselyn mail order catalog. Uncle Sam's partner was *Columbia* who was dressed in a star-sprinkled white dress. Her red striped hat matched *Uncle Sam's* pants.

MARKS: None on doll; hand-written tag said, "Uncle Sam//from//Daddy//Christmas 1940"
SEE: *Illustration 110.*
PRICE: $65-85
COMPANY: Attributed to Mollye.

Louise R. Kampes Studio (Kamkins)

The Louise R. Kampes Studio of Atlantic City, New Jersey, was a cottage-type industry. The studio supplied patterns and cloth to home sewers. They also made a line of clothing which could be purchased separately. They maintained a shop in Atlantic City, and children of families who vacationed there yearly looked forward to purchasing new doll outfits.

The dolls were sold in places other than Atlantic City. Riemann, Seabrey Co. advertised in *Playthings*, April 1920, that they were direct representatives of Kampes American Kiddies. In 1920 they wholesaled for $150 a dozen.

Boy in Checked Coat: 19½in (50cm); painted molded mask face; stuffed cloth body; deep color on face; kinky, curly hair; dressed in brown houndstooth, double-breasted wool coat with plain collar; flaps on two pockets; matching tam with brown ribbon trim; well-made white shirt with top-stitched trim; heavy white pants; leather shoes; white cotton socks; 1919 through 1920s.
MARKS: None
SEE: *Illustration 111. Betty Houghtailing Collection.*
PRICE: $1000-1200

Girl in Blue Coat: 19in (48cm); painted, molded mask face; stuffed cloth body; reddish-brown wig with straight hair and bangs; blue wool double-breasted coat with fur collar and tam; white leather shoes; white socks; 1920s.
MARKS: None on body
SEE: *Illustration 112. Betty Shriver Collection.*
PRICE: $1000-1200 +
$1600-1800 for 24in (61cm) doll

Karavan (Italy)

Swiss Girl: 10in (25cm); for general characteristics, see Identification Guide, page 231; dressed in black felt dirndl; white cotton blouse; white print skirt with black felt trim near bottom of skirt; green apron; black felt headpiece trimmed with high black pleated net; Lenci miniature look-alike; circa 1930s.
MARKS: "Karavan//Made in Italy" (cotton tag sewn into back of skirt); "Suizzera" (paper tag glued to underpants)

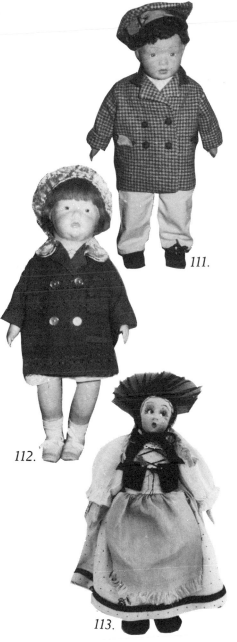

111.

112.

113.

SEE: *Illustration 113.*
PRICE: $25-50

101

Kimport Dolls

No book about cloth dolls of the 1920s and 1930s would be complete without mention of the wonderful dolls imported regularly from foreign lands by Kimport of Independence, Missouri. The newsletter that was published by the company was eagerly awaited by many doll collectors.

Usually the dolls were of the finest quality available and many people who could not afford to travel treasured these dolls. Several of the cloth dolls are shown in this book.

The author has found that many collections include one or more of the dolls tagged with the Kimport label.

King Innovations

114.

Rose O'Neill announced that King Innovations was the sole licensed manufacturer of the soft *Kewpie* and *Whoopy Clowny.* They were fully protected by copyrights, trademarks and U.S. Patent No 1,785,800.

The illustration shows Rose O'Neill with her *Kewpie* family at Toy Fair in February 1931.
SEE: *Illustration 114. Playthings,* March 1931.

The registered trademarks, the trademarks and copyrights appearing in italics/bold within this chapter belong to King Innovations.

Knickerbocker Toy Co., Inc.

Little Girl Cloth Dolls: Knickerbocker advertised cloth dolls with washable faces in *Playthings,* July 1935. They are very similar to Mollye, Georgene Averill and Krueger dolls.
SEE: *Illustration 115. Playthings,* July 1935.
Illustration 116. Playthings, July 1935.

Disney Dwarfs: Heavy oilcloth-type pressed mask faces; seam at sides of head; inside-out machine-stitching on

head; painted expressive face; body made from velveteen in various colors; back of body hand-sewn; legs part of structure of body; cardboard in bottom of feet to make them stand; arms stitched on at shoulders; cotton gauntlet hands; extra piece of velveteen at waistline to give illusion of belt and bottom of coat; embossed metal

The registered trademarks, the trademarks and copyrights appearing in italics/bold within this chapter belong to Knickerbocker Toy Co., Inc.

115.

buckle; slightly pointed brown velveteen feet, slightly curved upward; late 1930s-early 1940s.

Dopey: 11½in (29cm); large cotton ears; open mouth with teeth; lavender pants; yellow coat; blue felt belt; orange hat; "Dopey" painted in printed black capital letters; some letters on slight slant.

Sleepy: 12in (31cm); gray mohair beard; gray pants; pink coat; blue felt belt; lavender hat; "Sleepy" painted in

116.

printed black capital letters; some letters on slight slant.

Knickerbocker also made a similar composition dwarf.

MARKS: "Walt Disney's//Snow White and//the Seven Dwarfs" (one side of tag); "America's//Premier Line of//Stuffed Toys//Walt Disney's// Mickey Mouse//and//Donald Duck// Manufacturers//Knickerbocker Toy Co.,Inc.//New York City" (other side of tag)

SEE: *Illustration 117.*
PRICE: $150-200

117.

Mickey Mouse: In July 1935 the Knickerbocker Toy Co., Inc., advertised a *Mickey Clown* and *Two-Gun Mickey* in *Playthings*, April 1935. SEE: *Illustration 118. Playthings*, April 1935.

118.

Konroe Merchants

119.

The Parisienne: 25in (64cm); real wig; cigarette in mouth; suits of assorted bright colors; saucy facial expression; can be placed in many poses; 1924. SEE: *Illustration 119. Playthings*, November 1924.

The registered trademarks, the trademarks and copyrights appearing in italics/bold within this chapter belong to Konroe Merchants.

Krueger, Richard

Richard Krueger made many cloth dolls throughout the 1920s and 1930s under his company name. Mr. Krueger was also involved with other companies who marketed dolls, such as King Innovations (see page 102). The variety of dolls is amazing and excellent examples of his art are very collectible. They feature "stuffed ani- mal-type" toys, but they also made regular dolls. Many of his dolls used oilcloth for bodies, the costumes or both. Most of the time they are well marked. Look on the body of the doll or inside the clothing for labels.

The registered trademarks, the trademarks and copyrights appearing in italics/bold within this chapter belong to Richard Krueger.

104

Four Disney Dwarfs (from left to right): 12in (31cm); cloth pressed molded face; head has side seams and back seam sewn by hand; painted expressive face; plush beard; body made from velveteen in various colors; back of body hand-sewn; legs part of structure of body; cardboard in feet to make them stand; arms stitched on at the shoulders; polished cotton gauntlet hands; extra piece of velveteen at waistline to give illusion of belt and bottom of coat; felt buckle; brown velveteen feet rounded at the toes; circa 1940s.

Doc: Dark orange coat; gray pants and belt; yellow buckle; "Doc" painted on brown hat in printed capital letters.
Sneezy: Light orange coat; gray pants; yellow buckle; "Sneezy" painted on brown hat in printed capital letters.
Bashful: Lavender coat, light green pants; yellow belt and hat, purple buckle; "Bashful" painted on yellow hat in printed capital letters; longer beard than other dwarfs.
Happy: Dark tan coat with blue belt; bottom of coat is blue; light tan pants; lime green buckle and button; "Happy" painted on tan hat in printed capital letters.
MARKS: "AUTHENTIC//WALT DISNEY//CHARACTER//EXCLUSIVE//WITH//R.G. KRUEGER// NEW YORK" (cloth body tag)
SEE: *Illustration 120.* (Color Section, page *166).*
PRICE: $150-200

Cowgirl: 12½in (32cm); heavy buckram-type mask face with side seams; painted face; eyelashes above eyes; freckles over nose and under eyes;

pretty mouth; fleshtone soft cotton body and limbs; jointed at shoulders and hips; overcast hand stitches in seams of both head and body; mitt hands with no stitching to indicate fingers; feet are slim, pointed and turned up like elf feet; dressed in knit striped shirt and blue cotton pants; red felt cowboy hat with yellow felt trim; 1930s.
MARKS: "K Krueger// N.Y.C." (tag attached to clothing at waist)
SEE: *Illustration 121.*
PRICE: $50-75

121.

MARKS: "K Krueger//* N.Y.C."
(cloth tag)
SEE: Illustration 122. Vivien Brady-Ashley Collection.
PRICE: Rare doll and dog. Price samples unavailable.

Scootles: 10in (25cm) and 18in (46cm); blonde curly hair; side-glancing blue eyes; heavily painted eyelashes; tiny eyebrows over eyes; watermelon-type mouth; dimples in the middle of both cheeks; mitten hands with no seams for fingers; doll designed by Rose O'Neill; introduced for the first time in 1935.
SEE: Illustration 123. Toys and Novelties, October 1935.

Good Morning—Good Night (doll on left): 9½in (24cm); two-sided baby dolls; oilcloth body; painted face.
MARKS: "K. Krueger//N.Y.C." (tag)
SEE: Illustration 124. (doll on left).
Mary Tanner Collection
PRICE: $35-50

122.

Clown with Hoop: Shiny white mask face; curly wool hair; dressed in a white clown suit with red felt trim; red clown hat with white buttons; plush dog with red ears, paws and ribbon.

123. 124.

Girl: 7in (18cm); all-cloth (no oil-cloth); jointed at neck and arms; glazed cotton-type body; yarn hair; painted face; yellow organdy dress trimmed in lace; 1930s.

MARKS: "Krueger, N.Y.//Reg/U.S. Pat.Off//Made in U.S.A." (tag)
SEE: *Illustration 124* (doll on right). *Mary Tanner Collection.*
PRICE: $25-35

Käthe Kruse

At the beginning of the 20th century the winds of change challenged the art world of the Western countries. Käthe Kruse was part of this change. An actress in her teens, she became part of the German cultural world. She met sculptor Max Kruse and fell in love. She wanted to have children but she did not want to get married. She became one of the earliest "modern women" who juggled art, children and finally a career.

When her children wanted dolls, Max, who did not like the stiff china and bisque dolls available in stores, suggested that she make her own dolls. Her first doll was made from a towel filled with hot sand, knotted at the corners to make arms and a potato stuck into one end for a head. Her daughters loved this primitive doll. Challenged and interested, Käthe Kruse developed *Doll I* which was made into the 1930s.

By 1911 she had started a business which has lasted almost an entire century. Her primitive doll has turned into an "art" doll and is considered by many doll lovers to be one of the best.

Never an inexpensive doll, today's collectors seem willing to pay high prices as they vie for the few old Käthe Kruse dolls still in mint condition. They also pay high prices for the lovely new dolls being made each year.

Doll I Identification Features: 16in (41cm)-17in (43cm); washable cloth body; body has seven pieces; very wide hips; legs have five pieces; arms have two pieces; fingers individually stitched; thumbs sewn on separately; pressed cloth head; face hand-painted with oils; made from 1911 into the 1930s.
MARKS: "Käthe Kruse" in script (left foot)

Doll I Boy in Play Clothes: 16in (41cm); red cotton printed dress and tall hat; black feather stitching on front neck opening and cuffs of sleeves; white slip and underpants; red knit stockings; woven straw shoes.

The woven straw shoes and style of the boy's clothing help date this doll. Pictures from 1911 show this costume.
MARKS: "Käthe Kruse" in script (stamped on the bottom of the left foot)
SEE: *Illustration 125* (Color Section, *163*).
PRICE: $3000-3500 (recent auction prices have been high)

Doll I Soldier: For general characteristics, see above. Many of the #1 dolls measure 16in (41cm) instead of the advertised 17in (43cm).

The registered trademarks, the trademarks and copyrights appearing in italics/bold within this chapter belong to Käthe Kruse.

126.

MARKS: "Käthe Kruse" in script (stamped on the bottom of left foot)
SEE: *Illustration 126. Cohen Auctions.*
PRICE: $3000-3500

Doll II Schlenkerchen Identification Features: Also called *Little Floppy Doll;* 13in (33cm); cloth head with back seam; painted hair; one of the few dolls with painted eyelashes; only doll with smiling face; open-closed mouth; head covered with silk stockinette; legs loosely sewn on body; first produced in 1922; production stopped in 1930s.
MARKS: "Käthe Kruse" in script (stamped on bottom on left foot)
PRICE: $1000-1500+

Doll V and VI Identification Features: Two baby dolls used the same head; #V *Traumerchen* had closed eyes; #VI *Du Mein* had open eyes; #V was 18½in (47cm) and weighed about five pounds; #VI was 23in (58cm) and weighed about six pounds; heads were sewn on loosely so that they needed support; sand was used as a weight; at first the hair was painted but from 1930, hand-knotted wigs were used; in 1935 some dolls had a heavy cement-like head; cloth heads were made until 1940.
This doll is often called *Sandbaby.*
PRICE: $3100+

Doll VII Identification Features: 14in (36cm); small *Doll I* body with fewer seams; same sewn-on thumbs and wide hips; the second version of *Doll VII* in 1927 came at first with sewn-on thumb and wide hips; this changed to a slimmer version in the early 1930s. This doll is often confused with *Doll I.* *Illustration 127* shows both *Doll I* and *Doll VII.*

In January 1928, Käthe Kruse ran this advertisement in *Playthings.* She was still selling Series *IA* and *IB.* The

127.

advertisement says *Doll I* is 17in (43cm). Also pictured is *Style VII* which is 14in (36cm). Dolls in upper row from left to right: 1B-137 *Agnes;* 1A-132 *Nellie.* Dolls in lower row from left to right: 1A-131 *Bäbchen;* VII *Leopold; VII Anneliese;* 1B-136 *Kurt.* SEE: *Illustration 127. Playthings,* January 1928.
PRICE: $1200-1500 + (For Doll VII)
     $3000-3500 (For Doll I)

Doll VIII German Child Identification Features: 21½in (54cm); smooth painted mask face; first doll to have swivel head; slender body made with sturdy cotton; disc joint fastening on leg; one arm more crooked than the other; mitt hands with stitches indicating fingers; face modeled after Friedebald, Käthe Kruse's son; fashionable clothing; dolls were wigged to represent both boys and girls; their clothes included raincoats, long party dresses, sports clothes, sailor outfits and play clothes.

Doll VIII German Child: For general characteristics, see above; striped dress; hair in pigtails; high white socks.
SEE: *Illustration 128. Betty Houghtailing Collection.*
PRICE: $1000-2000 +

Doll XII Identification Features: *Hampelchen (Little Jumping Doll);* cloth head with three vertical seams on back of head; very loose legs; button and band on back helped make the doll stand; real hair wig; early 1930s through 1940s. There are several versions of this doll. Sizes include 18in (46cm), 14in (36cm) and 16in (41cm).

128.

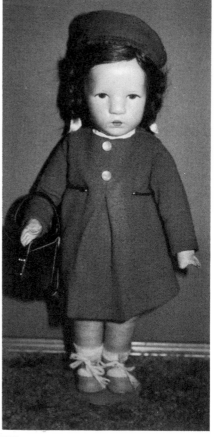

Doll IX Little German Child: 14in (36cm); small version of *German Child;* for general characteristics, see page 109; dressed in red coat and hat; black purse; introduced in 1929 and made into the 1930s.
SEE: *Illustration 129. Betty Shriver Collection.*
PRICE: $1000-1500

Doll X Identifications Features: Small version of *Doll I;* 14in (36cm); molded swivel head; circa 1935.

129.

110

Mme. Kuzara's Portrait Dolls

Art Dolls: According to *Playthings,* Mme. Kuzara's portrait dolls started an art vogue in the United States. She was the wife of a Bohemian inventor who made a series of caricatures of Bolshevist leaders. She also made mannequins for grown-ups. She was an early 20th century leader in the trend to use dolls for accessories rather than just for play.

SEE: *Illustration 130. Playthings,* October 1923.

130.

L.P.A. Bennett Couturier (France)

Girl in Silk Dress: 18in (46cm); hollow one-piece face mask covered with silk stockinette material; machine-stitching on back of head; inset blown glass eyes; painted face; open mouth; molded ears; elastic strung; jointed at neck, shoulders and hips; human hair wig; pink silk body and limbs; mitt hands with separate thumb; stitching indicates fingers; all-silk clothing including underwear and stockings; green dress with plaid trim at hem and collar; beautiful lace apron; silk net hat with ribbon trim; leatherette tie shoes.

MARKS: Picture of rising sun with bird flying in front of it. "L.P.A.//Bennett//Couturier//244.R.Rivoli Paris" (printed on back of doll)

SEE: *Illustration 131.*

PRICE: $250-350 depending on condition of silk clothes

131.

La Rosa Company, Milano-Corso Venezia (Italy)

132.

This company is known to have made *Rudolph Valentino* dolls marked with the company label on the bottom of the foot. The *Eagle* is attributed to La Rosa Company because of the doll's characteristics and labeling. The doll is well made and the costume is supurbly tailored.

Rudolph Valentino as the Eagle: 24in (61cm); mask face of unusual material which imitates felt; lips outlined in thin, deeper red; gray liner on lower lip; brown eye liner in upper eye; white highlight dot in each eye; molded cardboard stiff, hollow body with linen glued on it; arms have a felt-over-wire armature; legs are hollow cardboard; long, narrow felt fingers; second and third fingers indicated only by stitching; other fingers individually constructed; circa 1925-1928.
MARKS: "Made in Italy" (cursive print on a circle seal on the bottom of one foot); "Aquilla" seal (other foot) "Aquilla" is Italian for eagle.
SEE: *Illustration 132. Helen Krielow Collection.*
PRICE: $1400-1800+ (very few sample prices available)

The film *The Eagle* was released in 1925 by United Artists. It featured Rudolph Valentino, Vilma Banky, Louise Dresser, Albert Conti and James Marcus. *The Eagle* was the next-to-last film of Valentino and was an action, adventure film tailor-made for the star. Pictures from the film obtained by the doll's owner show the same costume that the doll is wearing.

Lang, Emile

Emile Lang of France manufactured cloth dolls with molded mask faces which were designed by Albert Guillaume and Jean Ray, well-known artists of the period. Some were dressed as soldiers in authentic costumes. The company had a stand at the Paris Toy Fair in 1917 which *Toys and Novelties* described as one of the most attractive displays. In 1918 they created two cloth dolls called *Little Godmothers of War.* They were named *Lily* and *Claudette.*

Emile Lang was associated with the S.F.B.J. organization although he kept his own independent workshop. Jean Ray created some doll designs for S.F.B.J.

Belgian Soldier: 14in (36cm); pressed mask face and head; oil-painted face and hair; inset tiny glass eyes; open mouth with painted teeth; sculptured ears on mask; papier-mâché hands; cloth body and legs; felt khaki coat; black felt pants with red stripes; leather boots; tiny brass buttons; wooden rifle; ceramic canteen with real cork; cloth bag; circa 1917-1928.

MARKS: "E.L.//Manufacture Francais//Jouettes Tissus//Systém Breveté//" (tag); "Belge" (handwritten on back of tag)

SEE: *Illustration 133* (Color Section, page *164*).

PRICE: $250-300

The registered trademarks, the trademarks and copyrights appearing in italics/bold within this chapter belong to Emile Lang.

Lenci Di E.Scavini (Italy)

From the very beginning of her career as a designer and maker of dolls, Madame Lenci had a vision of dolls which gathered together the trends of the art of the new 20th century. The lines and colors of the daring new art forms danced in her head. She took ideas from the paintings, sculptures, couturier designs, home decorations and architecture of the art deco period and added her own quixotic ideas to make dolls which have ever since danced in our minds and hearts. Starting in 1919 she introduced a line of unusual dolls which immediately became best sellers in Europe and the United States. They were expensive but they sold well, and they were widely imitated.

Her first advertising logo set her apart from earlier doll makers. What other company would design a doll logo showing an oriental doll with an opium pipe eyeing a harem dancer (see *Illustration 134*)?

Madame Lenci was a sophisticated lady with a sophisticated product. Decorators loved her dolls as accent pieces. Fashionable ladies carried her dolls and purses on the famous avenues of the big cities. However, she did not forget the children. In 1923 she advertised, "Develop artistic tendencies in your children. Buy a 'Lenci' Doll" (see *Illustration 168*).

The registered trademarks, the trademarks and copyrights appearing in italics/bold within this chapter belong to Lenci Di E. Scavini unless otherwise noted.

As the 20th century draws to a close, the art deco period is being seen in retrospect as a time of color, dash and fun. Madame Lenci's dolls have found their place in the art of the world. What the French bisque dolls were to the 19th century, the Lenci dolls are becoming to the 20th century.

Shown in the following pages are 70 illustrations and advertisements incorporating 90 dolls. There are many more Lenci dolls but, hopefully, through these pages the reader can learn to identify and appreciate the wonderful art of an inspired lady.

LENCI TABLE OF CONTENTS

The following sections will help you understand how to identify your Lenci dolls more accurately:

1. Company advertisements.
.........................Page *114-119*
2. Lenci novelty dolls. Page *120-122*
3. Illustrations of Lenci dolls by height. ....Page *122-147*
4. Lenci marks and tags. Page *147-148*
5. Chart of Lenci dolls by height including both photographed and unphotographed dolls.
.........................Page *148-149*
6. Body and clothing characteristics in *Identification Guide* at end of book. ....Page *224*

Early Logo: Elena Scavini was a lady ahead of her time. She was a leader in the art deco movement, and her doll art has been popular and widely imitated throughout most of the 20th century. The line of Lenci dolls today used the styles of the old dolls, yet they seem new and exciting.

Her logo was unique, clever and very daring. The doll on the right is smoking an opium pipe and eyeing a harem dancer on the left. **SEE:** *Illustration 134. Playthings*, January 1923.

Early Lenci Dolls Advertised in Playthings 1920-1921

101 Man in apron carrying a chicken
102 Dutch man character doll
103 Dutch girl carrying two buckets
104 Girl dancer in hula skirt
105 Indian
106 Cowboy
107 Bellboy
108 Large, plump, early toddler
109 Series of girl and boy dolls; early ones were coarse
110bis Large, thinner type girl doll than 108
111 Girls including Jump Roper
112 Black boy with grass skirt
113 Large Black man dressed as servant

134.

114 Man with feather in hat
115
116 Pierrot
117 Cartoon-type old man
118 Harlequin
119 Oriental man
120
121 Boy Winkers in several styles
122
123 Large Italian man comic character in pointed hat
124 Football player
125 Roly Poly Clown
126 Large policeman
127 Small girl with pocketbook
128 American Indian

Advertisement for 1921 Line of Lenci Dolls: 100 character dolls, children's dolls and animals were shown at the New York Toy Fair in February 1921. At this time Lenci was also making a line of music boxes in Switzerland.

Among the dolls were a *Harlequin, Pierrot, Islander* in grass skirt, several *Chinamen, Cowboy, Black Bell-*hop, a *Roly Poly Clown, Indian Chief, Sailor,* girl dolls with round faces, *Football Player, Dutch Girl with milk buckets, Old Man with Butcher Apron, Arabian Dancing Girls* and many others.
SEE: *Illustration 135. Playthings,* February 1921.

The first Lenci dolls were very different from the Lenci dolls that evolved a year or two later. However, they were eagerly purchased by quantity buyers at trade shows and retail sales soared. Both of the dolls shown in *Illustration 136* were on the top row of the *Playthings,* February 1921 picture. However, the *Toddler Doll* (on the left) has a white felt ruffled dress which was very attractive when new and sold well. The Dutch Girl carried milk buckets on her shoulders.

#108 Toddler Doll in White Dress: 16in (41cm); all-felt body; rounded, molded face typical of early

135.

136.

Lenci dolls; red mohair wig; flat nose; painted face; heart-shaped mouth; brown eyes with two white dots at upper right corner and lower bottom corner of pupil; tiny eyelashes above eyes; short neck sewn on the flat box-like top of the body; chubby arms and legs; mitt hands with thumb separate; fingers indicated by stitching only; back of head and tops of arms and legs have the familiar push-and-pull (zig-zag) Lenci stitching as does the crotch area; back and front seams are machine-sewn; original white felt dress with red felt piping; 1920-1921.

The simple dresses for these dolls usually had a tie top or a bodice without sleeves. Although lacking detail, they had the Lenci style (see *Illustration 135*).

#103 Dutch Girl: (Missing her wooden buckets and yoke) 16½in (42cm); six-piece cloth body; felt head, arms and legs; push-and-pull (zigzag) stitching on head, top of arms and legs; human hair wig; ears are single piece of felt, not double stitched; character face is more sculptured than *Toddler's*; painted side-glancing eyes with one highlight in upper left corner of pupil; upward slanting eyebrows; brown eyelashes above eyes; closed mouth with one white dot on lower lip; mitt hands with separate thumb; fingers indicated by stitching only; blue felt bodice; red and blue gored felt skirt; red felt trim at waist and collar; green scarf; white Dutch hat; white cotton apron with blue and white striped cotton inset at top; Lenci silver nail attached at bottom of apron; 1921.

This doll, and the other dolls in the bottom row of the Lenci advertisement, were simple by comparison with the later dolls. However, they have the Lenci charm and are easy to identify.

MARKS: None for the *Toddler*; silver nail on the apron of the *Dutch Girl* is engraved "Lenci"

SEE: *Illustration 136.*

PRICE: Not enough sample prices available

#106 Cowboy: 18in (46cm); early doll shown in October 1920 advertisement in *Playthings*; all-felt; felt mask face not pressed as hard in the mold as later dolls; mitt hands; red felt shirt; dark blue felt vest; blue kerchief; dark cowboy hat; leather and fur chaps; laced leather boots; 1920.

MARKS: Small Lenci silver nail attached to vest

SEE: *Illustration 137* (doll on right). *Eleanor Broden Collection.*
PRICE: $1500 up (very few sample prices available)

#116 Pierrot: 20in (51cm); early doll shown in October 1920 advertisement in *Playthings;* all-felt; felt mask face not pressed as hard in the mold as later dolls; expressive face; mitt hands; black and white *Pierrot* costume; carried string musical instrument; made in several sizes including 17½in (45cm) and 25in (64cm); also came in other colors including beige, green, red and orange; this doll has early beret cap without felt feather which came on later dolls; 1920.
MARKS: Small Lenci silver nail on bottom right edge of skirt
SEE: *Illustration 137* (doll in middle). *Eleanor Broden Collection.*
PRICE: $1500 up (very few sample prices available)

Opium Pipe Smoker: Approximately 18in (46cm); early doll; very thin all-felt body; felt mask face not pressed as hard in mold as later dolls; eyes almost closed; dreamy expression on face; third and fourth finger indicated by stitching only; stitching indicated toes; brilliant orange and light brown felt robe and turban; turquoise and orange undershirt with appliqued trim; white felt short pants gathered at knees; leg bracelets; early 1920s.
MARKS: Small Lenci silver nail on inside seam
SEE: *Illustration 137* (doll on left). *Eleanor Broden Collection.*
PRICE: $1500 up (very few sample prices available)

#108 Early Little Girl Dolls: 16in (41cm); all-felt; for general characteristics, see *Illustration 136* (doll on left). This was one of the very earliest of the Lenci advertisements, October

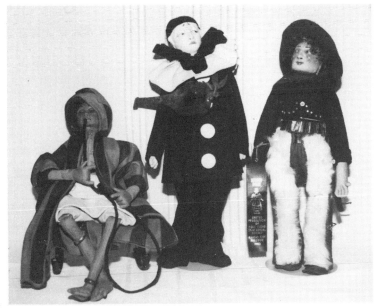

137.

SCAVINI DOLLS MADE IN TURIN, ITALY

These dolls are made of felt, hand painted and without any face seam. They are dressed in a great variety of styles. The finest cloths in bright colors are used.

Included in the line are Indians, Cowboys, Milkmaids, Fishermen, Pierrots, Harlequins, and many other odd and attractive figures.

138.   STUFFED ANIMALS OF UNIQUE DESIGN

1920. The dolls resembled the Campbell Soup Kids which were very popular at that time.

#110bis Girl: The larger girl is shown in the center of the picture in *Illustration 138.*
MARKS: Several of these dolls have been found with the Lenci nail somewhere on their clothes or body
SEE: *Illustration 138.*

#109 Boys and Girls (Upper row of advertisement): Series of boy and girl dolls.

#112 Black Boys (Upper row of advertisement): Black boy with grass skirt.

#121 Winker (Lower row of advertisement): From left to right, dolls #1, #3, #4 and #5; boys winking one eye; dressed in various boys' costumes of the period; bare feet; cap.

#107 Bellboy (Lower row of advertisement): From left to right dolls, #2 and #7; uniform with brass buttons.

#128 American Indian (Lower row of advertisement): From left to right dolls #6 and #8; dressed as Indians; long braided hair.
MARKS: These dolls usually have a silver nail with Lenci engraved on it fastened to their clothes or bodies
SEE: *Illustration 139. Playthings,* November 1920.

139.

Early Doll with Early Tag: One of the earliest known tags; long tag with fancy border.
MARKS: "Made in Italy//Lenci" in large script (tag on early doll)
SEE: *Illustration 140. Playthings, June 1923.*

Sports Series: 17½in (45cm); in 1929 Lenci advertised "The Classic in Dolls" when they introduced their *Sports Series.* These dolls were also made in other sizes. However, one of the most popular of the sizes was the #300. There were small changes in the costumes of individual dolls over the years.
SEE: *Illustration 141. Playthings, January 1929.*

140.

141.

142.

143.

Button (nail) Used on the Early Lenci Dolls: These were tiny silver-colored nails which were similar to the buttons used by Steiff. The buttons were placed in various positions on the bodies and/or clothing of the dolls. They were placed between fingers, fastening the tags on clothing, in the ear, between toes, on legs, and so forth. A large early sheriff doll had the button inside his gun holster which fastened the holster to the doll.

The very earliest Lenci dolls had a smaller button which had "Lenci" in engraved, capital letters (see *Illustration 136*).

MARKS: "Lenci" (engraved in script on the button)

SEE: *Illustration 142. Nancy Smith Collection.*

Novelty Heads: 1in (3cm)-2in (5cm); Lenci heads only; felt loops attached to hats; used for decorations in automobiles, homes, and so forth. Left to right:
1. Head of *Carbiniere* (policeman) (see *Illustration 148*) (Color Section, page 92).
2. *Man with Pipe* (possibly pirate); red hair and beard; black hat; wooden pipe.

3. *Bellhop* with red hair; rust-colored hat and neck piece.

All three dolls have wonderful expressive faces.

MARKS: "Lenci Torino" (ribbon tag)

SEE: *Illustration 143. Sherry Balloun Collection.*

PRICE: $75-80

144.

Novelty Heads Placed Inside Flowers in a Clay Pot: 1in (3cm)-2in (5cm); each head has a different color wig with a different hair style; felt flowers are shades of yellow, green and lavender.
SEE: *Illustration 144. Pat Vallancourt Collection.*
PRICE: $400-500

Head of Boy on Top of Wicker Basket: Head 2in (5cm); total height of basket and head 7in (18cm); blue and white golf hat; white collar; red tie.
SEE: *Illustration 144. Pat Vallancourt Collection.*
PRICE: $275-300

#287 Pincushion Fetish Pan: 7in (18cm); green pincushion and face; orange, rose, purple and red felt in layers for hat; yellow and green leaves; all original; original box has very early tag; 1922-1928.
MARKS: "Lenci (script) E.Scavini// Turin (Italy)//Made in Italy//287//Pat Sept 8-1921-Pat.N.142433//STE 8 G.D.G. x87395 BREVETTO 5173" (label on box)
SEE: *Illustration 145* (Color Section, page *92*). *Ester Borgis Collection.*
PRICE: $400-500

Pocketbook: 16in (41cm); all-felt lady; poke bonnet stitched together to form handle; painted face; side-glancing eyes; off-the-shoulder dress; light blue top and over ruffle; medium blue under ruffle; navy blue gathered skirt with strips of white felt trim; flowers on skirt have eight layers of felt including purple, dark red, light red, orange, peach, yellow, green and navy blue; green quilted leaves; bouquet has multi-colored flowers with five layers of felt; red quilted bows on skirt; imitation pin at neckline has five layers of felt; orange and gold poke bonnet; flowers on hat have four layers of felt; inside of purse lined in gold felt with pockets.

Many other manufacturers of felt dolls also made pocketbooks (see *Illustrations 82* and *288)*; vests (see *Illustration 221)* and other clothes for adults and children.
SEE: *Illustration 146* (Color Section, page *94).*
PRICE: $400-600 (rare; very few sample prices available)

Mascotte and Miniature Dolls: Although both types of dolls have similar paint on their faces; some of the dolls have thicker, wider eyelashes. This seems to change the expression on the face. The earlier dolls have more delicate eyelashes and general coloring. The author has seen only these two types of facial paint on the small dolls (see Title Page).

For other general characteristics, see page 149.

#2000C Mascotte Boy Selling Flowers: 8½in (22cm); loop at top for hanging doll; raised eyebrows; "surprised" look on face; tan jacket appliqued with green pieces of felt in crisscross pattern; tan pants with brown patches; blue scarf appliqued with green felt circles; brown felt clogs; woven felt basket; multi-colored felt flowers; white felt handkerchief with yellow crisscross design in pocket. This very early *Mascotte* is a wonderful example of the detailed art of Lenci.
MARKS: The tag is an earlier tag indicating the doll was made between 1922-1928. "Lenci (script) E. Scavini//Turin (Italy)//Made in Italy//2000c//Pat.Sept 8-1921-Pat.N.142433//STE 8 G.D.G. x87395 BREVETTO 5 1 173" (tag)
SEE: *Illustration 147* (Color Section, page *90).*
PRICE: $300-400

Mascotte Skier: 8½in (22cm); raised eyebrows; green ski jacket and pants with yellow crisscross trim on bottoms of pants and sleeves; white shirt; green vest with same crisscross trim; green army-style hat; yellow felt wig; white gloves tied with tan felt; heavy brown cobbled shoes; wooden skis and ski poles; late 1920s. Similar ski outfits were made in other styles and sizes (see *Illustration 190)*. The 12in (31cm) *Winker* also came with a ski costume. Lenci girl dolls had matching ski outfits.
SEE: *Illustration 148* (Color Section, page *92).*
PRICE: $300-400

Miniature Bersagliere (Soldier): 9½in (24cm); heavily raised eyebrows; dark green army uniform with pink felt epaulettes on black collar; black boots with felt uppers and black cobbled lowers; brass buttons; army hat with feather and insignia of Italy in

red, white and green felt; painted wooden dagger in sheath; very dark gray shirt; black tie; 1930s.
This doll was brought back to the United States by a family who traveled to Italy often in the 1930s.
SEE: *Illustration 148* (Color Section, page *92*).
PRICE: $300-350

Miniature Lombardia Girl: 9½in (24cm); for general characteristics, see page 149; thick, wide eyelashes; pink felt dirndl with light blue trim; lace trim at neck; black braided felt head cover; gold decorations on cover; white embroidered organdy apron with ruffle; 1930s.
MARKS: "Lenci//made in Italy" (ribbon tag); "Lenci//Torino//Made in Italy" (silver-colored tag)
SEE: Illustration on Title Page.
PRICE: $300-350

Miniature Carlos: 9½in (24cm); for general characteristics, see page 149; thin small eyelashes; black felt pants, coat and hat with red trim; white shirt; black tie; brown felt shoes; white socks with red trim at top; 1930s.
MARKS: "Lenci//made in Italy" (ribbon tag); "Lenci//Torino//Made in Italy" (silver-colored tag)
SEE: Illustration on Title Page.
PRICE: $300-350

Miniature Carabiniere (Policeman): 9½in (24cm); black police uniform of the period with red felt side stripes; the coat has "tails," red stripes outline these tails with embroidered black patches; two sets of buttons on coat; high collar with embroidered patches and metal stars; regulation police hats with blue and red feathers; hat has insignia of Italy in red, white and green; wooden curved sword in scabbard; 1930s.
SEE: *Illustration 148* (Color Section, page *92*).
PRICE: $300-350

Miniture Mountain Hiker: 9½in (24cm); slightly raised eyebrows; green felt jacket with tan trim; short tan lederhosen with dark blue suspender straps trimmed with felt stars; blue necktie; white felt shirt; brown backpack; Alpine flower in his hand; 1930s.
An Alpine outfit was used on different sizes and styles of Lenci dolls. They are not all exactly alike, but they are similar.
MARKS: "Lenci" (bottom of both feet)
SEE: *Illustration 149*.
PRICE: $300-350

There are many dolls which have stories. However, Lenci dolls seem to have collected special tales through the years. Here is one of them:

In the early 1930s Mussolini needed money. To win favor with the House of Savoy, Mussolini named a new luxury liner the *Conte di Savoia*. A costumed Sardinian doll was placed for sale in the ship's store for the maiden voyage in November 1932.

The famous movie star Gloria Swanson was a passenger on that first voyage and purchased the doll as a gift for her maid's daughter.

Late in the voyage, a turbine blew a hole in the side of the ship and the workers in the hold sent word to the captain that they only had about five hours until the ship would sink. How-

149.

ever, as in any really good story, a sailor managed at the last minute to get some wet concrete to plug up the hole and keep the water out for the last 900 miles of their journey to New York. The doll reached the arms of the little girl.

Fifty years later the doll stands proudly in the author's home. He is in a case with his other Lenci friends.

Miniature Sardinian Boy: 9½in (24cm); slightly raised eyebrows; black felt provincial coat and boots with orange trim; tan shirt and tan gathered pants; brass buttons; unusual

Sardinian black felt cap with brim; the long point of the cap comes down past his shoulder; 1932.
MARKS: "Lenci//Made in Italy" (ribbon tag in back of coat)
SEE: *Illustration 150* (Color Section, page *164*).
PRICE: $300-400

Army Mountain Soldier: 9½in (24cm) miniature; green Italian army uniform; dark gray shirt with black tie; lower pants wrapped in intricate pattern to permit easier mountain climbing; brass buttons; backpack with ropes for climbing on back; wooden dagger attached to belt; cobbled brown shoes with 12 cleats on each shoe for climbing; army hat with red pompon and feather.
There were many military dolls made with the Fascist uniforms of the Mussolini regime. Their tiny uniforms are very well-tailored.
SEE: *Illustration 150* (Color Section, page *164*).
PRICE: $300-350

Miniature Russian Girl: 9½in (24cm); nationality doll; orange heavily-embroidered felt jumper with white felt down center of jumper and around bottom of skirt; skirt further trimmed with edgings of yellow felt; white cotton blouse with blue and orange felt rickrack; sleeve hand-embroidered in buttonhole stitch; high felt headpiece trimmed with gray felt and white and blue pompons; many blonde curls over forehead and long braids; red felt embroidered boots; pants and slip edged in red rickrack; carried painted wooden pig; 1930s. This costume is used on dolls of differ-

ent heights including very large dolls.
MARKS: "Lenci (in script) Turin// Italy//Di E. Scavini//Made in Italy// L/131/Pat.Sept.8,1921- Pat.N142433//Ste8 G.D.G.X 87395 Brevetto 5016178."
SEE: *Illustration 151* (Color Section, page *167*).
PRICE: $300-400

American Indian: 11in (28cm); red fringed Indian outfit; white band around head; wide grinning mouth with teeth; large side-glancing black eyes; black "war paint" on face; long black pigtails braided with felt; early 1920s (see *Illustration 139*) (Advertisement).
MARKS: Silver nail in toe engraved with "Lenci"
SEE: *Illustration 152. Nancy Smith Collection.*
PRICE: $800-900+

Russian Boy: 10in (25cm); bright red hair; wide grinning mouth with four teeth showing; head fits into socket; body is jointed at neck, shoulders, elbows, hips and knees; rose felt jacket with white embroidered felt trim; brown pants; green embroidered boots; high brown Russian-style hat; early rounded mitt hands with three middle fingers indicated only by stitching; all original; holding wooden jar and musical instrument; early 1920s.
For information on *Indian* doll, see above; for information on *Islander* doll, see page 133.
SEE: *Illustration 152. Nancy Smith Collection.*
PRICE: $400-500+

125

152.

153.

Amore: 11in (28cm); beautiful blonde wig; gold bonnet; green felt bodice; pink, white and black plaid skirt; green ruffle with pink trim around bottom of skirt; white organdy ruffled sleeves with pink felt trim; carries red polka dot hatbox with "Amore" printed on it; late 1930s doll with smooth felt face and legs with single seam in back.
SEE: *Illustration 153. Pat Vallencourt Collection.*
PRICE: $800-900

Lenci Boy Winker: 11½in (29cm); closed mouth; right eye almost closed to give the appearance of winking; tan felt pants with brown felt patches at knees; black felt coat; red felt scarf; gold Tyrolean hat; black wig; 1920.

This was advertised in the November 1920 *Playthings* (see *Illustration 139*).

In the early 1930s a later version of the *Winker* was dressed in winter Alpine costumes.
SEE: *Illustration 154. Pat Vallancourt Collection.*
PRICE: $900-1000

Man Smoking Opium Pipe: 12in (31cm); oriental; almost closed eyes; tiny opening for opium pipe (missing from picture); dressed in yellow felt oriental coat with elaborate green trim; black pants with orange appliqued Chinese design; black hat; long queue; large green and yellow felt shoes which are large and flat enough to allow doll to stand alone; individually stitched fingers; used on Lenci trademark in 1922-1923 (see *Illustration 134*). Small metal teapot is not original.
SEE: *Illustration 155.* (Color Section, page *89*).
PRICE: $2200-2400+

Girl in Red Checked Dress: 12in (31cm); cotton checked dress; ruffle at bottom of dress; red felt hat, sash and slippers; white collar; felt face; mid 1930s-late 1950s.
MARKS: "Lenci//Torino//Made in Italy" (round silver cardboard tag); "Ti Porto Fortuna" (heart-shaped pretty paper tag with flower painted on it)

154.

156.

SEE: *Illustration 156. Esther Schwartz Collection.*
PRICE: $700-800+

#2000/E Girl in Coat and Hat Outfit: 12in (31cm); complete felt body; third and fourth fingers indicated by stitching only; reddish hair; tan felt coat and hat with maroon trim and buttons; tan slippers.
This doll has a tag that was used between 1922-1928.
MARKS: "Lenci (script) Di E. Scavini//Turin (Italy)//Made in Italy//2000c//Pat.Pending 8-1921 P.N. 142433//STE 8///G.D.G. X87395 Brevetto 5 1 173"
SEE: *Illustration 157. Pamela Farr Smith Collection.*
PRICE: $700-800+

157.

Child in Red Scarf: 12in (31cm); slightly rounded cheeks; slightly molded eyebrows; no stitching in ear; third and fourth fingers indicated by stitching; seam in back of leg only; seam at ankle; blue felt dress with pattern indicated by blue crisscross stitching; circle of same color felt sewn at intersection of each crisscross pattern; knee-length panties trimmed in red felt; half slip trimmed in red felt and attached to skirt; white apron with lace trim; red felt scarf; unusual Lenci-type socks with red stripes; wooden clogs with red felt strap which holds them on feet.
SEE: *Illustration 158. Helen Krielow Collection.*
PRICE: $700-800

158.

#111/5 Rope Jumper: 13in (33cm); one of Lenci Sports Series; green felt waisted dress; very full felt skirt in green and white checked design; large white bow in hair; stitching on toes; 1925-1926.

A Lenci dress with a waistline is less common than a yoked dress. Other styles for a *#111* doll included dresses with matching cloches, romper outfits and coat ensembles.

Other Lenci dolls with jump ropes include #109/30 22in (56cm); 32in (81cm); occasionally these dolls will have coiled braids at side of head.

SEE: *Illustration 159* (Color Section, page 91).

PRICE: $800-900

#450 0/S Girl in Blue: 13in (33cm); blonde hair; raised eyebrows; blue coat with brown and beige diamond-shaped felt squares at hemline; short pink dress trimmed with blue felt; blue felt cloche with rippled effect on brim; big blue felt bow on cloche; pink felt tie slippers; white Lenci socks; cloth body; stitching indicates toes; 1927-1930s.

This style number was made into the 1930s also using the same height. The dolls were costumed in many ways.

MARKS: "Lenci//Made in Italy" (ribbon tag)

SEE: *Illustration 160.*

PRICE: $700-800

Lombardia Girl with Spindle: 14in (36cm); Lucia face with raised eyebrows; white organdy apron and collar; carries wooden spindle with yarn; mid 1920s-1940s.

This doll also came in a miniature size without the spindle; (see title page).

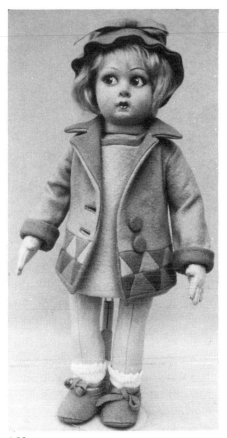

160.

MARKS: "Lenci//Made in Italy" (cotton ribbon tag)

SEE: *Illustration 161. Esther Schwartz Collection.*

PRICE: $1000-1500

Lucia Face Madame Pompadour Costume: 14in (36cm); historical costume; pink organdy ruffled dress; wide ruffled sleeves; ruffled panniers; varigated pink rope with green leaves down the front of dress; roses sprinkled individually on full skirt; head-

161.

163.

piece of matching roses; blonde hair inserted into felt head at hairline; wig pulled back into tight corkscrew curls at back of head; a curl on each side of face; raised eyebrows; no stitching on toes; 1930s. This costume, or a variation of the costume, was used on dolls of different heights. Usually the hair style was similar.

SEE: *Illustration 162* (doll) (Color Section, page *95*).

Illustration 163 (face) (Color Section, page 95).

PRICE: $1000-1500+

Lucia Face Dutch Costume: 14in (36cm); nationality costume; red felt skirt with band trimmed in red at bottom; red and white checked apron; heavily embroidered sleeveless red top; white blouse with red felt trim; white starched Dutch hat; wooden shoes; carried a flower pot with one large red and purple tulip; raised eyebrows; no stitching on toes; 1930s.

SEE: *Illustration 164* (Color Section, page *90* and front cover).

PRICE: $700-900

Not Photographed:
Smooth Lucia Face Doll: For general characteristics, see *Illustration 177*; 14in (36cm); smooth mask face that looks like composition; dusty pink and white cotton print dress; high yoke with full skirt with points at hem; organdy ruffle around pointed skirt; deep pink rickrack trim on skirt and teddy; Lenci-type teddy with attached petticoat; 1930s.

For a picture of the smooth mask that looks like composition, see *Illustration 177.*

MARKS: "Lenci//Made in Italy" (ribbon tag sewn on dress)

PRICE: $450-550

165.

Black Islander: 16in (41cm); large eyes and mouth; dressed in grass skirt; has early Lenci nail in ear; all original; 1920s.
MARKS: Silver nail in ear engraved "Lenci"
SEE: *Illustration 152. Nancy Smith Collection.*
PRICE: $900-1100 +

#149 Girl in Green: 16in (41cm); early Lenci doll with less sculptured and coarser felt face; curly hair; all-felt body; fingers indicated by stitching only; thumb separate; for other general characteristics, see Identification Guide, page 232; teddy trimmed in lace; separate slip with hemstitching;

Boy with Flowers: 14in (36cm); Lucia face; raised eyebrows; 1939-1941.
MARKS: "Bambola Italia//Lenci// Torino//Made in Italy" (red letters on white); used for this series of dolls in foreign clothes
SEE: *Illustration 165. Pat Vallencourt Collection.*
PRICE: $600-700

Boudoir Lady: 15in (39cm); long-limbed; dreamy, slitted eyes; long blonde pigtails; white dress with full ruffled skirt; ruffles caught up with large yellow butterfly; hat same color as butterfly; black ties on hat; yellow high-heeled pumps; 1920s.
SEE: *Illustration 166. Pat Vallancourt Collection.*
PRICE: $900-1100 +

166.

131

green felt dress with unusual pattern; front top and skirt panel cut in one piece; the other skirt panels are in two layers with the underskirt the same color as dress. The shorter overskirt is mustard color; matching cloche hat; hat and dress trimmed with multi-colored flowers; matching green shoes; Lenci short socks; stitching indicates toes; (see *Illustration 168* for advertisement of doll); 1923.
SEE: *Illustration 167* (Color Section, page 96).
PRICE: $800-1100

Advertisement "Buy a 'Lenci' Doll": The boudoir, or adult doll, was a hit in Paris, and doll makers in many countries were striving to be among the first to make them. Lenci advertised that they developed artistic tendencies in children and advised they could be placed on hassocks, lend color to the boudoir or decorate the corner of your limousine.

The small doll at the left wears the same style dress as the very early doll in *Illustration 167* (Color Section, page 96). The doll on the right is shown in *Illustration 192*.
SEE: *Illustration 168. Playthings,* May 1923.

#119 Chinese Man: Approximately 16in (41cm); blue embroidered felt coat with large applique; dark blue felt pants with light blue felt trim; gold shirt with Chinese writing on it; black Chinese hat; red wooden clogs; handlebar mustache; open mouth with teeth showing; ear has only single seam instead of regular Lenci double ear seam; all fingers defined by stitching only; 1920.
This doll was one of the first Lenci dolls advertised in *Playthings* magazine, October 1920.
MARKS: Lenci silver nail in ear inscribed with "Lenci"
SEE: *Illustration 169. Juanita Walker Collection.*
PRICE: $2500-3000

#300/63 Scandinavian Girl: 17½in (45cm); mohair wig; cloth body; third and fourth fingers indicated by stitching only; navy blue wool skirt with front panel of multi-colored hand-woven wool; white embroidered blouse with long sleeves; green flowered print jumper with red trim; hemstitched teddy and attached petticoat; separate hemstitched petticoat with crocheted lace trim; black felt pointed hat with red trim and pompons; no stitching on toes; cloth body; 1930s.
#300 was used for an international

168.

series of matching boy and girl pairs.
SEE: *Illustration 170* (Color Section, page 162).
PRICE: $850-950

#300 Girl in Green Coat with White Gloves: 17½in (45cm); green dress with white collar; green felt coat and hat trimmed with felt flowers; white gloves; circa 1925-1926.
The tag indicates that this is an early doll. However, the #300 series was not in the Lenci catalogs until 1925/1926.

MARKS: "Prodvzione//Orginale// Lenci" (cardboard tag on coat)
SEE: *Illustrations 171 and 172. Esther Schwartz Collection.*
PRICE: $2000-2750

171.

172.

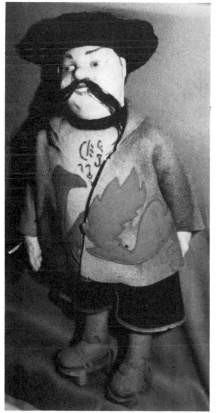

169.

#300 Mussolini Fascist Boy: 17½in (45cm); military-style uniform of the Jungvolk which was an organization preparing boys to become part of Fascist movements (Mussolini believed that a uniform effaced all individuality and could mold future generations of warriors); doll has swivel head; painted side-glancing eyes; mohair wig; dressed in gray wool short pants; black shirt with patch; blue kerchief; fez-style hat with tassel; cobbled leather shoes; late 1920s into the 1930s.

This costume was used on other dolls with different style numbers.

SEE: *Illustration 173. Richard Wright Collection.*

PRICE: $1100-1500

Dolls from Left to Right:

#1500 Pouty Girl: 17½in (45cm); highly sculptured face with plump cheeks, closed mouth; hollow body,

173.

174.

134

felt-covered plump torso; seam line at ankle; pierced ears and earrings; felt pink and white checked original dress; pink felt shoes; Lenci short socks; carries jump rope; shown in 1930 catalog.
SEE: *Illustration 174. Jeanette Fink Collection.*
PRICE: $1500-1800

#178K Smiling Fat-Cheeked Girl: 16in (41cm)-17in (43cm); slightly pigeon-toed; individual fingers; Bavarian dirndl; green felt jumper; white blouse with inset embroidered pink felt; blue and black striped felt apron; felt hat with embroidery trim; cobbled red and black leather tie shoes; carries basket with brightly-colored flowers; circa mid 1920s.
SEE: *Illustration 174. Jeanette Fink Collection.*
PRICE: $1800-2200

#300/S Tyrolean Boy: 16in (41cm)-17½in (45cm); felt lederhosen pants; green felt jacket with brown felt trim and brass buttons; blue felt Tyrolean hat with felt feather; blonde curly hair; 1927 into 1930s.
SEE: *Illustration 174. Jeanette Fink Collection.*
PRICE: $850-950

#178K Smiling Fat-Cheeked Girl: 16in (41cm)-17in (43cm); slightly pigeon-toed; individual fingers; white felt dress with large blue polka dots; black felt bolero; felt striped underskirt; white, yellow, and black felt checked kerchief; red hair; brown and black felt slippers; carries beautiful painted blue, red and yellow basket; circa mid 1920s.

175.

SEE: *Illustration 174. Jeanette Fink Collection.*
PRICE: $1800-2200

Back Row from Left to Right:
Oriental Dancer: (see *Illustration 195*)

#300/56 Lapland Girl: 16in (41cm)-17½in (45cm); white felt dress with red embroidered trim; white cotton underslips; red felt Laplander high hat with embroidered trim; blue felt and tan leather Laplander boots; 1927 into 1930s.
SEE: *Illustration 174. Jeanette Fink Collection.*
PRICE: $850-1000

#110 Girl in Pink: 18in (46cm); pink organdy dress with ruffles on skirt; white felt scalloped bolero which ties at neck; white felt bonnet with pink organdy trim on top; white leather tie shoes; beautiful wig with long curls; cloth body; third and fourth finger separated by stitching only.

This is an example of how similar styles with minor variations were used on dolls of different heights and style numbers (see *Illustration 186*).

SEE: *Illustration 175* (doll) *Illustration 176* (face) (Color Section, page *161*).
PRICE: $900-1100

#110 Smooth Face Girl: 18in (46cm); serene face; pressed felt mask face that looks like composition; delicately painted eyes and face; rosy cheeks; red felt dress with a band of green on the skirt and sleeves; white, yellow and gray flower on middle of skirt; same flowers around band on skirt; white felt collar; large red and green bow in hair; dark blue high Lenci-type socks; dark blue soft leather shoes with white stitching trim; late 1920s or early 1930s.

The Lenci company made this very smooth felt doll in other styles and size numbers. They were competing with the popular composition dolls.
MARKS: "Lenci//Made in Italy" (ribbon tag)
SEE: *Illustration 177*. (Color Section, page *94*).
PRICE: $800-1000 up

Man With Beard: 18in (46cm); hollow felt mask head; felt over armature body; very light stuffing; can be posed; black fur hat and beard; unusual side-glancing painted eyes; eyebrows have three slanted lines; unusual red felt mouth, circle cut like a "lifesaver" placed over a black painted line; one upper tooth; one lower tooth; black and white knitted sweater; black felt pants and moccasin-type shoes are part of body construction; mitt hands with separate thumb; circa late 1930s into the 1950s. A very similar rag-type doll has been available in the 1980s line of Lenci dolls.
MARKS: "L 8000//2 44 06" (blue and white sticker on Lenci box)
SEE: *Illustration 178* (Color Section, page *162*).
PRICE: $150-200 (rare; very few sample prices available)

Dickens-type Boy: 18in (46cm); brown suit and top hat; maroon vest and tie; white shirt; spats; carrying a wooden cane; 1920s-1930s. This was also made in other sizes including 23½in (60cm) which is tagged #174.
SEE: *Illustration 179. Richard Wright Collection.*
PRICE: $850-1050

Girl Carrying Basket: 19in (48cm); blue and dark orange plaid skirt; embroidered blue felt top with lace collar; two strands of metal beads; 1940s. This doll was made in several sizes.
MARKS: "Modello Deposititato// Lencis//Torino//Made in Italy" (square white tag with green print; doll on tag has checked skirt)
SEE: *Illustration 180. Esther Schwartz Collection.*
PRICE: $850-1050+

Duck Figure: 19in (48cm)-20in (51cm); white felt animal with burnt orange legs; deep rose cloak; purple

136

shield trimmed in rose with appliqued cross; carries metal sword; large green and purple cavalier hat with large plume; 1940s.

The Lenci company made many types of novelty items. There are many imaginative animals that today are difficult to identify because they have lost their Lenci tags.

MARKS: Red print on white background tag "Modello Depositato// Lenci//Torino//Made in Italy" (figure of doll in background)

SEE: *Illustration 181. Elliot Zirlin Collection.*

PRICE: $1000-1300

180.

181.

179.

183.

182.

Tag: Red print on white background; figure of girl doll in background. This tag was found on a sword-fighting cavalier duck (see *Illustration 181*).
MARKS: "Modello Depositato// Lenci//SA//Torino//Made in Italy"
SEE: *Illustration 182. Elliot Zirlin Collection.*

Widow with Terrier: 20in (51cm); googly glass eyes; individually sewn fingers; mourning dress; wig has long blonde curls down the back; black hat with net trimmed with red flowers and green leaves; white and gray terrier; mid 1930s.
MARKS: Dolls usually had round silver tags "Lenci//Torino//Made in Italy"; tags were used from the mid 1930s
SEE: *Illustration 183. Gloria Robinson Collection.*
PRICE: $2200-3000

#500 Girl in Blue Coat: 21½in (55cm); later doll with smoother felt face; blonde pigtails; blue coat with red, white and blue plaid trim and red buttons; matching plaid skirt; has look of an older child; late 1930s-early 1940s.
MARKS: Tag with green print "Modello//Depositato//Lencis//Made in Italy"; picture of doll in checked skirt

184.

SEE: *Illustration 184. Christine Lorman Collection.*
PRICE: $1100-1200

#500 Boy in Leggings: 21in (53cm); green embroidered jacket; tan sweater and pants; green cap; 1930s.
Boy dolls were only about ten percent of the Lenci production.
SEE: *Illustration 185. Esther Schwartz Collection.*
PRICE: $1100-1200

#109 Girl in Pink: 23in (58cm); pink organdy dress with rows of ruffles on the skirt; pink felt bolero jacket which ties at neck; pink felt rickrack trim on jacket; pink felt bonnet with pink organdy trim; pink felt tie shoes; third and fourth fingers separated by stitching; older felt faces; 1925-1928. This is an example of how similar styles with minor variations were used on dolls of different heights and style numbers (see *Illustration 175*).
SEE: *Illustration 186. Richard Wright Collection.*
PRICE: $1200-1400

#109/107 Tennis Player: 23in (58cm); variation of popular tennis player of the Sports Series; long beige pants; knit sweater; all original in box; 1925/1928.
MARKS: "Lenci Turin (Italy)//Di E. Scavini//Made in Italy//#107// Pat.Sept. 8-1921-PAT N. 142423// STE S..G.D.G.X 87395 BREVETTO 5 1-173" (paper tag)
SEE: *Illustration 187. Esther Schwartz Collection.*
PRICE: $2800-3000+

#109/79 Girl: 23in (58cm); white organdy dress with large dark blue polka dots; dark blue coat and shoes;

185.

186.

139

187.

188.

dark blue matching hat with red ribbon trim; side-glancing eyes; reddish hair; late 1920s to early 1930s.

The #109 doll was one of the most popular dolls. There were approximately 135 different outfits over a long period of time.

MARKS: "Lenci (script)//Di E Scavini//Turin (Italy)//Made in Italy //109//79//Pat. Sept.8-1921.- Pat.N.142433//STE 8 S.G.D.G. x87395 Brevetto 501 178"

SEE: *Illustration 188. Richard Wright Collection.*

PRICE: $1200-1400

#109 Girl with Vegetables in Basket: Short brown hairdo; white cotton blouse; dark green vest with red ties; bright multi-colored skirt made with strips of felt; Lenci socks; black slip-on felt shoes; holding sturdy basket filled with felt vegetables; 1940s.

MARKS: "Modello Depositato// Lenci//Torino//Made in Italy" (green and white tag with figure of doll wearing a short checked skirt)

SEE: *Illustration 189. Esther Schwartz Collection.*

PRICE: $1750-1850

Boy Skier: 24in (61cm); dark blue ski pants; green and white sweater with triangle pattern; matching ski hat; striped socks; cobbled shoes; thick, sturdy skis and ski poles.

MARKS: "Lenci//Made in Italy" (ribbon tag)

SEE: *Illustration 190. Countess Maree Tarnowska Collection.*

PRICE: $4500+ (very few sample prices available)

Boudoir Doll: 24in (61cm); slitted eyes; open mouth with painted teeth;

Madame Pompadour hair style, but a different style dress; white organdy dress with full sleeves; lovely felt flowers appliqued on skirt; pink sash; white organdy headpiece with ruffles; carries a powder puff; 1920s.
SEE: *Illustration 191. Pat Vallancourt Collection.*
PRICE: $1800-2100

190.

189.

191.

Boudoir Lady with Apron: 24in (61cm); blue felt dress; full skirt with two scalloped ruffles; white apron; white trim at neck and bottom of sleeves; picture hat with inner ruffles; hat trimmed with flowers; normal side-glancing eyes; bouquet of felt flowers in her hand; costume was first advertised in *Playthings*, May 1923 (see *Illustration 168)*. This was a popular costume and it was made in many different style numbers and heights. SEE: *Illustration 192. Shirley Buchholz Collection.* PRICE: $1500-1800

#165 Blonde Boudoir-type Doll: 24in (61cm)-25in (64cm), depending on how the doll is measured; pink organza dress; scalloped collar with felt rickrack trim; felt flowers at belt line and scattered over full skirt; pink picture hat trimmed with pink felt rickrack; sultry, slitted eyes; third and fourth fingers indicated only by stitching; pearls. SEE: *Illustration 193. Nancy Smith Collection.* PRICE: $1400-1800

Fad-ette: 25in (64cm); cloth body with felt over upper body; felt head, arms and legs; curly blonde mohair wig sewn on in strips; double-stitched ears; painted felt mask face; slitted eyes; thick eyebrows; thin eyelashes below eyes; red heart-shaped mouth with hole for cigarette; jointed at head, shoulders, waist and hips; also stitching makes elbows and knees jointed; handsewn onto arm separately; individual thumb and fifth fingers; middle three fingers indicated by stitching only; black felt pantsuit with turquoise and black striped trim;

192.

193.

turquoise felt buttons; pearl necklace; high-heeled soft leather shoes; 1923.
SEE: *Illustration 194* (Color Section, page 93).
PRICE: $1000-1800+ depending on condition (very few sample prices available)

Oriental Lady: 26in (66cm); very slim body and head construction; felt face; cloth body with swivel waist; painted Oriental features; illusion of elbows and knees with use of stitching; first, second and third fingers sewn together; felt dress with cream-colored top with dark red trim; dark red skirt with appliqued figures in various earth-tone colors; high-heeled feet and shoes; unusual pointed head-dress; circa 1921-1924.
This type of doll was dressed in several different ethnic costumes. For body construction, see Identification Guide, page 232.
SEE: *Illustration 195* (Color Section, page 96). *Jeanette Fink Collection.*
PRICE: $2200-2500

Googly-Eyed Girl: 26in (66cm); rare painted googly eyes looking straight ahead; peach organza dress; very long green organza scarf tied in bow around neck; green organza ruffled head-piece; fingers sewn separately; probably one of the *Seasons Series* (see page 159).
SEE: *Illustration 196. Countess Maree Tarnowska Collection.*
PRICE: $2700-2800

196.

197.

143

#165/21 Madame Bovary: 27½in (70cm); slightly slitted eyes; polka dot full skirt; white top; string of pearls; bluish-green sash, cape and feathered hat; carries a parasol; 1927-1928. **SEE:** *Illustration 197. Fran Tillotson Collection.* **PRICE:** $1500-2000

#165/15 Lolita: 27in (69cm); boudoir type; slitted eyes; Spanish-style curl in the middle of the forehead; gold dress; lace ruffles at bottom of full skirt; lace mantilla; fan; 1927-1928. **SEE:** *Illustration 198. Fran Tillotson Collection.* **PRICE:** $1500-2000

Boudoir Type: 28in (71cm); slitted eyes; white organdy dress with rose, pink, and tiny yellow flowers; green leaves on skirt; long blonde curls; face is reputed to be a model of Lillian and Dorothy Gish; late 1920s. **SEE:** *Illustration 199. Pat Vallancourt Collection.* **PRICE:** $1500-2000

Russian Cossack: 28in (71cm); special extra piece at neck which allows the head to move freely; unusual swivel joints at shoulders and waist which allow these dolls to be posed freely; seam at elbows; third and fourth fingers indicated by stitching; same face as Oriental doll (see *Illustration 195*, Color Section, page 96); the painted eyes are wide open; thin, pointed face and nose; red hair; blue felt tunic and top of hat; black felt pants and band on hat; replaced boots (the original were white leather with red piping; well-known costume; (see

198.

199.

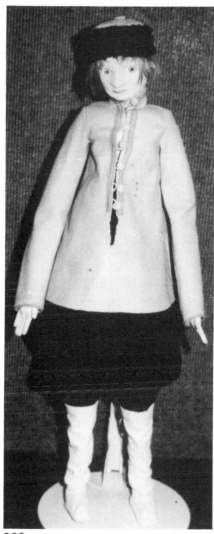

200.

Identification Guide, *Illustration 306* for undressed doll showing unusual construction).
SEE: *Illustration 200. William Zito Collection.*
PRICE: Not priced because of condition of doll

201.

Closeup of Rudolph Valentino Doll and Two Boudoir Dolls: From an advertisement showing the permanent showroom at 167 Madison Avenue in New York City. Other dolls can be seen in cases.
Rudolph Valentino: 29in (74cm); beautifully sculptured face; dressed in beige felt pants; lushly appliqued short jacket and wide belt; red and beige striped coat; dark, long turban; intricate decorations on leather boots with tassels; 1928.
SEE: *Illustration 201. Playthings,* March 1928.
PRICE: $12,000-$15,000

Lady in Pink Ruffled Dress: 38in (96cm); boudoir-type doll with long legs; pensive look on face; normal side-glancing eyes; brown hair with long curls; deep ruffles on skirt; ruffles trimmed with pink felt rickrack; short puffed sleeves; black felt ribbon around neck; pink felt bonnet with white inner ruffles; yellow and white felt flowers on hat; 1925-1926. This may be one of the #180 Series.

145

202.

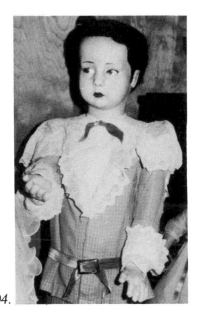

204.

203.

SEE: *Illustration 202. Countess Maree Tarnowska Collection.*
PRICE: $2900-3100

#800 Girl with Yellow Braids: Calf-length white organza dress with hoop; white organza scarf; red flowers in hair; black sash; black low-heeled wooden clogs with yellow flower trim; ruffled pantalets; side-glancing eyes; face has "scared" look.
MARKS: "Lenci" (on foot)
SEE: *Illustration 203. Vivien Brady Ashley Collection.*
PRICE: $2000-2600

Boy Mannequin: 41in (104cm); swivel head; brown side-glancing eyes; dark eye liner; white eye dots; red dots in nose; closed mouth; brunette mohair wig; felt covered wooden torso; felt-covered metal arms and legs, separately attached; adjusts to various poses; intricate pivot torso attachment under costume; boy wears period suit

146

with lace-collared shirt; blue and white checkered suit; 1920s.

MARKS: "Lenci Torino" (inscribed on wooden base); "Kirsh and Reale, New York" (metal label on wooden base of body)
SEE: *Illustration 204. Betty Shriver Collection.*
PRICE: $3000 up (very few sample prices available)

Ways Lenci Marked Their Dolls

1. Silver nails inscribed with Lenci in either print or script used in very early dolls; circa 1921-1922.
Found on different parts of the body or on clothing.
(See *Illustrations 136* and *142*).
2. Tag with fancy border used on very early dolls; circa 1921-1923.
"Made in//Italy//Lenci" (printed on tag)
(See *Illustration 140*).
3. Tag with fancy border; circa 1923.
"Provdvzione//Original//Lenci"
(See *Illustration 172*).
4. Tag on doll or glued on box; used for most of the 1920s.
"Lenci di E. Scavini//Turin(Italy)//Made in Italy/(Number of doll)//Pat.Sept.8,9121,Pat.N.142433//Bre SGDG x87395. Brevetta 501.178"
(See *Illustrations 145* and *187*).
5. Cotton ribbon attached to clothes; circa mid 1920s-1950.
This is the most common Lenci tag. "Lenci//made in Italy"; sometimes there is also a round silver-colored Lenci tag with this ribbon tag.
(See illustration on Title Page).
6. Tag on doll; circa 1930s.

"Bambino No.2//Lenci Turin//Italy//Scavini//Pat.Sept.8,1921//Pat.N. 142433//Bre. S.g.d.g. x87395 Brevetto 501.178"
7. Tag on doll; circa 1930s.
"Provduzione//Originale//Lenci//Torino//Made in Italy"
8. Black ribbon tag with silver letters; circa mid 1930s-early 1940s.
"Ars Lenci//Made in Italy Torino//New-York. Paris. London"
9. Pretty heart-shaped tag on doll; mid 1930s through 1940s.
Painted with pretty flowers and designs; "Ti Porto Fortuna;" other tags may have "Piena dei Greci" or name of doll or place of costume.
(See *Illustration 156*).
10. Silver-colored tag; circa mid 1930s through to 1960s; some of the small hard plastic dolls have this tag.
"Lenci//Torino//Made in Italy"
(See *Illustration 156*).
11. Flowered tag with green border; circa late 1930s.
Name of provincial costume on tag.
12. Large square tag; circa late 1930s-early 1940s.
"Bambola.Italia//Lenci//Torino//Made in Italy"
(See *Illustration 165*).
13. Square tag with doll wearing checked skirt and large bow in hair, holding flowers; tag came in several colors; circa 1940s.
"Modello Depositato//Lencis//Torino//Made in Italy"
(See *Illustrations 180* and *182*).
14. Purple or black stamp on bottom of foot; circa 1930s.
"Lenci" or "5"
Many collectors believe that it is not a Lenci unless it has this

stamp on the foot. However, this stamp wears off quickly. The author has only seen it a few times. For more identification features, see Identification Guide, page 230.

Height Chart for Identification of Lenci Dolls

It is recommended that readers first check their unidentified cloth doll, point by point, with the list of Lenci characteristics (see Identification Guide, page 232). If there is a chance that the doll might be a Lenci, this Height Chart will help the reader narrow down the possibilities. HOWEVER, IT IS IMPORTANT TO REMEMBER THAT THIS IS NOT A COMPLETE LIST. Lenci made many dolls and novelties through the years and different ones seem to appear regularly.

Because of the method of manufacture and the differences in costumes of the dolls, measurements cannot always be accurate. In checking the height of your doll, please check the lists 1in (3cm) more and 1in (3cm) less than your own measurement.

If a particular doll costume was a best seller, it was often used on dolls of different heights and models. Only a few of these are listed in the following chart.

1in (3cm)-2in (5cm)

There are many tiny heads of Lenci dolls made as decorative hangings or novelties for homes or automobiles (see *Illustration 143* and *144).*

6½in (17cm)

A few dolls similar to the *Mas-* *cottes* and *Miniature* dolls can be found in this unusual height. An example is a tiny caddy to a *Mascotte* golfer.

7in (18cm)-7½in (19cm)

1. Although smaller than the *Mascottes,* a few of these types can be found in this height. Examples are tiny girls and a very small prizefighter.
2. *Fetishes* very often represented *Pan* or other Greek gods. They were considered good luck tokens. They were hung in homes and automobiles in both the United States and Europe. Their heights ranged up to 10in (25cm).
3. #276 *Cupid.*

8in (20cm)-8½in (22cm)

Mascottes:
1. There is usually a felt loop for hanging it as a decoration.
2. *Mascottes* usually have a better quality than the *Miniatures.*
3. The eyeballs are not quite as round as the *Miniatures.*
4. Their faces have a surprised look.
5. They have raised, sculptured eyebrows.
6. There is stitching to indicate toes.
7. The body pattern has slightly more shaping.
8. They have most of the Lenci characteristics (see Identification Guide, page 230).

Many thousands of these small dolls were manufactured as the demand for the larger dolls decreased during the depression years. Many of these dolls were imported into the United States by mail order companies such as Kimport and Elsie Krug. Along with the later *Miniatures,* in the 1930s these small dolls provided a good share of the company business.

1. Most of the *Mascottes* are dressed in foreign or provincial costumes and often came in pairs.
2. Some *Mascottes* are dressed in the same styles as the larger dolls. These are rarer and usually command higher prices than the provincial dolls.
3. Some of the *Fetishes*, such as *Pan* and #297, a Satyr, are this size.
4. *Mascottes* often have accessories that, in themselves, are pieces of art (see *Illustration 147* and boy in Title Page, felt flower basket and *Illustration 148* skis).

Unusual *Mascottes* include:

1. #309 Doll seated on a tortoise.
2. #310 Doll seated on a shell.
3. #604 Workbag made in shape of a rose with a doll's head in it.
4. #612 Workbag doll wearing a regional costume.
5. #2000 This number was given to several different sizes and styles of dolls (see *Illustration 147*).
6. #3005 and #3007 Girls with short skirts and panties showing.
7. #3011 Boy in blue suit trimmed with roses.
8. #3014 Drummer Boy.

9in (23cm)-9½in (24cm)

Miniatures:

1. These dolls seem larger than their height indicates.
2. Their faces have a "surprised" look.
3. They have a sturdier body when placed beside a *Mascotte*.
4. They have raised, sculptured eyebrows.
5. They usually do not have the felt loop for hanging.
6. Many of them wore provincial or nationality costumes.

7. Often they have the same costumes and accessories as the dolls in other sizes (see *Illustration 175* and *186*).
8. Many of the *Miniatures* carried a heart-shaped tag indicating that they were made in the late 1930s or later (see *Illustration 156*).
9. They have most of the Lenci characteristics (see Identification Guide, page 230).

10in (25cm)-10½in (27cm)

1. *Russian Boy:* Has wooden jar and musical instrument; (see *Illustration 152*). This costume can be found on dolls in larger sizes.
2. #206 *Roly Poly Woman:* Dressed in Russian costume; flat bottom with no legs; high headpiece with shawl; happy smiling face; 1925-1926.
3. #211 *Dutch Girl:* Flat-bottom doll in Dutch costume; 1925-1926.
4. #262 *Madonna:* Lady with downcast eyes; red embroidered skirt; white shawl over head; blue heavily embroidered outer shawl trimmed with jewels; 1925-1926.
5. #280 Felt Frog: 1927-1928.
6. #281 Felt Grasshopper: 1927-1928.
7. #564 *Mariana:* Dressed in Dutch costume; 1927-1928.
8. Girls: Dressed in organdy dresses and felt bonnets; versions of the Pompadour look.
9. *Clown Puppet:* Red hair, tiny derby hat; black bolero with lavender trim; yellow and lavender puppet dress; lavender gloves and bow tie.
10. *Marottes.*

11in (28cm)-11½in (29cm)

1. *Fetishes.*

149

2. #160 Early Girl: Non-sculptured face.
3. #265 *Winkers:* Dolls have one eye closed to make them appear to be winking; winter sports outfits; 1930s. They sometimes measure 12in (31cm)-12½in (32cm) (see *Illustration 154*).
4. #265F *Mountain Climber Winker:* Carries rope on back and has ice axe in his hand; 1930s.
5. #265G *Boy Pulling Sled:* Winker; 1930s.
6. #265H *Skier:* Skis and ski poles; winker; 1930s.
7. #360 Girls: Dressed in pretty dresses with high waists and full skirts; 1930s.
8. Ethnic and Nationality Costumed Dolls.
9. Character Ethnic Dolls: (see *Illustration 152, Indian Doll*).
10. Line of Small Dolls with Versions of Popular Costumes such as *Amore* (see *Illustration 153*).
11. Mussolini's *Fascist Boy:* Small version (see *Illustration 173* for same uniform on larger doll).
12. Plush Rooster: Plush and felt rooster.
13. Winker Puppet: Black hat; red puffed dress; lace ruff.

12in (31cm)-12½in (32cm)
1. #190 Oriental *Fukuruko:* Chinese character with long forehead; 1925-1926.
2. #209/A-D Black Babies in Diapers: Ethnic characters; 1925-1926.
3. Little Girls: Dressed in fancy organdy ruffled dresses.
4. Hand puppets.
5. *Opium Smoker:* Early Lenci logo doll (see *Illustration 155*).

6. *Goosegirl:* Heart-shaped tag; 1930s.
7. #2000 Children: Several different types of dolls have been tagged with this number (see *Illustration 157*).
8. *Girl with Jump rope:* Braided hair in buns on side of head; some of these dolls were imported to England by "Liberty" and tagged both "Liberty" and "Lenci."

13in (33cm)-13½in (34cm)
1. #111/5 *Rope Jumper:* (see *Illustration 159*); other 111 styles included dresses with matching cloches; romper outfits; coat and dress ensembles; 1925-1930s.
2. Oriental Japanese Girl.
3. #264 Barefoot Street Vendor.
4. #450 Child: Raised eyebrows; muslin body; had approximately 25 outfits; many of the costumes had short matching dresses, coats, hats. (See *Illustration 160*).

14in (36cm)-14½in (37cm)
1. *Lucia Face:* Doll was made in 1930s with a slightly smoother felt face and raised eyebrows. This size doll sold well and it was often used for the popular costumes used on other dolls. It was also dressed in provincial (see *Illustration 161*) and other nationality clothes (see *Illustration 164*). It was also used for many historical and fictional costumes such as *Mozart, Rapunzel* and *Pompadour.* (See *Illustration 162*).
2. #114 Chinese Man: Early 1920s.
3. #117 Old Man: Early cartoontype; 1920s.
4. #600 Workbag: Lady dressed in period costume with poke bonnet (see *Illustration 146*).

5. #610 Workbag: Has elf-like head.
6. #900 Older Girl: Long legs.
7. *Miss Muffet:* Half doll on matching felt-covered tuffet.
8. Oriental girl with Dolly Face: Unusual painted eyebrows; 1930s.

15in (38cm)-15½in (39cm)

1. Child with Felt Ball: Wears tam.
2. Italian Provincial Doll.
3. Boudoir-type Doll: (See *Illustration 166.*) This also came in nationality costume dresses. Example: Spanish.
4. Boudoir-type doll: Dressed like *Winter.* This is the same type dress used on the popular glass-eyed Seasons Series.
5. *Mozart.*

16in (41cm)-16½in (42cm)

1. #102 Dutch Man: Character type; 1920-1921.
2. #103 Dutch Girl: Character type (see *Illustration 136);* 1920-1921.
3. #108 Early Child Doll: All-felt (see *Illustration 136).*
4. Marionettes.
5. #149 Early Doll with All-Felt Body: Often had fuzzy-type hair; some had large hair bows; 1923-1926; 1927-1928 doll is 16½in (42cm).
6. Sports Series Rope Jumper: Smooth hair.
7. #475 Little Girl: Dressed in felt.
8. Black Islander Girl: With ethnic features.
9. Baby (rare size).
10. #119 Oriental Man: (See *Illustration 169);* early 1920s.
11. #159 Girl with Chubby Cheeks; 1927-1928.

12. #400 Older Girl with Slender Legs: Felt arms and legs.
13. #609 Workbag: Girl carrying a muff; girl in bonnet with full skirt.

17in (43cm)

1. #178 Chubby Child: Cheeks and hair styled to emphasize this chubbiness; one model carried knitting needles and ball of yarn; another model came with flower pot (see *Illustration 174).*
2. Dark-skinned Indian Squaw with Papoose on Back.
3. Baby with Bent Knee.
4. Pouty-faced Dolls: Dressed like women or older girls.

17½in (45cm)

1. #101 (height approximate) Man in Apron Carrying Chicken: Character face; 1920-1921.
2. #104 (height approximate) Oriental Girl Dancer: Character face; 1920-1921.
3. #116 (height approximate) *Pierrot* with Musical Instrument: Painted mask face; felt rotating joints on shoulders and hips; (see *Illustration 137);* 1920.
4. #118 (height approximate) *Harlequin:* 1920-1921.
5. #300 This was a very popular number from the 1925-1926 catalog into the 1930s; approximately 110 different costumes; many boy dolls have this number.
   A. *Foreign Boy and Girl Series:* Argentinian; Dutch; Eastern European (two different sets); Lapland (see *Illustration 174);* Oriental, Russian; Scandinavian (see *Illustration 170);* Scottish; Spanish; Turkish; Tyrolean

(see *Illustration 174)*; and others.

B. Boys and Girls: Dressed in street clothes of the era.

C. Girls: Dressed in party clothes.

D. Boys: Dressed in party or historical clothes; example, boy dressed in Edwardian costume with monocle.

E. Girl Dressed in Pompodour-styled dress: Tag says, "Bambole Italia, Lenci."

F. Nationality children with Accessories: Example, girl with chicken.

G. Sports Series (see *Illustration 141)*.
#1000 croquet player with mallet.
#1001 soccer player with ball.
#1002 golfer with club.
#1003 oarsman with oar.
#1004 tennis player with racket.
#1005 boxer with boxing gloves.
#1006 basebell player with bat.

H. #300/7 Drummer Boy: Military uniform; high leggings.

I. #300/12 Girl: Wearing large hat; carrying a rake.

J. #300/60 Oriental girl.

K. #300 Fascist boy: (See *Illustration 173)*.

6. #613 Workbag: In form of Russian lady.

7. #614 Workbag: In form of French lady.

8. #615 Workbag: In form of old-fashioned lady.

9. #1500 Girl: Chubby pouty face; similar to #178 but hair not so fuzzy at sides; 1930.

1. #106 *Cowboy:* Early doll (see *Illustration 137)*; 1920-1921.

2. #110 popular series: Had approximately 120 costumes. In 1925-1926 it was 18in (46cm). In 1927-1930s it was 19in (48cm).

A. #110 Girl: Dressed in all-felt; also dressed in combinations of felt and organdy (see *Illustration 175)*.

B. #110 Girl: Also came in 1930s with a smooth felt mask face which is usually mistaken for composition (see *Illustration 177)*.

C. #110 Girl: All-felt very early doll; felt on face is coarser than later versions; came with metal and cloth tags; 1921-1922.

3. #178L Girl: Poke bonnet; checked felt skirt; holding flowerpot.

4. #573 Black Doll: Dressed as little girl; 1930s.

5. #575 Black Doll: Short skirt; holding palm tree and plume; 1930s.

6. #8000L 2 44 066 Man: Novelty rag doll type; large fur hat; made entirely of felt (see *Illustration 178)*.

7. Dickens-type Boy: Came in several sizes; (see *Illustration 179)*.

8. Opium Pipe Smoker: (see *Illustration 137)*.

1. Oriental Girl: Similar to #300 Oriental girl; dressed in felt oriental dress; black felt jacket with blue felt trim; center of jacket has round patch with Oriental characters.

2. Boudoir-type Doll: Lace umbrella; lace gloves; similar to #165.

3. #565 *Maria:* Black barefoot girl; skirt with vertical stripes.

19½in (50cm)

1. Liberty Doll: Lenci label; organdy and felt dress.
2. #554 African Native Boy: Knock-kneed; several of wire necklaces around neck; matching earrings; black wig with large spit curl on forehead; grass-type skirt with pseudo-bone trim; barefoot.
3. #566 *Amor:* Black Cupid with wings; high hat; knock-kneed; barefoot; girdle of roses around hips.
4. Russian Girl: For same costume, see *Illustration 151.*
5. Provincial Costumed dolls: Late 1930s and early 1940s; (see *Illustration 180).*

20in (51cm)

1. Googly-eyed dolls that have painted or glass eyes.
   A. Lady in Scottish outfit: Brown felt short coat; felt plaid skirt; Scottish hat; glass eyes.
   B. Widow with Black Outfit and Dachshund: Came with glass or painted eyes.
   C. Widow with Black Outfit and Terrier: Came with glass or painted eyes (see *Illustration 183).*
   D. Girl in Blue: Organdy dress with many white ruffles; small hat; glass eyes.
   E. Girl in Felt and Organdy Costume: Glass eyes.
   F. Tyrolean Girl: White blouse; felt skirt; Glass eyes.
2. Babies: circa 1930.
3. Workbag (pocketbook): Russian

lady; French lady; 19th century lady.

4. Oriental Lady: Slim body; (also in 23in (58cm) size).
5. #350 Older Child: Eyes not side-glancing; some have pigtails.
6. Duck Dressed as Cavalier: Novelty animal carrying a metal sword (see *Illustration 181).*
7. Indian Girl: Dark skin; side-glancing eyes; slim body; black hair in bangs; Indian costume; heavy beads.
8. #116 *Pierrot:* (see *Illustration 137).*
9. #252 *Mozart.*
10. #253 *Maria-Teresa.*
11. #3100 Candy Box: Spanish lady.
12. #3100 Candy Box: 1860s lady.
13. #3101 Candy Box: 18th century lady.

20½in (52cm)

1. #602 Workbag: White-haired old lady with checked skirt.
2. #350 Older Child: Eyes not side-glancing; some have pigtails.

21in (53cm)-21½in (55cm)

1. #500 Girls and Boys: Felt coats, hats and leggings; late 1920s (see *Illustrations 184* and *185).*
2. #500/0 Child: Pajamas with "Nini" on them; tiny teddy bear in pocket.
3. Girl: Carrying a basket.
4. Girl: Reputed to be Mary Pickford; dress with felt yoke; organdy skirt with felt flowers; pink, blue and gold cloche with same flower trim found on skirt.

22in (56cm)

The 109 mold is one of the earliest and most popular of all the Lenci dolls. It was advertised as early as 1923, and it was one of the most photographed dolls in the 1925-1926 catalog. The earliest ones have a less sculptured face and an all-felt body. Their mitt hands have only stitching to represent fingers. The thumb is separate. Later dolls have a more sculptured face, cloth body and different fingers; approximately 135 costumes.

1. #109 Boys and Girls: Dressed in various street clothes; some have on coats and hats (see *Illustration 186* and *187*).
2. #109/40 Golfer: Named *Plucci* from the Sports Series; dressed in dusty pink and white checked pants and golfer's hat; white shirt; matching sweater with white felt stripes around the bottom; matching knit socks; cobbled brown shoes; golfer dolls were made in other sizes also.
3. #109 Smooth Felt Face: Made to resemble composition.
4. #109 Girl: Romper suit and shovel.

23in (58cm)

1. #109 mold: Changed to 23in (58cm) in later models.
2. #188A *Le Tia Guai:* Oriental with slanting eyes; coolie hat; wooden clogs; carrying a lamp.
3. #188 *Dschang-go* Oriental Boy: Heavily embroidered red felt kimono; blue and gold felt trim; short hair; came with stringed oriental instrument; 1925-1926.
4. #189 *Madame Butterfly:* Blue or green heavily embroidered kimono; felt trim comes in several colors on different dolls. 1925-1926.
5. Geisha Lady: Black heavily embroidered kimono; pink trim and sash; high black hairpiece; three

middle fingers indicated by stitching; thumb and little finger separate.

6. #251 *Hu Sun* Opium Smoking Woman: Long hair; orange felt kimono with felt applique and embroidery; circa 1925.
7. #255 *Tsau Guo Giu:* Green kimono; blue overpiece; white embroidered overjacket; unusual black headpiece with heavy red tassel; 1925-1926.
8. Workbag: Topped with Oriental doll with almost closed eyes; felt hairpiece; red felt kimono with blue high-necked yoke.
9. Long-limbed Lady Boudoir-type Doll: One version with hip-length braids reputed to be Lillian Gish; another version with fancy dress and bonnet reputed to be Dorothy Gish; partially closed eyes.
10. #563 *Bellhop:* Carrying a round box of flowers.

23½in (60cm)

1. #601 and #603 Workbag: Doll dressed in Eastern European clothes; 1927-1928.

24in (61cm)

1. #165 Slim Lady Dolls: Fancy costumes with ruffled dresses and high-heeled shoes; four of these ladies in 1930 catalog; similar dolls came in taller sizes also.
2. Flapper-type Doll: Dressed in red felt and organdy costume; picture hat; bobbed hair.
3. Blonde Lady Doll: Pink organdy garden dress; wide collar trimmed in rickrack; picture hat trimmed in felt rickrack; pink gloves; pearl necklace (see *Illustration 193*).
4. #576 *Pierrot:* Costume trimmed

with felt circles; wide pleated felt neck ruff and cuffs; large hat turned up in front; carried mandolin and bouquet of roses.

5. Boy Skier: Dark blue ski pants; green and white sweater with triangle pattern; matching ski hat; striped socks; cobbled shoes; thick, sturdy skis and ski poles (see *Illustration 190*).

6. Boudoir Lady with Apron: Blue felt dress; full skirt with two scalloped ruffles; carries a bouquet of flowers; advertised in *Playthings* in May 1923 with a headline saying, "develop artistic tendencies in your children//Buy a 'Lenci' Doll"; came also in 13in (33cm) size (see *Illustration 192*).

24in (61cm)-28in (71cm) SPECIAL LENCI SERIES

There is a series of unusual Lenci dolls with slim, stick-like figures and swivel joints at neck, shoulders and waist that enable the dolls to be placed in unusual poses. They have different sizes depending on their costumes. The eyes are painted differently depending on the nationality costume worn by the doll. Some have heavily slitted eyes. A sewn seam at elbow simulates jointed arms. They may be a part of the #165 series.

1. Oriental Dancer: Same body form; red, dark blue, beige and orange costume beautifully blended together; unusual spire-like headpiece; slitted eyes (see *Illustration 195*).

2. Spanish Dancer: Same body form; large black Spanish-type hat with beautiful felt flowers; black felt around neck; red felt dress; slitted eyes.

3. Russian Cossack: Same body form; (see *Illustration 200*).

4. Lady in Riding Costume: Same body form; wig with long curls; 19th century equestrienne style; wood riding crop with felt handle; eyes not heavily slitted.

5. #165/30 Lady: Same body form; high red felt hat with narrow brim; white dress trimmed with red felt flowers and black leaves; skirt has three ruffles and is shorter in front; red high-heeled shoes; five-strand pearls around neck; carries bulldog; 1930.

There are other dolls in this series.

25in (64cm)-25½in (65cm)

1. *Butterfly:* Oriental similar to 23in (58cm) size; carries baby; dressed in blue jacket; black, red and white trousers; in 1927-1928 catalog.

2. *Pierrot:* There are several different styles and colors of this costume in this size; came with mandolin (see *Illustration 137*).

3. *Fad-ette:* Slim boudoir doll; jointed at waist; blonde curly wig; smokes a cigarette (see Illustration page 93).

26in (66cm)-26½in (67cm)

#165 Boudoir-type: This popular doll came in several variations in the 25in (64cm)-26½in (67cm) height range.

1. #165/4 *Colombina:* Dressed as a shepherdess with walking stick. There are variations in the color of the costumes.

2. #577 Flamenco Dancer: White dress with red dots; red roses in dark hair; high-heeled shoes; large earrings; carries a mandolin; 1930.

3. #585 Lady: Period-style dress in black, mauve, green and yellow

plaid on white background; green jacket; white bonnet with mauve feather on top; doll has a parasol.

4. #587 Lady: White dress trimmed with red and yellow dots; yellow ruching; green bonnet with red flowers; carried basket of flowers.

5. Unusual Googly-type Doll: Painted eyes; peach organdy dress with ruffles on skirt; light green hat and scarf tied in bow (see *Illustration 196*).

27in (69cm)-27½in (70cm)

1. #165/21 *Madame Bovary:* Dotted dress with poke bonnet; dark wig parted in center; carries parasol; 1927-1928. (See *Illustration 197*).

2. #165/16 *Madame de Pompadour:* Beautiful pink organdy dress with rows of pink ruffles; low neckline; felt pink and blue flowers on skirt and bodice and in hair; small curls down the back of head; pearl necklace; slitted eyes; 1927-1928. (See *Illustration 191* for similar costume).

3. #165/17 *Rosina:* Dressed in period country costume; gray and green dress with green and yellow striped polonaise; white apron and neck piece; pink bow on tiny hat; 1927-1928.

4. #165 *Contessa Maffei:* Brown jacket with black felt trim; green and blue striped skirt; 1925-1926.

5. #165 Provincial Dolls: Costume of Roma and others.

6. #165/15 *Lolita:* Wears black lace mantilla; fan; 1927-1928 (see *Illustration 198* for similar costume).

7. #165/20 *Fiorella:* Dressed as a red rose.

28in (71cm)-28½in (72cm)

1. #165/1 *Mara:* Dressed in nationality black costume with white blouse; appliqued flowers on skirt and hat; streamers hanging from hat; 1925-1926.

2. #950 Series of Girls: 1927-1928.
   A. *Bimba:* Ruffled dress.
   B. *Bibi:* Coat and hat.
   C. *Beppe.*

3. #268 Slim Lady Doll in Modern Street Clothes: Fashionable hat of period; light skirt; dark jacket; carrying a large black and white dog.

4. #263 *Raquel Miller:* Dressed in white and green outfit with three large ruffles in skirt; a bouquet of large pink roses with green leaves is on skirt; straw hat with large pink rose at side of head; white parasol; riding crop; black high-heeled shoes.

5. #569 Bobbed Hair Lady: Shades of green ruffled skirt; pink roses used as shoulder straps; green high-heeled shoes; triple string of pearls; 1930.

6. #570 Lady with Short Hair: Three-strand necklace; dark paneled skirt trimmed with figures of man in uniform, two clowns, man with striped trousers; 1930.

7. #586 Lady: Low bodice trimmed in green; rose-colored ruffled skirt; large rose at waistline; green bonnet, gloves and shoes; two-strand pearl necklace; black lace fan; 1930.

8. #578 Lady: Dress trimmed with large flower appliques; 1930.

9. #579 Lady: Straight, black bobbed hair with bangs; sleeveless red dress; large rose at waistline;

full skirt; holds a rose; smokes a cigarette; 1930.

10. #582 Spanish Dancer: Has castanets; 1930.

11. #584 Doll with Fishing Basket and Rod: 1930.

29in (74cm)-29½in (75cm)
The style number #165 has many variations in height and costume. They are high-heeled dolls and have normal eyes unless otherwise noted. They were among the most popular Lenci dolls.

1. #165/3 *Susie:* Short bobbed hair; very large picture hat; sleeveless dress; short vertically striped skirt; choker of large beads; 1925-1926.

2. #165/5 *Bergere:* Short shepherdess-type dress; striped underskirt; 18th century-type overskirt and top; felt roses trimming skirt; white organdy apron and trim on neck; carries a walking stick and a basket of flowers; 1925-1926.

3. #165/6 *Miss Sweet-Flower:* Demure lady with felt dress with horizontal striped trim on sleeves and neck; deep ruffles on the full skirt; picture hat tilted over her face trimmed with flowers and ribbon; carries a handkerchief; has two long blonde curls at each side of face; 1925-1926.

The following dolls are large long-limbed art dolls of the boudoir type with their eyes half shut. The dolls of this type have high-heeled shoes. There are variations in the color and costume in some of the style numbers. Dolls in other heights have similar descriptions:

1. #250 *Mimi:* Lady with polka dot hatbox; 18th century costume; striped panniers; pantalets; felt hat trimmed with flowers; 1925-1926.

2. #256 *Musette:* Feathered bonnet matches a gown of French blue felt; full skirt with narrow crossbars of magenta felt; low neckline trimmed with ruffle of magenta; leg-o-mutton sleeves; silk-embroidered, yarn fringed shawl of white cashmere; hoopskirt; garters of felt roses; 1925-1926.

3. Spanish Dancer: Black print skirt with very large flowers in pink, orange, yellow, blue and white; black off-the-shoulder top; lace mantilla; carries fan.

The following dolls are from the 1930s. They are still the long-limbed boudoir dolls with wonderful costumes. The shape of their eyes is unknown.

1. #580 Spanish Dancer *Lagartera:* Dark full skirt, accordion-pleated apron, kerchief on head; carries a scarf or bag over her arm; 1930s.

2. #581 *Salamanca:* Fringed, embroidered shawl and apron, ball-like earrings; three strands of beads; crucifix; long hat which extends down back; 1930s.

3. #583 Lady: Tall bishop's hat trimmed with beads; scalloped skirt with heavy embroidery; carries an ewer; 1930s.

4. #588 Lady: Dress of 18th century style; ruffled petticoat trimmed with roses; blue robe with ruching down the front; white tucker and full undersleeves below short sleeves of robe; wide-brimmed hat with flowers on top; pink high-heeled shoes.

5. #750 Lady: Felt dress with high waistline; organdy bodice; short puffed sleeves; full skirt with appliqued flowers; ruffles at bottom; slipper-type shoes with no strap; felt flowers on bonnet; 1930s.

6. #752 Lady with Short Bobbed Hair: Skirt with scallops at bottom; large two-color sash; sleeveless bodice; upper skirt and bodice trimmed with appliqued flowers; 1930s.

7. #753 Lady: White full skirt with scallops at bottom; pantalets with red flowers at knees; plaid sash of orange, yellow and white; wide-brimmed yellow hat trimmed with red flowers, black lace mitts; carries a diabolo game; 1930s.

30in (76cm)-30½in (78cm)

1. #560 *Rudolph Valentino:* Elaborate reproduction of costume worn in the movie, *The Sheik;* beige embroidered pants; embroidered jacket under white and red striped Moorish cloak; red felt turban with rope trim; dagger on leather belt; all-felt (see *Illustration 201*).

2. Flapper Smoking Cigarette (Marlene Dietrich look-alike): Deep turquoise flapper dress with flounced, ruffled skirt; deep neckline with strap high across neck; two-strand pearl necklace; ruffled turquoise petticoat; turquoise ruffled garter.

31in (79cm)-31½in (80cm)

1. #257 *Katinka:* Russian costume; full skirt with large appliqued flowers; long embroidered jacket with no sleeves; blouse with long sleeves; high rectangular embroi-dered Russian hat; long pigtails; high-heeled boots.

2. #260 *Sam:* Turkish (or Arab) boy; black felt body; heavily embroidered harem pants; each finger is sewn separately; striped turban; pointed felt slippers; dagger in belt; fetish on chain; large bead necklace.

3. #261 *Kufi:* Large black girl with checkered felt dress; chubby face; large eyes and lips; fuzzy-type black hair which is wide at cheek line; large hairbow; buttoned felt slippers; no socks; 1926-1927.

32in (81cm)-32½in (83cm)

1. #561 *Carmen:* Spanish costume; yellow dress with appliqued red poppies; high-heeled red shoes; high red comb; carries a basket with red apples; 1927-1928.

2. *Shirley Temple:* Swivel joints on neck, hips and shoulders; stuffed felt body; very curly hair sewn to head; orange organza dress trimmed at scalloped hemline with felt flowers; black oilcloth shoes; white socks; 1930s.

3. Lenci with Jump Rope: Very large doll; painted blue eyes; pigtails in buns on side of head; small felt bows on hair; pinafore with red felt skirt; red and white checked band around hem; top of pinafore is same red and white check; holds jump rope.

35in (89cm)-35½in (90cm)

There are approximately 25 style variations of #169.

1. #169/J Large Long-limbed Older Girl: Organdy dress and bolero; brunette wig.

2. #169/L Large Long-limbed Older Girl: Pleated felt skirt; sleeveless jacket embroidered

158

with chicken-like figure; large felt tam; carries tennis racket.

3. #556 *Kigan:* Nationality doll; wears a jacket and pants; carries a curved-end spear; big toe is separate from other toes; 1927-1928.

4. #700 *Little Miss Muffet:* Green and white checked dress; solid-colored yoke; scalloped felt band with black dots at hemline; comes with large spider; 1927-1928.
This type of dress is seen in many other style numbers. It is often in red and white.

5. Russian Male Dancer: Red hair; character face; open mouth with teeth showing; black pants and boots; green heavily appliqued jacket with brown trim; white gloves. (See *Illustration 152* for doll in smaller size.)

37in (94cm)-37½in (95cm)

1. #700 *Tilde:* Braids over ears; wears red and white dress with high waistline and full skirt that covers her knees; her dress is similar to *Little Miss Muffet* but is a different color; 1927-1928.

2. #700/1 *Rita:* Braids over ears; wears dress with high waistline that covers the knees; 1927-1928.

3. #700/2 *Edvige:* Braids over ears; wears dress with high waistline that covers the knees; 1927-1928.

4. #700/3 *Flora:* Wears dress with high waistline that covers the knees; 1927-1928.

5. #700/4 *Dina:* Wears dress with high waistline that covers the knees; 1927-1928.

6. #700/5 *Nene:* Wears dress with high waistline that covers the knees; 1927-1928.

38in (97cm)

1. Lady in Pink Ruffles: Pink organdy dress with deep scalloped ruffles; trimmed in pink felt rickrack; pink puffed sleeves; white organdy around neckline; black felt ribbon around neck; pink felt bonnet with white inner ruffles; yellow and white felt flowers on hat; normal side-glancing eyes; 1925-26 (see *Illustration 202*). This is probably the same series as #180bis.

40in (100cm)

1. #180bis Girl with Bobbed Brunette Hair: Dress of ruffled organdy trimmed with colored felt scallops; black felt ribbon around neck; normal side-glancing eyes; flower and leaf trim on skirt; hair parted down the middle in unusual style; 1925-1926.

2. #186 Russian Man: Wears black felt pants; black leather Russian boots; heavily embroidered green jacket; gold felt blouse; belt with wooden tassels; white gloves in belt; red hair; character face; open mouth with teeth showing; brown Russian-style cap; 1925-1926. (See *Illustration 152* for similar smaller doll.)

3. #187 Russian Lady: Heavily embroidered orange skirt with white felt in front and on bottom edge of skirt; blue jacket with dark pink trim; peasant blouse trimmed with felt rickrack on top of sleeve; fan-type Russian headdress; long blonde pigtails; normal side-glancing eyes; 1925-1926. (See *Illustration 151* for smaller version of same costume.)

4. #562 *Kamimura:* Lady doll; wears a dark kimono with designs

in shades of lavender; white trim on kimono; white Japanese-style pants; black Japanese-type felt clogs; gold Japanese ornament in short black hair; circa 1928.

SEASONS SERIES
Similar costumes to these 40in (100cm) dolls can also be found in some of the other doll sizes.

1. *Autumn:* Light peach and green organza dress with many layers of petaled ruffles; a bright red and purple cluster of grapes with green and blue leaves trim the skirt; bright red hair decorated with a cluster of various shades of grapes which drops down over the dress; glass or painted googly eyes; surprised expression on face; all five fingers sewn separately; green one-button slippers; 1929-1930.

2. *Winter:* Full white cape over white dress trimmed with large white felt circles to resemble snowdrops; cape, dress and hat trimmed with white fur and holly; brown hair with center part; white leggings over black slippers; glass or painted googly eyes; surprised expression on face; fingers sewn separately; 1920-1930.

Liberty of London

The Liberty of London Company made handmade needle-sculptured cloth dolls which were dressed in English historical and storybook costumes. The facial sculptures were amazing likenesses of the real people depicted. They made dolls in the 1930s, 1940s and 1950s. A partial list of their dolls includes:

1. Anne, Queen of England
2. Albert, Consort to Victoria
3. Baa, Baa Black Sheep
4. Beefeater
5. Churchill, Winston
6. Copperfield, David
7. Coronation Group of 1937
8. Drake, Frances
9. Duke of Wellington
10. Elizabeth, Princess
11. Elizabeth, Queen Mother
12. Elizabeth I
13. Elizabeth II
14. Elizabeth II and Prince Phillip in Coronation costumes of 1953
15. Father Christmas
16. George III
17. George VI
18. Grenadier
19. Henry VIII
20. Humpty Dumpty
21. Irish man and lady
22. James I, Mary's son
23. James VI of Scotland
24. Joan of Arc
25. Lord Nelson
26. Margaret Rose, Princess
27. Mary, Queen Mother
28. Mary, Queen of Scotland
29. Mother Goose
30. Mr. Micawber
31. Mr. Pickwick
32. Raleigh, Sir Walter
33. Richard III
34. Richard the Lion Hearted dressed as a Crusader
35. Shakespeare, William

The registered trademarks, the trademarks and copyrights appearing in italics/bold within this chapter belong to Liberty of London.

Continued on page 169.

Lenci #110 girl in pink
(see page 136).

Lenci #300 Scandinavian girl
(see page 133).

Lenci man with beard (see page 136).

Käthe Kruse Boy (see page 107).

Lenci miniature *Sardinian Man* and *Soldier* (see page 125).

Emile Lang *Belgian Soldier* (see page 113).

164

Chad Valley *Boy Blue* and *Bo Peep* (see page 52).

Krueger *Dwarfs* (see page 105).

Liberty Coronation dolls (see pages 169 and 170).

Lenci Russian Girl with pig
(see page 125).

Royal Society *Pierrette* (see page 196).

Gre-Poir cowboy and girl in green (see pages 81 and 82).

Liberty of London
Continued from page 160.

36. Victoria, Queen of England
37. Welsh man and lady
Doll Questers was a mail order company in Coral Gables, Florida. In September of 1953 they put out a newsletter telling about items they had for sale for the Coronation of Elizabeth II. Among the many items was a *Yeoman of the Guard (Beefeater)*.
Yeoman of the Guard: 9in (23cm); all original.

The uniform was designed during the Renaissance and has changed very little through the centuries. The doll's costume was made of felt with black and yellow felt trim. King George's cipher is embroidered on the tunic. The hose is red and there are rosettes on his garters and shoes. The black felt hat is a type of beret with a brim. The doll's face is made of stockinette over a mold. It has gray hair, beard and mustache. A halberd is in his hand.
MARKS: "Liberty//Made in England" (cloth tag sewn in coat)
SEE: *Illustration 205.*
PRICE: $80-90
Coronation of George VI: This group of dolls is one of the most famous made by this English company. The Coronation was in 1937 and the dolls were made shortly thereafter. They were sold in England and abroad. Kimport sold out quickly. They were made entirely of cloth. The face was a miracle of needle-sculpture. The individual dolls really do look like their real-life counterparts.
(From Left to Right)
Knight of the Garter: 9in (23cm); white rayon pants; black felt coat with gold trim; red velvet robe with white felt trim; white felt coat with black

205.

stitching to simulate fur; red velvet crown with white felt and gold ribbon trim; leather shoes; seam in center of face.
Princess Royal: 9in (23cm); red velvet dress with front lace inset; lace cuffs on sleeves; white felt trim on dress; red velvet robe with white felt trim; silver leather slippers; no seam in center of face.
King George VI: 9in (23cm); white silk knee pants and stockings; long lavender coat with gold braid trim; blue chest ribbon; gold garter on left leg; purple velvet robe with gold trim; robe edged with white felt with black stitching to simulate fur; white felt cape with black stitching; jewels and sequins at neckline; white ribbon bows; purple velvet crown with jewels and sequins; black leather shoes; seam in center of face.

Queen Mother Mary: 9in (23cm); gold brocade dress with sewn-on pearls; gold slippers; purple velvet robe with gold braid and felt trim with black stitching to simulate fur; white felt cape with black stitching; three strings of pearls; blue ribbon across chest; decorations on chest; jeweled crown and earrings; white mohair wig; no seam in center of face.

Princess Elizabeth (now Queen Elizabeth II): 6½in (17cm); blue organdy skirt and puffed sleeves with blue rayon bodice; lace gloves; pink roses at waist and in hair; high white socks; blue rayon shoes; blonde mohair wig; no seam in center of face.

Queen Elizabeth: 9in (23cm); white satin dress with heavy gold embroidery; lace sleeves; white silk slippers; purple robe with gold embroidery; felt trim embroidered with black stitching to simulate fur; white felt cape with black stitching; purple velvet crown with jewels and sequins; no seam in center of face.

Chancellor of the House of Commons: 9in (23cm); black pants; red coat with white felt trim and gold braid; red felt cloak with white felt trim; black felt ribbons at shoulders; lace jabot; white wig; seam in center of face.

Not Shown in Picture
Archbishop of Canterbury, Speaker of the House of Commons, Archbishop of York and *Princess Margaret Rose.*

MARKS: *Knight of the Garter:* "Liberty//Made in England" (tag sewn on robe). *King George VI:* "Liberty//Made in England" (tag sewn on robe); Kimport dolls//Independence, Mo.// This Doll Was Made in England" (tag sewn on robe). *Queen Mother Mary:* "Liberty//Made in England" (tag sewn on robe). *Princess Elizabeth:* "Liberty//Made in England" (tag sewn on underpants). *Queen Elizabeth:* "Liberty//Made in England" (tag sewn on robe).

SEE: *Illustration 206* (Color Section, page 166).

PRICE: $75-125 each

Live Long Toys

Beginning in 1923 this company made a line of stuffed oilcloth-type dolls. The main product was a line of cartoon dolls made with permission of popular cartoon artists.

1923
1. *Skeezix* made as a baby in red rompers; 13in (33cm).
2. *Uncle Walt:*
   MARKS: "Uncle Walt" (printed on lower back)
3. *Chester Gump* made by Fleming: 13in (33cm); red hair; long nose; polka dot shirt; wide collar; large tie; short trousers; short boots.

MARKS: "Chester Gump//by Sidney//Smith" (printed on doll)
1924 Dolls Added to the Original Line
1. *Skeezix* made as boy in blue suit with short pants: 14in (36cm).
2. *Auntie Blossom* (Mrs. Blossom).
3. *Rachel:* Black doll; printed clothes; striped skirt, apron, cap.
4. *Teenie Weenies:* Cartoon characters representing a boy, lady, Black

The registered trademarks, the trademarks and copyrights appearing in italics/bold within this chapter belong to Live Long Toys.

person, Chinese person, Indian and policeman.
5. *Ester Starring* by Penny Ross (from the cartoon "Mamma's Angel Child").
Chester Gump was continued in his original form.

1925 Dolls Added to the Original Line
1. *Little Orphan Annie* drawn originally by Harold Gray: Several sizes up to 16in (41cm).
2. *Sandy* (Little Orphan Annie's dog).
3. *Herby* (Smitty's little brother): 11in (28cm); small boy in red coat.
   MARKS: "Herby" and "Walter Berndt" (printed on doll)
4. *Puff:* Cat in "Gasoline Alley Cartoon."
5. *Pal:* Dog in "Gasoline Alley Cartoon."
6. *Red Grange:* Wears football suit with "77" printed on doll; carried a miniature football.

1926 Dolls Added to the Original Line
1. *Emily Marie:* Character in cartoon "Little Orphan Annie."
2. *Smitty:* Character by cartoonist Walter Berndt.
   MARKS: "Smitty" and "Walter Berndt" (printed on doll).
3. *Kayo:* 11in (28cm); character in "Moon Mullins" cartoon.
4. Three flower dolls including *Tulip, Morning Glory* and one other.
5. *Skeezix:* Wearing overalls, pajamas or a bathing suit.
6. *Chester Gump:* 13in (33cm); designed by Eileen Bernoliel; looks like a small boy wearing a red and blue suit.

1927 Dolls Added to the Line
1. *Skeezix:* 10in (25cm) and 11½in (29cm).
   MARKS: "Skeezix//Reg.U.S. Pat.Off//Feb.27,1923."
2. *Little Orphan Annie:* In two sizes this year.
3. *Moon Mullins:* 19in (48cm); wore a derby and had a cigar in mouth.
   MARKS: "Moon Mullins" and "Frank Willard" (printed on doll)

1928 Dolls Added to the Line
1. *Corky* (Skeezix's baby brother): Wore a long baby dress.
2. *Kayo* (from "Moon Mullins" cartoon): Dark shirt; one suspender; long polka dot trousers; derby hat.
3. *Jane.*
4. *Humpty Boy.*
5. *Clown.*
6. *Baby Bibs.*

1929 Dolls Added to the Line
1. *Pat.*
2. *Jean.*
3. *Harold Teen:* 15in (38cm); spring in leg; yellow sweater; blue pants.
4. *Perry Winkle:* Character in "Winnie Winkle" cartoon by artist Martin Branner; two versions; 13in (33cm); red suit with Eton jacket and no hat. 11in (28cm); blue suit with Eton jacket and wide-brimmed red hat.
5. *Freckles:* From cartoon "Freckles and His Friends" by Merrill Blosser; had freckles; print shirt; short trousers; striped stockings; big shoes.
6. *Smitty:* 10in (25cm); printed blue coat; removable cap and necktie.
7. *Skeezix as Baby:* Two sizes — 9in (23cm) and 13in (33cm).

207.

8. *Skeezix:* Standing on two legs.
1930 New Lines Added
Children of Today: Boys and girls; hands snapped so they could hold hands; they could then stand by themselves; some dolls had voices.

Gasoline Alley Dolls: Various sizes; stuffed oilcloth; bright colors; *Uncle Walt; Skeezix* (boy); *Skeezix* (baby); *Mrs. Blossom; Rachel; Pal; Puff; Jean.* **SEE:** *Illustration 207. Playthings*, January 1925.

Ilse Ludecke (Germany)

The dolls in *Illustrations 208* through *211* were purchased in Dover, Ohio, from an antique dealer who said that she found them wrapped in a 1917 paper. During the early part of this century many artists were creating wonderful dolls in the manner of the Munich Art Dolls and Käthe Kruse. As new methods were found for molding and sculpturing cloth, many artists in European countries turned to the new medium.

One such artist was Ilse Ludecke. Not much is known about her except that the mayor of Schwetzingen, West Germany, said in 1988, "Ilse Ludecke is just living." A letter to her known address was not answered, but it also was not returned. Each of her dolls was well sculptured, dressed and tagged. They are Steiff look-alikes.

Each of the dolls is 15½in (39cm) tall. They are mounted on wooden

208.

The registered trademarks, the trademarks and copyrights appearing in italics/bold within this chapter belong to Ilse Ludecke.

209.

211.

stands which are stamped with, "Ilse Ludecke//Trachtenpuppen//Schwetzingen Deutschland//Schleßsplatz Frhorinzen.
Clock Seller: Dressed in a black felt suit with red trim; blue stockings with red trim; small goatee; glasses; carry-ing wooden clocks on his back; also carried a stout walking stick.
SEE: *Illustration 208* (front). *Illustration 209* (back). *Eleanor Guderian Collection.*
PRICE: $75-250 (depending on the costuming)

210.

Resl: The tag on the doll says: "My name is *Resl* and I come from the Berchtesgaden Area, a special picturesque landscape with the famous Lake Konigee and the Mount Walzmann. Please, notice me, and you will see a typical Upper Bavarian costume on a characteristic peasant lass.

"We have to dress suitable for the mountainous climate, but not too warm for summer wear. You see, our dresses do not differ much from one area to another. In some parts, there is a difference between maid and married woman. The colour of the skirt

may be green, blue, or red. But they wear the long sleeves and blouses more frequently with the latter 2 colours. A black velvet bodice of heavy silk, closed with silver chains, is matched with a silk scarf and apron." SEE: *Illustrations 208* and *210. Eleanor Guderian Collection.*
PRICE: $75-250 (depending on the costuming)

Seppl, a Bavarian Mountain Hiker: The tag on the doll says, "He wears a white shirt and leather pants, the usual dress for most Bavarian boys and men in the mountains. For these people the Rueksack will replace the suitcase.

"The Lederhose has now become international, but something special are the short woolen stockings without feet which are worn to keep warm in great heights!

"On the hats they wear the usual Alpine flowers; the white Edelweiss, the red Alpenrosen (alps rose) and the blue Enzian, sometimes a Gamsberth, not a shaving brush or an eagle feather.

"Seppl comes right from the mountains. He has a mountainstick (bergstock) in his hand and is biting on a flower. The Rusksack is empty, probably he is hungry! Ilse."
SEE: *Illustration 211. Eleanor Guderian Collection.*
PRICE: $75-250 (depending on the costuming)

Bagpiper: 12in (31cm); unstiffened muslin face with seam down the middle; hand-painted face with delicate strokes; open mouth with teeth and a hole where the bagpipe is inserted; machine-stitched down back of neck and back; body not jointed; dressed in Scottish men's costume; red felt coat; red, white and green plaid skirt; fur sporran; real leather leggings and shoes; bagpipe; doll mounted on small wooden square; doll brought to the United States in the 1930s.
MARKS: "Ilse" (written on bottom of wooden stand)
SEE: *Illustration 212.*
PRICE: $150-160

Magis
(Italy)

The ornate spelling on the Magis tags makes them very difficult to decipher. They have been spelled various ways in the doll literature. Recently, most authors have written "Magis." There is another tag on the doll in *Illustration 216* with the distinct spelling Magit; the T is definitely crossed. Those tags have "Torino" on them. The only Magis labels that this author

212.

174

has seen have the city "Roma" on them. Another Magit company has been reported in France as well as a second French doll company with dolls marked "Magati." Do any of our readers have any information on these companies?

Girl with Violets in Roma Costume: 10½in (27cm); for general characteristics, see Identification Guide, page 235; dressed in green felt skirt with red and yellow ribbon trim; blue leatherette vest; white cotton blouse; red felt headpiece with lace trim; orange felt apron with yellow felt border and trimmed with white ribbon with felt flowers; embossed oilcloth-type shoes tied with red thread up to the knees; late 1930s-early 1950s.
MARKS: "Magis//Roma" (embossed gold tag); map of Italy//"Made in Italy" (second tag of blue embossed with gold)
SEE: *Illustration 213.*
PRICE: $40-50

Girl in Red Felt Dress: 14in (36cm); for general characteristics, see Identification Guide, page 236; pretty sculptured hands with red painted fingernails; beautiful black mohair wig with braided buns at each side of head; bright red felt dress with yellow felt trim and applique; white ruffled collar; lace trimming on cuffs and upper collar; ornate black felt coiled headdress trimmed with yellow felt strips and gold ribbon; red felt pieces fall to each side of headpiece; red oilcloth-type slippers; white handkerchief trimmed with lace; late 1930s-early 1950s.
MARKS: Illegible numbers printed on bottom of shoe

Shoes: Usually made of embossed oilcloth-type material; often red; two main types of shoes:
1. Slipper-type as shown in *Illustration 215;* cardboard sole.
2. Shoe folded over the toe and fastened with tied thread up as high as

213.

214.

the knee (see *Illustration 213*).
MARKS: At one time there were probably style or other pencil marks on shoes. However, most of these marks have worn off or are illegible. **SEE:** *Illustration 215.*

Magit (Torino, Italy)

215.

Girl in Pink: 20in (51cm); for general characteristics; see Identification Guide, page 236; dressed in pink jumper with white felt trim at edge of neck and hem; white cotton blouse with long puffed sleeves; underpants trimmed with felt edging; white felt daisies on jumper; pink felt slippers trimmed with white felt; button and thread closing similar to Poir shoe; white Lenci-type socks; early Lenci look-alike; circa 1924-1930.
MARKS: "Bambole Artistiche// Magit//Torino Italia" (tag fastened to jumper with metal nail, similar to Lenci)
SEE: *Illustration 216* (Color Section, page 218).
PRICE: $350-400

Messina-Vat

217.

About 1924 the Messina-Vat company started to produce cloth dolls in Torino, Italy. This was also the home of the Lenci company. The Messina-Vat dolls competed with Lenci and made wonderful, carefully-constructed dolls. The costumes were also excellent. The line included black dolls, men dolls, Pierrots and other favorites of the period.

Along with dolls of various styles and sizes, the company also made colorful felt coats, vests and other items of clothing for women and children.

They continued making dolls and clothing into the early 1930s.

Girls in Advertisement: Messina-Vat made dolls in the late 1920s and they did not advertise very much in the United States later. Their dolls were made in Torino, Italy, the home of the

219.

220.

Lenci factory. There are many similarities in the construction of the dolls of both companies. The design and construction of the Messina-Vat dolls are excellent, as are the Lenci dolls. **SEE:** *Illustration 217. Playthings,* February 1927.
PRICE: $350-450

Girl in Red Coat with White Dots: 18in (46cm); all-felt body; pressed felt mask face; hand-painted; brown eyes with large white dot, small white dot and light brown highlights; lips have lighter red spot in middle; applied ears made of single piece of felt; unusual bump for chin; mohair wig put on in strips; mitt hands with separate thumb; stitching indicates fingers; jointed at neck, shoulders and legs; leg seams in front and back; no seam in ankle; for more information, see Identification Guide, page 237; circa late 1920s.

MARKS: " *A* " (bottom of foot)
SEE: *Illustration 218* (Color Section, page 219).
PRICE: $350-450

Organ Grinder with Monkey: 17in (43cm); mask face; no ears; stitching on back of head imitated Lenci; gray suede jacket; dark red pants and bag; gray felt vest with red buttons; white beard and eyebrows; mitten hands with stitching indicating fingers; gray hat with red trim and red and green feathers; well-cobbled walking boots; late 1920s to early 1930s.
Tiny Monkey on Back: Felt; black wig; dressed in matching felt clown-like costume.
MARKS: "Vat//Made in Italy// Torino"
SEE: *Illustrations 219 and 220. Gigi Williams Collection.*
PRICE: $500-700

Group of Felt Dolls: Advertisement in *Playthings*, January 1928, shows group of Lenci look-alike dolls with felt hats and costumes; advertisement was placed because of mistake in December 1927 *McCall's* and an advertisement in Rotogravure Section of the *Sunday New York Times*, *Chicago Tribune* and other publications; both the dolls and felt coats on the models were made in Itàly by Messina-Vat instead of France as stated in the advertisement.
SEE: *Illustration 221*. *Playthings*, January 1928.

221.

Methodist Dolls

222.

Missionary Dolls: "Dolls designed by a group of religious artists in hope of marketing them to raise money for missionary purposes. The group was working in conjunction with the Epworth Herald," according to *Toys and Novelties*, September 1932. The dolls were very similar to Lenci and other art dolls of the period.

The Epworth League is the National Methodist Youth Organization.
SEE: *Illustration 222*. *Toys and Novelties*, September 1932.

Meyer & Lorang

Felt Dolls: Natural hair; washable faces; eyes look straight ahead; arms slightly bent; mitt hands with thumbs separate; stitching indicating fingers; felt clothes; brimmed hat; felt shoes with large bows at ankles; Lenci look-alike; circa 1929-1931.

Some of these dolls came with a trunk and wardrobe. The trunk was marked "Cass Toys Athol, Mass//Toys of Quality Made in U.S.A."
SEE: *Illustration 223. Playthings*, October 1929.

223.

Modern Toy Co., Inc.

Buttercup: Soft, cuddly doll; cartoon character from the comic strip "Toots and Casper;" manufactured by permission of Jimmy Murphy, creator
SEE: *Illustration 224. Playthings*, August 1924.

Mollye

Mollye Goldman's business began in the early 1920s in her home. She hired neighborhood women as seamstresses for the clothes and dolls that she designed. She later designed clothes for many of the large and small doll companies of the time.

She competed with Georgene Averill and each company issued a popular series of international dolls. Each company also marketed many other types of cloth dolls.

Two of her most beloved dolls were *Raggedy Ann* and *Andy* which she designed in conjunction with Johnny Gruelle, the author of the fa-

BUTTERCUP

Copyright, 1924, by King Features Syndicate, Inc.

"THE DOLL OF THE HOUR"

SO COMICAL, SOFT and CUDDLY YOU CAN'T RESIST IT

MANUFACTURED BY PERMISSION OF JIMMY MURPHY, CREATOR OF THE FAMOUS
TOOTS and CASPER COMICS

Which are being read daily by twenty million people all over the country

YOUR TOY DEPARTMENT WILL BE INCOMPLETE WITHOUT "BUTTERCUP"

MODERN TOY CO., INC.
Sole Licensees and Manufacturers

Factory and Main Offices:
181 BELMONT AVENUE, BROOKLYN, N. Y.

Chicago Representative:
C. A. RIDD

New York Salesrooms:
1133 Broadway
Room 28—Smith Bldg., Wheaton, Ill.

224.

mous book. Other cloth dolls included *Muffin, Raggi-Muffin, Beloved Belinda, Kate Greenaway* and *Little Louisa.*

225.

226.

Raggedy Ann and Raggedy Andy: 17in (43cm) — 19in (48cm); painted faces; red hair; solid red heart on body beside mark; all original clothes; cotton print dresses and aprons; *Andy* has red and blue shirt and solid blue pants; 1935-1938.
MARKS: "Raggedy Ann and Raggedy Andy Dolls//Manufactured by Molly-'es Doll Outfitters" (cloth tag on doll)
SEE: *Illustration 225. Candy Brainard Collection.*
PRICE: $325-375 each.

TAGS: Mollye had at least three different series of international dolls with different tags.
1. *Roumanian Doll* (see *Illustration 226*).
2. *Rosita of Mexico* (see *Illustration 227*).
3. *Margot of Tyrol* (see *Illustration 228*).

Ileana the Roumanian Girl (spelled as appeared on label): 15in (38cm); white piqué skirt with red and white embroidered trim; blue, pink, yellow and white printed blouse; red felt apron with black, white and green felt trim; red rayon head scarf; 1938.

Other dolls in this series included dolls from Russia, Bulgaria, Bavaria, Spain, England, Prussia, Switzerland, Norway, Denmark, Serbia, Greece, Turkey, America, France, Belgium, Scotland, Sweden, Holland, Austria, Ireland, Italy, Tyrol, Poland, Hungary, Mexico and Czechoslovakia. There was also a *Sleeping Beauty* and a *Gypsy*.
MARKS: None on doll; "Ileana the Roumanian Girl No. 2956//A// Molly-'es//Doll//copyright 1938

180

Molly-'es" (on wrist tag booklet)
SEE: *Illustration 226.*
PRICE: $75-110

Rosita of Mexico: 13in (33cm); green organdy skirt trimmed with lace; white cotton blouse; multi-colored belt and straps; blue print seersucker triangular hat with white felt brim; has Mollye characteristics; for general characteristics, see Identification Guide, page 226; circa 1937-1943.

Dolls in the series included England, Switzerland, France, Sweden, Holland, Mexico and Czechoslovakia, according to the tag.
MARKS: "Created by Mollye//International Doll Co.//Philadelphia, Penna." (on wrist tag booklet)
SEE: *Illustration 227.*
PRICE: $75-220

227.

Margot of Tyrol: 13in (33cm); straight yellow yarn hair; dressed in blue skirt with yellow and red bias trim; yellow apron with red and blue bias trim; white print blouse; red vest with blue ties; green felt Tyrolean hat with feather; has Mollye characteristics (see Identification Guide, page 226); circa 1937-1943.
MARKS: "Margot of Tyrol//Manufactured by//Molly'es, Inc.//Made in U.S.A." (on wrist tag booklet)
SEE: *Illustration 228.*
PRICE: $75-110

Marassa of Russia: 14in (36cm); red peasant skirt trimmed with braid and lace; white cotton embroidered blouse; red high boots; high Russian headpiece trimmed with felt symbols; Mollye characteristics (see Identification Guide, page 226).
MARKS: "Molly-'es//Doll//Copy-

228.

right 1938 Molly'es" (tag)
SEE: *Illustration 32* (Averill Section; doll on right).
PRICE: $90-135

Moravian Dolls

For over 100 years, since 1872, Moravian women have gathered together to make dolls which have been sent all over the world. Today in Bethlehem, Pennsylvania, women in several church groups still meet to sew the beloved *Polly Heckewelder, Benigna* and *Anna Nitschmann* dolls which are sold to raise money for many Moravian purposes. Throughout the years, the dolls have been lovingly handmade with beautiful materials and tiny detailed stitches.

The Sewing Society of the Central Moravian Church created the *Polly Heckewelder* doll in 1872 to honor Johanna Marie Heckewelder after her death. She was known more familiarly as Polly. Polly was the daughter of John Heckewelder, a missionary in Salem, Ohio, at the time. She was the second white child born in Ohio.

The same patterns have been used over the years for the 15in (38cm) cloth doll. Thousands of these dolls have been made. *Polly* is dressed in either a pink or blue checked dress. If she has brown hair and brown eyes, she will be wearing pink. If she is blonde with blue eyes, her dress will be blue. This is the type of dress that little girls wore in the early days of Bethlehem.

The faces on these dolls are beautiful. They are painted on white nainsook by skilled members of the group. The general features are always the same but because they are individually done, each doll has her own personality.

The double bonnet is very important. The inner bonnet is cloth with lace trim; the outer bonnet is carefully crocheted with the same pattern and number of stitches for each doll.

The doll in *Illustration 229* was made in the 1930s but the ones made today are the same. In fact, this doll was missing her outer bonnet and when she was taken to visit Mrs. Alice Knauss, who heads the sewing committee today, she was given a new bonnet by Mrs. Knauss, and it fits perfectly.

MARKS: None
SEE: *Illustration 229.*
PRICE: These dolls can rarely be purchased. They are usually sold to members of the Moravian Society and handed down from generation to generation.

Another group of women from the Bethel Circle of King's Daughters of the first Moravian Church of Bethlehem originated and made a small 6in

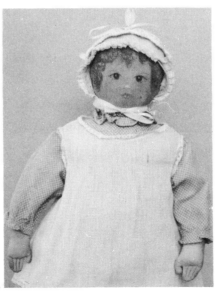

229.

(15cm) doll. Like the *Polly* doll, each doll is carefully created with exquisite detail in both the sewing and the painting of the tiny face. Each dress is made of cotton and trimmed with a white organdy collar and apron. This doll was also made in the 1930s, although similar dolls are still being made today. Each doll carries a bag with the following message written in beautiful script so tiny that it must almost be read with a magnifying glass:

"This doll is named *Benigna*, the founder of the first Protestant boarding school for girls in America. At the age of 16, she accompanied her father, Count Zuizuedorf to Bethlehem. The dress is copied from those worn by Moravian ladies long ago. The color on the cap signifies the choir to which the doll belongs: White — widow; blue — married sister; pink — single sister; cherry — little girl."

230.

MARKS: None on doll
SEE: *Illustration 230.*
PRICE: These dolls can seldom be purchased. They are mostly sold to members of the Moravian Society and handed down from generation to generation.

Mutual Novelty Corp.

The advertisement in *Playthings* said, "Our undressed Boudoir Dolls are steady sellers throughout the year." Some of their dressed dolls came with cigarettes in their mouths and wore pantsuits; some of the dolls had silk embroidery thread hair; some of the heads were composition.

In 1926 they advertised an Egyptian doll dressed in silk ruffled pajamas.
SEE: *Illustration 231. Playthings,* January 1927.

231.

For "MUTUAL" Reasons
See Our

BOUDOIR DOLLS

You will find our special designs very attractive

Our undressed Boudoir Dolls are steady sellers throughout the year.

We also manufacture a number of exclusive

MAMA DOLLS

All Our Dolls Retail at a Popular Price
See Them During the Toy Fair In
ROOM 1026—TOY MART
315 FOURTH AVENUE

MUTUAL NOVELTY CORP.
15 E. 26TH ST.,   NEW YORK CITY

N.A.T.I.
(Novedad Arte Tomalidad Ingenio) (Spain)

232.

around the world but not so well-known in the United States.

Until recently, their prices have been very low. However, prices have been climbing quickly and the collector will find both high prices and great bargains until prices stabilize.

IDENTIFICATION FEATURE FOR N.A.T.I. DOLLS: Stiffened mask faces are made from a unique large weave muslin.

Male Spanish Dancer with Castanets: 9in (23cm); for general characteristics, see *Illustration 233;* doll is made with same fine attention to detail as larger dolls; Lenci Mascotte-type doll; gray felt bolero suit with black felt buttons and trim; handsome brown cobbled shoes; wooden castanets tied to wrists; maroon cummerbund; thread wig; ear is single piece of gathered felt; circa 1930s.
MARKS: None on doll: "N.A.T.I.// Madrid//Lema//Novedad Arte// Made in Spain" (box)
SEE: *Illustration 232.*
PRICE: $100-175 (sample prices vary widely)

Girl in Green Dress: 14in (36cm); stiffened muslin mask over shaped cardboard head; sculptured eyes; painted eyelashes above eyes; gray eye liner; raised eyebrows painted black; bow mouth; no ears; jointed at neck

Recently, collectors have been discovering the wonderful dolls from Spain. Like the Italians, the Spaniards have been producing excellent dolls for many years. They not only have made cloth dolls, but they have produced dolls in such materials as hard plastic, vinyl, celluloid, and so forth. There has also been interest in their doll artists and recently doll publications have been focusing on their creations. In the past few years N.A.T.I. dolls have won awards in doll shows in England and the United States.

N.A.T.I., like other Spanish, French and Italian companies, made both art dolls and inexpensive tourist dolls. Their dolls are well-known in the Spanish-speaking countries

The registered trademarks, the trademarks and copyrights appearing in italics/bold within this chapter belong to Novedad Arte Ingenio unless otherwise noted.

and shoulders; pin-jointed at hip; overcast seam at arm; hollow muslin body and limbs; third and fourth fingers sewn togehter; green organdy dress; white organdy collar and ruffles on sleeves, hemstitched trim on skirt; green felt tam; felt roses on trim around skirt; Lenci-type socks; unusual cobbled shoes; white cotton teddy; green organdy pants and slip. MARKS: None on doll: "N.A.T.I.// Madrid//Lema//Novedad Arte// Made in Spain" (paper tag); "N.A.T.I." (box)
SEE: *Illustration 233* (Color Section, page 223).
PRICE: $200-400 (sample prices vary widely)

Girl in Gold Dress: 14in (36cm); for general characteristics, see *Illustration 233;* Lenci look-alike; dressed in vibrant gold brocade dress; net apron decorated with colored sequins; gold felt hat; costume trimmed with felt flowers; circa 1930s and possibly later.
MARKS: None on doll: "N.A.T.I.// Madrid//Lema//Novedad//Arte// Made in Spain" (box)
SEE: *Illustration 234. Joane C. Hise Collection.*
PRICE: $100-250 (sample prices vary widely)

Winker Girl: 26in (66cm); stiffened muslin mask face; bow mouth; heavy muslin body; blonde wig; cloth arms and legs; costume has blue felt top and hat; bright yellow organdy skirt trimmed with blue felt; cobbled blue shoes; circa 1930s.

This doll has two levers in the back. One turns the head, the other lowers the lid over the eye.

234.

235.

The Nelke Corporation

Let's Go!

NELKE DOLLS

Nelke Soft Dolls get the right of way —every time! See how innocent that puppy looks? Even the Nelke Cop—the newest arrival in the Nelke Family—hasn't the heart to stop him!

That's just the way Nelke Soft Dolls win their way into the affections of kiddies everywhere! They're so soft, so cuddly, so lovable, you can't resist them. Not a button or pin anywhere. Lovely, bright colors—but absolutely fast! Boys and girls, clowns, puppies, kittens, rabbits—and now, to make them all behave, a Nelke Cop!

Leading department, drug, notions and specialty shops everywhere sell Nelke Soft Dolls at 50c and up. A woven label with our diamond trade-mark identifies the genuine. Send for our free booklet "The World's Happiest Family", in full colors! We'll appreciate your mentioning the name of your dealer.

The Nelke Corporation
10th and Norris Streets   Philadelphia, Pa.

236. *Look for this Trade* NELKE *Mark*

Nelke was the name of a company which made lisle underwear for men and women. About 1917 they started to make a line of animal and doll characters for children in a soft knit material.

In 1919 they made a *Romper Girl* dressed in pink, blue or white cotton crepe rompers.

In the 1920s they made 4½in (12cm) brown stockinette *Gold Dust Twins* used as premiums by the Fairbanks Soap Co., makers of Gold Dust Soap Powder.

In 1923 they advertised the *Nelke Cop* as the latest arrival in the Nelke Family. That year they also made clowns, puppies, kittens and rabbits. The *Nelke Cop* was supposed to make them all behave. It is reported that 400,000 dolls were made in 1923.

In 1929 *Cuddles* was the trade name of a jersey cloth doll with hand-painted features and hair. It had a one-piece body.

The company advertised that all the dolls were tagged with a woven label with the diamond-shaped Nelke trademark for easy identification (see *Illustration 236*).

Advertisement that Appeared Regularly through 1923: Knit fabric dolls; no buttons or pins for safety; both animal and human characters; 1917 and into the 1920s.
MARKS: Woven label with diamond trademark.
SEE: *Illustration 236. Playthings,* January 1923.

In *Playthings,* January 1928, The Nelke Corporation reported that they had changed the stockinette material to a new knitted material made of "powder puff" and silk with particular appeal to infants.

The registered trademarks, the trademarks and copyrights appearing in italics/bold within this chapter belong to The Nelke Corporation.

Ninon
(French Fashion Importing Co.)

The French Fashion Importing Co. advertised that they were importing the "Family 'Ninon' Beautiful French Dolls." They said these dolls had human expression, were lifelike in appearance, were unbreakable and washable and absolutely sanitary.

Ninon Dolls: 11-23in (28-58cm); felt; mitt hands with fingers indicated by stitching; thumb separate; slight curve in the arms; some came with glass eyes; felt shoes were tied at ankles. The doll was reported to be made by Bonin & Lefort.

SEE: *Illustration 237. Playthings*, February 1931.

Novelty Dolls

Flapper Handkerchief Holder: 9½in (24cm); body of doll in two pieces of flesh-colored felt sewn together to form a pocket; the front has the design of the doll imprinted in red and black ink; the head is a piece of imprinted cotton and a piece of felt sewn together and slightly stuffed; the imprinted felt hat fits over the head; felt loop for hanging or carrying; snap holds handkerchief in place.

MARKS: "Patented 1-3-28" (printed on felt back of doll)
SEE: *Illustration 238.*
PRICE: $20-25

Pocketbook Doll: 9½in (24cm); for general characteristics, see Identification Guide (Eros), page 229; doll and costume made of heavy pink felt

237.

238.

239.

which forms purse; zipper in back of skirt is opening for purse; skirt decorated with strips of blue felt and appliqued colored felt flowers; pink felt hat; hand-crocheted lace used for cuffs, collar and hat decoration; long pink felt strip attached for carrying straps; circa late 1930s-1940s. The doll has "Eros" characteristics; however, a marketing company may have purchased the heads and made them into pocketbooks.

MARKS: None
SEE: *Illustration 239.*
PRICE: $25-35

João Perotti Manufactura Orbis (Brazil)

During the late 1920s and early 1930s, a Lenci designer is reputed to have immigrated to Brazil where he started a doll company. These dolls are truly "art dolls" and resemble Lenci dolls, except for the color of their skin.

The quality of the costumes is excellent. The quality of the doll is poor.

Although the people and language of Brazil are Portuguese, bullfighting is a national sport. This matador is dressed in his "suit of lights." The details of his costume are exquisite.

Matador: 16in (41cm); for general characteristics, see Identification Guide, page 237; pressed felt mask face with side seams; no ears; painted face; red dots on the inside corners of eyes; thin eyelashes above and below eyes; two-tone lips; embroidered velvet pants and coat; red and black embroidered felt cape; black matador hat with pompons; 1929-1935.

MARKS: "Manufactura Orbis//João Perotti-St. Paulo//Industria Brazileira" (paper tag glued on cape)
SEE: *Illustration 240* (Color Section, page 220).
PRICE: $500-600

Gaucho (Cowboy of the Brazilian Grasslands): 18in (46cm); for general characteristics, see Identification Guide, page 237; felt pressed mask face with side seams; no ears; handsome hand-painted face; heart-shaped lips; felt wig; dressed in blue felt gaucho pants tucked in boots; black boots with the wooden high heels; red, yellow, blue and white checked shirt; red silk scarf around neck; leather belt with red felt trim and large metal medallions hanging down on belt extension; white felt poncho over shoulder with intricate felt trim; black felt gaucho hat. The following is a description of the clothing of a Brazilian gaucho. This doll has most of the details. Over his left arm hangs a whip of leather thongs which is comparable to our lasso. He uses it to trip the feet of cattle instead of lassoing them. In his right hand is a gourd with a sipper which contains maté, his native drink.

He has a poncho around his shoulders. Soft wool trousers have pleat inserts and buttons down each side. His leather belt has front pockets and a sheath for a short knife.

This *Gaucho* has a different paper tag from the other Perotti dolls that the author has seen. There is no indication that Orbis is the manufacturer, and it may have been an early Perotti. The mask face is sculptured with the rounded look of the early Lencis.

MARKS: "Joâo Perotti//R. Dr. Joao Alves de Lima, 309//S. Paulo Ind. Brasileira" (paper tag glued to felt belt)

SEE: *Illustration 241.*

PRICE: $500-600

Bahai Boudoir-Type Doll: 18in (46cm); for general characteristics, see Identification Guide, page 237; dark felt mask face with center seam only at back of head; heart-shaped mouth; beautifully painted face and eyes; black thread wig with side part; mitt hands with very large separate thumb; stitching indicating individual fingers; dressed in provincial costume of Bahai; white rayon dress, apron and scarf; multi-colored felt appliqued on

241.

dress with fancy stitching; green pleated organdy trim around apron and bottom of skirt; blue cotton pants with blue felt trim; extra long legs; felt slippers with high heels; red rayon scarf; various felt fruit, including bananas in woven straw basket on her head; wooden beads; brass earrings; circa 1930s.

MARKS: "Manufactura Orbis//Joâo Perotti//S. Paulo//Industria Brasileire" (paper tag glued to underpants)

SEE: *Illustration 242* (doll on left); (Color Section, page 221).

PRICE: $175-225

The two dolls in the illustration come from the province of Bahai on the Atlantic coast of Brazil. Here people of all nationalities and races live in harmony in one of the nicest climates on earth.

Bahai Girl in Original Box: 13in (33cm); for general characteristics, see Identification Guide, page 237; dark felt mask face with side seams; heart-shaped mouth; beautifully painted face and eyes; black thread wig with center part; mitt hands with very large separate thumb with stitching indicating individual fingers; dressed in the provincial costume of Bahai; red felt skirt with multi-colored pieces of felt forming large flowers; blue rayon apron with same type of felt applique as skirt; both skirt and apron have blue pleated organdy trim with felt borders; blue rayon blouse with puffed sleeves; pink scarf with red and blue yarn trim; red rayon scarf; felt fruit including bananas in woven straw basket on her head; wooden beads; brass earrings; wooden clogs with felt up-pers; felt flowers on toes; circa 1930s. **MARKS:** "Manufactura Orbis//Joâo Perotti s. Paulo//Industria Brasiliera" (paper tag glued to underpants); "Orbis//Original//Bahiana" (label on box with beautiful Indian design) **SEE:** *Illustration 242* (doll on right standing on box); (Color Section, page 221). **PRICE:** $200-250

Dolls Not Photographed

Perotti made a line of girl dolls not dressed in provincial clothes. They had the dark skin of the other dolls, but were dressed very much like the Italian Lenci dolls in organdy and felt. They had dark Spanish-type hair. Some of them were large dolls similar to the Lenci 109 series.

Ronnaug Petterssen (Norway)

243.

Provincial Girl: 15in (38cm); pressed mask head; cloth body; jointed at neck, shoulders and hips; legs have center seams; stitched fingers; arms attached with material for easy movement; black felt skirt with green trim; white blouse; red felt jumper top with colored beads; red felt hat with black felt trim; felt shoes; white cotton stockings; white cotton panties trimmed in rickrack; white cotton apron; 1930s. **MARKS:** None on doll **SEE:** *Illustration 243. Diane Domroe Collection.* **PRICE:** $500-600

The registered trademarks, the trademarks and copyrights appearing in italics/bold within this chapter belong to Ronnaug Petterssen.

190

Boy with Horn: 18½in (47cm); felt head; cloth body; open mouth with painted teeth; poodle-type mohair wig; royal blue suit with white trim and buttons; blue socks and shoes; all original; 1930s.
MARKS: Blue and silver tag "Made in Norway" on one side; silhouette of Laplander on other side.
SEE: *Illustration 244. Mary Tanner Collection.*
PRICE: $500-600

Pierrette

Pierrette: 27in (69cm); cloth mask face with back seam only; white mo- hair wig; side-glancing dark blue eyes with white dot and light blue curved line under eyes; dark eye shadow above eye; poorly sewn cloth body; black and white Pierrette costume with white pompons; late 1920s-early 1930s.

Many companies made very inexpensive "French-type" boudoir dolls. Many home sewers bought a mask face and made a cloth body from one of the commerical or magazine patterns readily available. This may have been one of these non-commercial dolls.
SEE: *Illustration 245.*
PRICE: $75-100

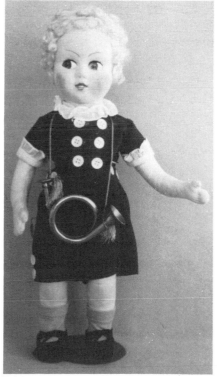

244.

245.

Pinky Winky Products Co., Inc.

Ma-Ma-Doll: 19in (48cm); fiberoid face; rolling eyes; dresses of pink and white voile; says "ma-ma;" cotton stuffed.

Created by Mme. Georgene Averill, originator of the soft stuffed walking doll. Other Ma-Ma dolls by this company were made with composition heads.

SEE: *Illustration 247. Playthings, September 1924.*

The registered trademarks, the trademarks and copyrights appearing in italics/bold within this chapter belong to Pinky Winky Products Co. Inc.

247.

Poir

Company listed under Gre-Poir (see page 81).

Poupées Nicette

246.

Gast Perrimond made cloth dolls with felt faces in the 1920s and 1930s. They were considered art dolls in France and they were used for children's play dolls, export and decorations.

Girl from Provence: 9½in (24cm); painted felt mask face joined in back of head only; beautifully hand-painted face; tiny eyelashes above eye; pinkish eye shadow around entire eye; eyebrows painted with very fine line; two-tone lips; brown wig; cloth body; mitt hands with no stitching indicating fingers; metal pin joint at shoulders and hips; seam in front and back of legs; no seam at ankle; dressed in the pink candy-striped skirt of

Provence (Mediterranean province of France around Nice); black felt trim; black apron; white blouse trimmed with lace; printed scarf; gold cross at neck; black felt shoes.

MARKS: "Poupèes Nicette//Paris Nice//Made in France" (gold and black tag)
SEE: *Illustration 246.*
PRICE: $75-85

Presbyterian Dolls

In the 1880s the women of the Church Society of the First Presbyterian Church of Bucyrus, Ohio, made cloth dolls to raise money to help build the church. They originally sold for $1.00.

The Society had records of the early project but the pattern and the most of the dolls had disappeared. Periodically, there was talk of revival. During one of these occasions in the late 1950s, an elderly lady in the church remembered that she was an excellent seamstress as a young girl and had helped with the sewing of these dolls. One of the older ladies had given her the pattern to save "because sometime the Presbyterian ladies may want to make them again to raise money for the church."

The fragile pattern was recovered and since there was a need for money in the 1960s to renovate the parsonage for a Sunday School, another committee was formed to make the dolls. A loving history of the dolls was written to be included with each of the later dolls. Such a history came with this doll.

The original pattern allowed the cloth doll to sit easily. This was innovative for the time. The second doll was carefully crafted to have the characteristics of the old ones. During this second period, at least one of the old

248.

dolls was found in an old trunk in Bucyrus.

1960s Presbyterian Doll: Cloth body lacquered; dressed in red dress and bonnet with white dots; organdy apron with lace; hand-crocheted collar; carefully painted face; bright red shoes.
SEE: *Illustration 248. Thelma Purvis Collection.*
PRICE: $250-300

Ravca
(France)

249.

Old Couple with Hurdy-Gurdy: 18in (46cm); needle-sculptured cloth faces; man dressed in black pants; jacket; shirt; red polka dot tie; wooden-type shoes; carrying a hurdy-gurdy which plays the French National Anthem; monkey with red vest and blue cap sitting on hurdy-gurdy; woman dressed in green felt skirt; beige felt jumper top; white blouse; carrying a straw doll; 1930s. These dolls were part of the Pryor collection (see page 5).
MARKS: "Made in France, Ravca" (tag).
SEE: *Illustration 249. Diane Domroe Collection.*
PRICE: $200-250 each

Les Poupées Raynal
(France)

250.

The Raynal dolls are made of both cloth and/or felt. They may have a celluloid head. The fingers are often a squared-off mitten type. They also used celluloid for some of their hands. Usually they have side-glancing eyes. There may be two highlights on the lower lip.

The dolls had beautiful clothes which sometimes imitated the Lenci look.
UNUSUAL IDENTIFICATION FEATURE: Eyebrows are very wide on the forehead.

Girl in Blue Dress: 14½in (37cm); beautifully painted silk mask face;

194

251.   252.

face oil painted; blue eye shadow under eyes; brown side-glancing eyes; painted upper lashes only; unusual wide eyebrows; two-tone lips with two white highlights on lower lip; pink cotton body; legs sewn up the back only; blue party dress; blue felt shoes with same buttons as on back of dress; circa early 1930s.
UNUSUAL IDENTIFICATION FEATURE: Very wide eyebrows.
MARKS: "Les Poupées//Raynal" (box)
SEE: *Illustration 250. Childhood doll of Margaret Mandel.*
PRICE: $500-600+

Girl: 18in (46cm); beautiful color on silk mask face; face oil painted; blue eye shadow under eyes; brown eyes; unusual slanted eyebrows; small painted eyelashes at outer edges of upper part of eye; two-tone lips with no highlights; fingers are squared-off mitten type; legs sewn up front; teal blue skirt with checkerboard inset of contrasting felt; bright pink bodice; for further information, see Identification Guide, page 238; 1925-1930s.
MARKS: "Les Poupèes Raynal//Narque Deposee/Made in France" (tag sewn to front of dress)
SEE: *Illustration 251* (doll). *Jeanette Fink Collection. Illustration 252* (closcup of face). *Jeanette Fink Collection.*
PRICE: $500-700+

Royal Society

Pierrette Laundry Bag: 28in (71cm); soft muslin face; orange and blue broadcloth body (laundry bag); muslin hands and feet; painted cheeks and lips; embroidered eyes and trim on suit and hat; orange hat; 1926.

The Royal Society supplied art needlecraft for home sewing for many years at the beginning of the 20th century. This Pierrette was cut, embroidered and packed away incomplete. Recently completed, the colors are still vivid.

195

MARKS: "Royal Society//Attractive Novelty//Pierrette Laundry Bag//Orange and Blue Linette. Hand//Tinted. Unbleached for Face.//Ready to Embroider in Black" (printed on package front)

SEE: *Illustration 253* (Color Section, page 168).
PRICE: $30-40 with packet of directions

The Rushton Company

254.

By 1929 the dolls had voices and in 1930 the variety of materials used for the creations included velveteen, terry cloth and stockinette. A heavy canvas was used for the face and they were hand-painted in oil.

Mawaphil Dolls (Snuggle-Ups): Created by Mary Waterman Phillips; handmade and hand-painted; materials included plush, rayon and stockinette.
SEE: *Illustration 254. Toys and Novelties*, April 1932.

In 1920 a line of dolls designed by Mary Waterman Phillips was started by The Rushton Company. The line is known as "Mawaphil," an acronym of the creator's name. The dolls were made well into the 1930s. Made of stockinette, these art dolls came in many different styles of both child and animal figures. There were nursery rhymes and ethnic characters as well as other figures. There were as many as 20 different characters created each year.

Mawaphil Dolls: Made of stockinette, terry cloth, velveteen and rayon plush; new line included spring and holiday lines; displayed at New York Toy Fair in 1931.
SEE: *Illustration 255A. Playthings*, February 1931.

Little Tommy Tucker (Mawaphil Line): 15in (38cm); head and body made of an oilcloth-type cloth; face is

The registered trademarks, the trademarks and copyrights appearing in italics/bold within this chapter belong to The Rushton Company.

255A.

pressed, molded and brightly painted; real eyelashes; white curly floss hair; mitt hands with no stitching to indicate fingers; no stitching to indicate toes; ankle seam in front and dart at ankle line at back; unusually small and neat hand-sewn, overcast stitches on back body and head; yellow corduroy suit trimmed with pleated lavender organdy; white organdy shirt trimmed with same pleated lavender organdy; lavender molded felt hat with yellow trim; white shoes and socks; 1930s.
IDENTIFICATION FEATURE: The doll is easily confused with Averill dolls but the oilcloth-type head and body and the stitching on the back and head are very different.
MARKS: None on doll or clothing; "Little Tommy Tucker//The Rushton Co.//Atlanta, Florida" (paper tag attached to wrist)

255B.

SEE: *Illustration 255B*
PRICE: $75-100+ (very few sample prices available)

S.F.B.J.
(Société Francais Fabrication Bébés et Jouets) (France)

By the early 1920s, S.F.B.J. realized that they must begin to make dolls of varying materials. Always resourceful, in 1923 they offered a partnership to Emil Lang who had been experimenting with cloth dolls since 1914. He had been making boudoir dolls, animals and other dolls with his new methods of hot molding and gluing fabrics.

Emil Lang accepted their offer and this gave S.F.B.J. designs by Jean Ray who had designed early boudoir-type dolls. Lang helped set up a stuffed doll department and dolls were produced under old and new patents. The new patents were issued under the S.F.B.J. name. It is known that they made cloth girl and boy dolls and boudoir dolls for various French department stores.

Emil Lang left S.F.B.J. about 1928; he and his son formed a new company which continued to make boudoir dolls, pincushion dolls, animals and other novelties.

Dolls with felt or cloth heads and stuffed fabric bodies were made from the 247 mold.

197

S & H Novelty Co.

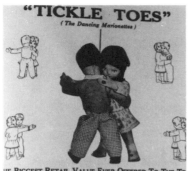

256. HE BIGGEST RETAIL VALUE EVER OFFERED TO THE TR

Tickle Toes, the Dancing Marionettes: Can be snapped together for dancing or unsnapped for regular play; held by a string; dressed in a variety of costumes; cloth faces and bodies; 1929.

The advertisement gave a warning, "The 'Dancing Marionettes' are fully covered by applications by U.S. Letters Patent and makers of infringing items will be vigorously prosecuted."
SEE: *Illustration 256. Playthings*, January 1929.

Schoen and Yondorf Company, Inc.

257.

Helen and Maria: 17in (43cm); double-faced doll; one side has golden hair of wool, body of sanitary oilcloth, cotton stuffed; the other side has dark wool hair; dark oilcloth body; can be carried by a slender strap at the top of the head.

Other novelties which were available in 1924 included *Mistah Sunshine, Jiggles the Clown, Beansie the Dog* and *Teddy in Boots*.
SEE: *Illustration 257. Playthings*, September 1924.

Silk Novelty Dolls

Czechoslovakian Girl: 14in (36cm); pink mask face; pink muslin body; painted face; Averill look-alike; dressed in ethnic costume; long black shirt trimmed with same material as sash and decoration on head scarf; late 1930s.
MARKS: "Character Doll//Silk Novelty Co.//N.Y.C." (printed on gold paper tag)

SEE: *Illustration 258. Marie Ezzo Collection.*

PRICE: $50-70

GENERAL CHARACTERISTICS:

1. Push-and-pull hand-sewn seam on back of head.
2. Hand-sewn overcast back seam extends only half way down the back.
3. Hands and legs are cut out with body in one piece.
4. Head is machine-stitched to body.
5. Mitten hands have no individual fingers.
6. Side-glancing eyes have white dots for highlights.
7. Red dots are painted on nose.

258.

Steiff (Germany)

For over 100 years, the dolls of Margarete Steiff have been popular with children and collectors. Today they are still being sold and enjoyed by the present generation.

The concept of an impish, character face with a seam down the middle has been imitated by many companies (see Identification Guide, page 249), and many authors have used pictures of these dolls as illustrations of their stories. Some of the dolls closely resemble characters from fiction or cartoon characters. Their stylized animal figures are very popular. Felt was often used for the basic doll and/or clothing.

These cloth dolls are very much a part of the dolls made during the 1920s and 1930s. However, the identification of the hundreds of these dolls is not within the scope of this book. Presented here is a picture of a group of dolls which is part of the collection of Nancy A. Smith. It shows a variety of Steiff dolls for anyone who is unsure

259.

of their identification. An unidentified Steiff-like doll can be found in *Illustration 271.*

SEE: *Illustration 259. Nancy A. Smith Collection.*

199

Strobel & Wilken Co., Inc.

260.

261.

The registered trademarks, the trademarks and copyrights appearing in italics/bold within this chapter belong to Strobel & Wilken Co., Inc., unless otherwise noted.

Strobel & Wilken was a Cincinnati, Ohio, importing company which had ties to Germany, especially Sonneburg. As early as 1913, they advertised *Käthe Kruse* dolls. They had exclusive rights to the American Art Dolls with their *Susie's Sister* line, *Tootsie* line and others.

Katrina and **Hendrik:** 11in (28cm); dressed in Dutch costumes; other dolls in the series are also dressed in nationality costumes; stuffed with soft cotton; durable heads; movable arms and legs; 1931.
SEE: *Illustration 260. Playthings,* April 1931.

Susie's Sister: 17in (43cm); cloth; painted face; jointed arms and legs; dresses came in assorted colors; pleated cap; apron; shoes and stockings.
SEE: *Illustration 261. Playthings,* October 1915.

T.A.F. (Talleres de Arte Fusté) (Spain)

In 1934 the T.A.F. company in Madrid issued a sales catalog of the lovely dolls in their line. There were 32 pages showing over 200 dolls with stunning costumes and accessories. The pictures were actual brown-tone photographs which were so popular in Spain during that era.

Over a four-year period, the author was unable to find more than one doll that was in this catalog despite having advertised widely. That doll, a

Gallegos Boy, is shown in *Illustration 262* with his page from the catalog. He is beautifully crafted with life-like details.

Only five pages of this catalog can be shown in this book, but the rest of the dolls are equally beautiful and show the provincial and urban culture of Spain of the 1930s. It is hoped that

The registered trademarks, the trademarks and copyrights appearing in italics/bold within this chapter belong to Talleres de Arte Fusté.

more of these art dolls can be identified.

The dolls range from 10in (25cm)
to 32in (81cm) and include play dolls,
provincial dolls, boudoir dolls, novelty
dolls, holiday dolls and cartoon-type
dolls similar to Klumpe dolls.

Like Lenci and other cloth companies in the different countries,
T.A.F. offered a sports series, dolls
with the latest swim wear and dolls
representing various vocations such as
musicians, priests, cowboys, dancers,
farmers, and so forth.

Some of the dolls mirrored the
wonderful adult fashions of the Art
Deco era which were designed by the
courturiers of the international style
centers.

There are similarities between the
N.A.T.I. and the T.A.F. dolls. Both
were made in Madrid. However, the
author has not been able to connect
them in any way.

Gallegos Boy: 14in (36cm), very firm
body; stiffened fine muslin painted
mask face; side-glancing eyes; painted
eyelashes above eyes; light eyebrows;
bow mouth with cloudy white dot in
center; applied ears similar to Alma;
black plush wig; neat hand-sewn seam
in head, no side seams; jointed at
shoulders and hips only; arms operate
together when moved; unusual
widely-spaced fingers with second and
third fingers indicated only by stitching; first, little finger and thumb more
pointed than fingers of other cloth
dolls; body and limbs of fine woven
muslin; dressed in Gallegos musician
costume; white muslin shirt with
cuffs open; front of vest is maroon felt
with white felt in back; black felt
knee-length pants with white cloth inset at hem; black high felt boots with

felt buttons; blue cotton cummerbund; brown felt provincial hat with
black felt brim and pompons; 1934.

The catalog shows that the boy
was carrying a bagpipe. This boy is
from the Galicia province of north-
west Spain. The population traces its
roots to the Celts and bagpipes are a
common musical instrument. The region is poor, agricultural and heavily
populated. The climate is different
from most of the rest of Spain because
it gets more rain. However, over the
years, the land has been divided into
very tiny impoverished farms.

The catalog page shown in the illustration is one of three which pictures the "Munecas Regionales//Serie
R."

From left to right it shows a pair of
dolls from Castellanos and Rondenos
(top row) and Abulenses and Gallegos
(bottom row). Other regions shown in
the catalog include Catalanes, Valen-
cianos, Andaluces, Charros, Alcar-
renos, Vizcainos, Aragoneses and
Lagarteranos.
MARKS: "Talleres De Arte//Fuste//
Impuesto De Lujo Ametalico//Per-
miso No. 359//Factura No.1107"
(sticker on bottom on left foot)
SEE: *Illustration 262* (Color Section,
page *222*).
PRICE: $250-275 up

**1934 Catalog Page Munecas Hispa-
nia:** 10in (25cm).
Dolls No. 9-16 show ornately costumed Spanish provincial dancing
dolls.
SEE: *Illustration 263.*

**1934 Catalog Page Huevos de Pas-
cua:** 12¾in (33cm)
Novelties 4-6 show Easter egg with
three different designs; center egg is

9   13   10   14   11   15   12   16

14   15   16

263.

264.   17   18   19

open to display a doll which was packaged in egg.
SEE: *Illustration 263. T.A.F. Catalog, 1934.*

1934 Catalog Page Series E: 21in (54cm); (dolls from left to right). (14) Girl in crocheted dress with large

bow in hair. (15) Girl in party dress with large hat. (16) Girl in school skirt and vest carrying a book.
SEE: Illustration 264.

1934 Catalog Page Series E: 21in (54cm); (dolls from left to right). (17) Boy in provincial costume with fez-type hat. (18) Oriental boy with heavily-embroidered costume. (19) Girl in garden-type dress with large straw hat.
SEE: *Illustration 264.*

1934 Catalog Page of Large Boudoir-type Dolls Series J: 32¼in (82cm). Doll in upper picture is romantic version of traditional Spanish ruffled dancing costume; ornate sleeves and headdress.
Doll in lower picture is wearing a romanticized hunting costume of the 17th century; skirt is appliqued with large hunting scenes; elaborate tricorn hat.
SEE: *Illustration 265.*

265.

1934 Catalog Page Series C (upper row left to right): 16in (41cm); (10) Girl in long dress carrying a straw hat. (11) Boy with golf club. (12) Girl in party dress. (13) Girl in jodhpurs. **SEE:** *Illustration 266.*

1934 Catalog Page Series D (lower row left or right): 19in (48cm); (1) Girl in party dress. (2) Girl in bathing suit and beach coat. (3) Girl in pinafore with large ribbon in hair. **SEE:** *Illustration 266.*

The 1934 T.A.F. catalog pictured 20 cartoon dolls. They are similar to the 1950s Spanish Klumpe and Roldan dolls. They, too, are clever and well-made.

Munecas Humoristicas Series T: 15in (38cm); 9-20 pictured and 1-8 listed only; cloth over an armature; felt heads.

10   11   12   13

1   2   8

266.

267.

203

UPPER PICTURE FROM LEFT TO RIGHT

9. Gardener with a hoe.
10. Skier.
11. Golfer with a golf club.
12. Man with towel over his shoulder.
13. Tennis player with tennis racket.
14. Man with fishing pole.
15. Boxer with boxing gloves.
16. Man with serape.

LOWER PICTURE FROM LEFT TO RIGHT

21. Clown.
17. Man with tall hat and bolero.
22. Chef with food.
18. Man in plaid pants.
23. Man with walking stick.

19. Man with checked pants.
24. Sailor.
20. Man in smock.

NOT PICTURED BUT IN 1934 CATALOG

1. Guitar player.
2. Male singer.
3. Matador (several with different costumes).
4. Picador.
5. Spanish male dancer.
MARKS: Possible sticker on foot
SEE: *Illustration 267.*
PRICE: No sample prices
It is hoped that some of our readers can help us identify these dolls.

Unique Novelty Doll Co.

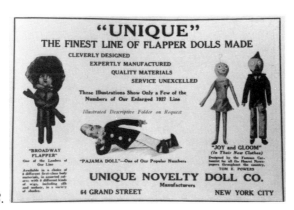

268.

Boudoir Dolls: 32in (81cm); silk and mohair wigs in a variety of shades.

Broadway Flapper: Silk and mohair wigs in a variety of shades; six different body materials in different colors; came undressed.

Pajama Doll: One of the popular bag-type boudoir dolls.

Joy and Gloom (In Their New Clothes): Designed by Tom E. Powers, the cartoonist for all Hearst newspapers throughout the country.
SEE: *Illustration 268. Playthings,* January 1927.
PRICE: $80-125

Unknown

The 1920s and the 1930s were two different decades in history. In the 1920s money was easy and both large companies and single artists with an idea for a doll made a prototype, rented a booth and showed their doll at one of the toy fairs in this country and abroad. Each one hoped that his doll would "make it big." Sometimes only a few dolls were made and they were often unmarked.

In the depression of the 1930s, the need to "make it big" was even more important to faltering companies and unemployed artists. It was necessary to economize and the dolls of this decade are not as well made. Often the dolls were sold unmarked and untagged.

The government tried to help the struggling unemployed through the WPA in the middle 1930s and, since government money was involved, it insisted that these dolls be marked well. Collectors and researchers can be happy about this.

There are still many unmarked dolls from the 1920s and 1930s in spite of a diligent search. Three such dolls are pictured in this book. They are particularly appealing dolls and perhaps one of our readers can help identify them.

Winking Boy with Cigarette: 12in (31cm); painted stockinette face; muslin arms and legs; double-stitched ears; red lock of hair peeping out from green felt cap; left eye winking; right eye wide open with prominent brown eyelashes above eyes; curved eyebrow; green felt shirt and shoes; black short pants; cigarette in left corner of side-

269.

curving mouth; box is covered with bright red cherries; circa 1920s.
MARKS: None
SEE: *Illustration 269. Margaret Benike Collection.*
PRICE: $600-850+

Baby: Treated gauze face; sturdy cotton body; delicately painted face; blue glass eyes; leather arms; mohair wig; pink and white striped cotton dress; beige ribbon sash; sunbonnet style hat.
MARKS: "au Main Bleu//Paris//Bd des Capuchnes27" (on shoes)
SEE: *Illustration 270. Elizabeth Martz Collection.*
PRICE: $250-300

Sheik: 20in (51cm); all felt; U-shaped ear; blown glass eyes; beard; seam down the center of face; red felt coat and cape; red cummerbund; white riding breeches; real leather shoes; metal curved sword.

The doll is well made and the costume is beautifully tailored. **MARKS:** None on doll **SEE:** *Illustration 271. Margaret Benike Collection.* **PRICE:** $700-900

270.

271.

A. Alberani Vecchiotti

Provincial Girl Campania Sessa Aurunca: 12in (31cm); for general characteristics, see page 238; dressed in blue felt skirt and vest with painted gold design; gold trim and red felt around bottom of skirt; light blue silk rayon overskirt; black felt short coat with pink felt trim; black underapron trimmed with gold braid; pink double overapron with gold embroidery; long blue beads; short silver beads; silver ornament holds white cotton and lace headpiece; holds red flower with green leaf in her hand with divided fingers (thumb and first finger separate; second, third and little finger indicated only by stitching). **MARKS:** "A. Alberani Vecchiotti// Milano" (cloth tag sewn in skirt); "Bambola 13/15//Campania Sessa aurunca" (separate gold medallion tag) **SEE:** *Illustration 272.* **PRICE:** $80-85

Venus (France)

Brittany Girl with Quimper Provincial Costume: 16in (41cm); pressed mask head; painted face; cloth body; jointed at neck, shoulders and hips (no pins showing); dressed in fine wool blue dress; rayon apron; silk printed shawl; organdy and lace headdress; circa 1930s.

This doll is from the Pryor Collection and is not marked. However, another doll in the collection with the same characteristics was labeled "Venus." Adrien Carvaillo was the maker of the *Venus* doll. Bon Marché, a department store in Paris, distributed them.

MARKS: None on doll

SEE: *Illustration 273. Diane Domroe Collection.*

PRICE: $400-450

The registered trademarks, the trademarks and copyrights appearing in italics/bold within this chapter belong to Venus.

273.

272.

WPA (Works Progress Administration)

In the middle and late 1930s Franklin Roosevelt sponsored the famous Works Progress Act (WPA) which was passed to help citizens who were out of work. This Act also helped artists who had difficulty making a living. Projects included the making of dolls. These dolls were often historical characters, international dolls, storybook characters and others which could be used by schools, libraries and museums for teaching children. They were also used for displays. Each project was different. Today these dolls, puppets and marionettes that were made in the Depression have become very collectible.

The dolls in this book are cloth. However, many other doll projects included dolls of papier-mâché, unusual composition, pottery and glazed china. Some of the papier-mâché dolls had a layer of cloth glued on the bodies and heads.

WPA Macon, Georgia Project

274.

Scarlett O'Hara Mammy Dolls: Made in Macon, Georgia; an article was written about them in the June 1937 issue of *Toys and Bicycles* magazine.

"*Scarlett O'Hara Mammy Dolls*, inspired by the best selling novel *Gone with the Wind*, are being made by a

WPA project in Macon, Ga. The doll was originated by Mrs. M.H. Parham, WPA sewing class teacher.

"*Mammy* is being built along generous lines both as to clothing and figure. She wears a starched calico dress, white apron and cap. Like her outer garments, her underclothes are also practical and old-fashioned. There are the old time pantalettes and a full petticoat. The shoes are made from black typewriter covers."

"The WPA women also make another type of *Mammy* doll, with a pine straw basket of clothes balanced on the head. With the approach of the movie 'Gone with the Wind,' these dolls will probably enjoy a large sale. Full details can be had by writing Mrs. Matile D. Bennett, Supervisor, Home Economic Department, Works Progress Administration of Georgia, 356 Cherry St. Macon, Ga."

SEE: *Illustration 274.*
PRICE: $300-450

WPA Michigan State Project

Dutch Boy and Girl: 15in (38cm); legs and body cut together; arms attached to body; seat gusset to allow dolls to sit; Steiff-like face with seam down the middle; oil-painted face; yarn hair; boy dressed in blue cotton and red necktie; girl dressed in same blue top, white and blue striped skirt, white apron and Dutch hat; girl has three muslin petticoats; 1930s.
MARKS: "Michigan State Wide// WPA Toy Project//Sponsored By// Michigan State College."

SEE: *Illustration 275. Geri Gentile Collection.*
PRICE: $200-300 each

Little Bo Peep: 13in (33cm); oil-painted face; mohair wig; pink and white candy-striped skirt with white blouse; black laced weskit; white apron; high-laced shoes; stitching indicates fingers on hand; late 1930s.
MARKS: "Michigan State//WPA Project//Made By//......(last line illegible)" (stamped on doll)

275.

SEE: *Illustration 276. Tory Scelso Collection.*
PRICE: $250-300

276.

WPA Milwaukee Wisconsin Project

277.

Polish Peasant: 23in (58cm); oil-painted mask face; multi-striped cotton skirt and apron; white and black weskit; white blouse with beautiful embroidery on sleeve; cloth boots; jewelry of crocheted twine; peasant kerchief covers yarn hair arranged in pigtails; unusual leg joint with the date January 26, 1939, printed on the inside.
MARKS: "W P A //Handicraft//Project//Milwaukee//Wisconsin//sponsored by//Milwaukee//County and// Milwaukee State Teachers//College" (stamped on back)
SEE: *Illustration 277. Marianne Gardner Collection.*
PRICE: $1100-1300 up

Norah Wellings

Norah Wellings started manufacturing dolls in Arleston, England, in 1926 with her brother, Leonard, as a partner. She had wonderful ideas in her head and she had had experience designing dolls for Chad Valley. Today many doll collectors smile when they encounter Norah's dolls with their impish grins; they cannot resist taking them home to join their collection. Her dolls sold originally in many countries of the world, especially those in the British Empire.

While many of Norah's novelties are small, her dolls range from 6in (15cm) to 36in (91cm) and include hundreds of different types. They are made of excellent quality material with great attention to detail. Many were presented to English royalty as gifts.

Most of the Norah Wellings dolls are well tagged, but occasionally the tag has been cut off or lost from the body. A detailed study of the Wellings identification features can be found in the Identification Guide, pages 239 and 240. In some ways the Wellings dolls follow the Lenci sewing details more than most of the other Lenci look-alikes. An example is the double-stitched ear. However, the actual sculpture of the faces is entirely different.

After the war, the Wellings Toy Works continued and Norah produced novelties which were similar to the prewar models. However, after her brother died, she closed the business in 1960 and lived in retirement at her home in Arleston where she continued with her "art" by painting lovely pictures. Today the wonderful novelty dolls with the gamin grins and their bright cheerful costumes continue to bring smiles to the faces of collectors in many parts of the world.

English Garden Girl: 18in (46cm); felt head, arms and legs; cloth body; for body characteristics, see Identification Guide, page 239; white, green, pink and yellow printed voile dress; ruffles on sleeves and skirt; pink felt bonnet with green felt ties; carries a gilt basket with multi-colored flowers; pink snap felt shoes; 1930s.
MARKS: "Made in England//by// Norah Wellings" (cloth tag on arm)
SEE: *Illustration 278* (Color Section, page *220*).
PRICE: $450-550

Scottish Girl of the International Series: 12in (31cm); stockinette mask face; painted features; mohair wig; cloth body; mitt hand with separate thumb; stitching indicates fingers; front and back seams in legs; white rayon blouse; tartan skirt and tie; black felt shoes; 1930s.

Although this is an inexpensive "tourist-type" doll, it is very well made and very collectible now.
MARKS: "Made in England//by// Norah Wellings" (cloth tag sewn to wrist)
SEE: *Illustration 279.*
PRICE: $100-150

Old Couple: 27in (69cm); made of felt; unusual sculptured, painted eyes which makes them very realistic;

The registered trademarks, the trademarks and copyrights appearing in italics/bold within this chapter belong to Norah Wellings unless otherwise noted.

man's whiskers cleverly attached to his jowls; lady's felt skirt has a blocked pattern which resembles a Lenci design; lady carries a basket; the old man carries a walking stick; 1935.

The *Old Couple* was displayed at the British Industry Fair in 1935.

MARKS: "Made in England//by// Norah Wellings" (cloth ribbon sewn to wrist)

SEE: *Illustration 280. Margaret Benike Collection.*

PRICE: $1600-1700 pair

Large Bed Doll: 36in (91cm); long limbs; high-heeled shoes; jointed at shoulders and hips; pink and gray ruffled dress; 1930s.

MARKS: "Made in England//by// Norah Wellings" (cloth tag sewn into wrist).

SEE: *Illustration 281. Celina Carroll Collection.*

PRICE: $850-1000

279.

280.

281.

282.

283.

Tourist Novelties Sold Around the World: 6in (15cm); left to right *Mountie, Islander, Welsh Girl.*

These and other tiny dolls were sold by the thousands around the world. They were sold on ships at sea including the *Queen Mary* and the

Queen Elizabeth and liners on the Orient run. The Canadian steamship lines sold *Little Pixie People* for $1.75. Many of the *Mounties* were sold in gift shops of the Pacific Railway Company hotels at Banff and Chateau Frontenac. This Canadian *Mountie* was purchased in Montreal, Canada, in 1953 as a special coronation souvenir. Tourists found many types of Norah Wellings' dolls in shops in the Caribbean islands.

MARKS: All three dolls have unusual cloth tags which say, "Made by Norah Wellings//Wellington, England."

SEE: *Illustration 282. Lois Janner Collection.*

PRICE: $40-75 each

Islander in Yellow Striped Pants: 12in (31cm); velvet head and body; brown velvet coat and yellow and brown striped pants are part of body construction; yellow velvet hair; big smiling mouth with white painted teeth; multi-colored bow tie; 1930s.

SEE: *Illustration 283. Angela Tillman Collection.*

PRICE: $125-200

212

Islander Doll: 36in (91cm); brown velvet head and body; side-glancing eyes; wide, toothy grin; straw "hula-type" costume; lifelike expression on face. Norah Wellings was famous for her *Islander* dolls which were sold around the world; 1930s.
SEE: *Illustration 284. Marvin Cohen Doll Auctions.*
PRICE: $700-900

Gripsholm Sailor: 13in (33cm); the uniform forms the body; smiling sculptured mask face; double seamed ears; side-glancing eyes with one white dot; painted reddish brown hair; blue felt uniform with yellow felt trim and brass buttons; matching sailor cap with "Gripsholm" embroidered on it in yellow; felt hands which are wired to hold bouquet of flowers. A tag with the flowers says, "With compliments//Swedish American Line."
284.

Norah Wellings made many sailor dolls which were sold aboard ships. The *Gripsholm* was a passenger and cruise ship which was commissioned in 1924. During World War II, it served as a peace ship exchanging diplomatic representatives of the warring countries.
SEE: *Illustration 285* (Color Section, page *217).*
PRICE: $150-200

West Indian Policeman: 14in (36cm); head and body made of velvet which is incorporated into costume; black curly mohair wig; unusual character face for *Islander* doll; wide smiling mouth with painted teeth; laughter lines sculptured into face; blue velvet coat; painted gold buttons; white felt skirt; brown velvet legs and
286.

288.

289.

Pirate: 15in (38cm); velvet mask head; double stitched ears; hand-painted face; velvet body incorporated as part of costume; jointed at neck, shoulders, hips and knees; black felt knee-length pants; red velvet stockings; felt shoes with large buckles and bows; yellow felt over shirt; green felt coat with red felt trim; silk bandana print scarf around neck and on head; brass buttons on coat; felt tricorn. This is an excellent example of the brilliant sculpture techniques of Norah Wellings. He has deep "character" lines on his face and forehead which make him look almost real; 1930s.
MARKS: "Made in England//by// Norah Wellings" (cloth tag sewn on bottom of foot)
SEE: *Illustration 287* (Color Section, page *222*).
PRICE: $300-400

Spanish Girl Purse: 11in (28cm); felt face; velvet upper body; skirt and sleeves made of brilliant black satin with a pink, red, yellow and green print; canary yellow fringed scarf and belt; skirt sewn together at bottom and lined to make a purse-bag; 1930s.
MARKS: "Made in England//by Norah Wellings" (cloth tag sewn in bottom in skirt)
SEE: *Illustration 288.*
PRICE: $50-75

feet; toes indicated by stitching; red felt belt and chest ribbon; white chevron marks painted on right sleeve; 1930s-1950s.
MARKS: "Made in England//by// Norah Wellings" (cloth tag sewn on bottom of foot)
SEE: *Illustration 286.*
PRICE: $75-85

MILITARY DOLLS

The English people especially loved the Norah Wellings felt and velvet military dolls. She tried to recreate the uniforms as authentically as possible. During World War II the Wellings' doll production was severely cut back. Their showrooms in London were bombed, and they no longer had their export trade. However, she did manage to make a few dolls. The most shining example was *Harry the Hawk* (see *Illustration 289*). Today it is especially nice to visit museums in the outlying lands of the old English Empire and greet the beloved uniform dolls of Norah Wellings (see *Illustrations 291 and 292*).

Harry the Hawk: 10in (25cm); velvet face; body is the beige twill aviator's uniform; wonderfully sculptured, smiling face; side-glancing brown eyes; leatherette goggles; brown velvet hands and feet; dark beige parachute strapped to chest; mohair "fur" collar; early 1940s.
MARKS: Tag states, "Made by Norah Wellings//By arrangement with the Royal Air Force Comforts Committee an agreed percentage of the manufacturers sales of these R.A.F. mascot doll is contributed to the Royal Air Comforts Fund"; "Made in England//by// Norah Wellings" (cloth tag on foot)
SEE: *Illustration 289.*
PRICE: $250-300

290.

292.

291.

215

RAF Girl: 10in (25cm); velvet head and body; glossy paint used for eyes and mouth; brown hair painted with unusual small brush strokes which is identified with Norah Wellings; white shirt with painted black tie; blue military jacket; blue slacks which are part of the body; dark blue shoes which are part of body; RAF marked cap is made of felt and velvet with leatherette visor; cloth mitt hands with fingers indicated by stitching; 1939-1945.
MARKS: "Made in England//by//Norah Wellings" (cloth tag sewn on bottom of foot)
SEE: Illustration 290.
PRICE: $75-100

Uniformed Dolls: Hanging from the rafters of the House of International Dolls on tiny Prince Edward Island in Canada are two groups of dolls. They include dolls in the uniforms of the British Army, Air Corps and Boy Guides. Due to the excellent quality of the material, their uniforms are still crisp and tailored. They preside over a collection of dolls from around the world. 1940-1945.
SEE: Illustration 291. House of International Dolls.
Illustration 292. House of International Dolls.

Wolf Doll Co., Inc.

The Wolf Doll Company was a "Verliger" company with offices in Sonneberg, Nürnberg, Boston and New York. They produced and distributed many types of dolls including bisque, composition and cloth.

In 1922 they started to make

Dutch peasant dolls dressed in "brilliantly colored felt." They also made a 2-in-1 Aunt Jemima (doll on right).
SEE: Illustration 293. Playthings, June 1923.

The registered trademarks, the trademarks and copyrights appearing in italics/bold within this chapter belong to Wolf Doll Co., Inc. unless otherwise noted.

293.

216

Norah Wellings Gripsholm Steward (see page 213).

Magit girl in pink (see page 176).

Fascist boy (see page 21).

Messina-Vat girl in red (see page 177).

Perotti matador (see page 188).

Norah Wellings garden girl (see page 210).

Perotti Bahai dolls (see pages 189 and 190).

Norah Wellings pirate (see page 212).

T.A.F. Gallegos boy (see page 201).

N.A.T.I. girl in green (see page 185).

Crowley Milna & Co. flapper dolls (see page 57). *Joe Golembieski Collection.*

Identification Guide Table of Contents

1. Body Identification 225
2. Cloth Used in Doll Construction ..
   240
3. Countries (Lists of Cloth Dolls) 242
4. Criers 246
5. Ears 246
6. Elastic Strung Bodies 246
7. Eyes 246
8. Hair 247
9. Look-alikes 248
10. Types of Cloth Dolls 249
    A. Animals 249
    B. Aunt Jemima and Mammy-type
       Dolls 249
    C. Babies 250
    D. Boudoir Dolls 250
    E. Cigarette Dolls 251
    F. Cowboys, Cowgirls, Gauchos ....
       252
    G. Matadors 252
    H. Military Dolls 252
    I. Novelties - Workbags,
       Pocketbooks, Pillows, Clothes, etc.
       252
    J. Pierrots and Pierrettes 252
    K. Religious Dolls 253

Identification Guide

All of the names in italics/bold appearing in the following section are protected names. The legal protections were left off for the readability of the charts and price guide.

Alma General Characteristics

Alma dolls have the same type of elastic stringing as the Altman dolls. However, their characteristics have some differences.

1. Elastic-strung body.
2. Mohair wig sewn onto head in strips.
3. Painted side-glancing eyes with two white dots connecting light brown curved line under each eye.
4. Thin painted eyelashes on outside of each eye.
5. Two-tone lips on closed mouth; on larger dolls with teeth showing, the lips are the same color.
6. Ear is single piece of felt slightly gathered and sewn on head.
7. Hollow felt-covered torso.
8. Felt is lighter skin tone than many other Italian dolls.
9. Legs and arms have no stitching on top.
10. Seam on back of neck resembles a ladder.
11. Felt clothes are beautifully made.

SEE: *Illustration 294.*

Altman Dolls (Possibly Alma) General Characteristics

Very few cloth dolls are strung with elastic. The author has located only two types of dolls with this characteristic. (1) Alma (2) Altman. The Alma characteristics are listed above.

The Altman Department Store in New York City imported cloth dolls made by several different doll manufacturers from several countries. The dolls have only the label "B. Altman//(the country of manufacture)."

The *Girl with Oranges* has this label (see *Illustration 13*). The *Lady with Fan* has the same characteristics but it has no label (see *Illustration 14*).

1. Pressed silky cloth mask with no side seams or ears.
2. Welt-like hand-sewn overcast seam on back of head.
3. Mohair wig.
4. Beautiful hand-painted face.
5. Heavy brown eyelashes over eyes (see *Eros* Characteristics, page 229).
6. White dot at left of pupil of eye and slight blue curved line underneath.
7. Bright red one-tone mouth.
8. Bright red cheeks.
9. Hollow pink body with no center front seam; machine-sewn; back seam; slight dart at bottom between legs; upper body is covered

294.

225

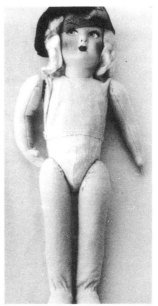

295.

with same thin, felt-like material that covers the lower body.

10. Hollow legs covered with same soft felt-like material.
11. Unusual foot seam with seam at ankle in front and bottom of heel in back.
12. Felt stuffed arms with mitt hands; shoulder seams closed by uneven overcast hand-sewing.
13. Mitt hands with separate thumb; fingers indicated by stitching.
14. Although the body characteristics of Alma and Altman dolls are similar,there are differences, especially in the head sculpture.

SEE: *Illustration 295.*

Averill and Mollye Comparison of General Characteristics

The cloth dolls of Averill and Mollye are often hard to distinguish, especially the International Series. How-ever, each artist had her own body characteristics which can be used to identify the dolls. They are shown in the following illustrations.

Faces

Both designers used mask faces with painted features. Averill used two types of lashes (1) thick, bold, painted lashes (2) real eyelashes applied to the eye (see *Illustration 314).* Mollye used only painted eyes with smaller eyelashes.

The mouth of the Averill doll is a wider, smiling mouth, while Mollye's mouth is pouty.

SEE: *Illustration 296.* Averill doll is on left.

Mollye doll is on the right.

Bodies

The cloth dolls of both artists are sewn up the back of the body. Those of Mollye are machine-sewn. Those of Averill are hand-sewn with an overcast stitch.

The doll on the left has a typical mohair wig used by Mollye. However, Mollye sometimes did use yarn hair. The blonde doll on the right has the kinky yarn hair used quite often by Averill.

SEE: *Illustration 297.* Mollye doll is on left.

Averill doll is on right.

The flags of both doll artists are distinctive. The flags of the Averill dolls have a tiny ball on the top of a metal pole. The flags of the Mollye dolls have a wooden pole.

Chad Valley General Characteristics

1. Seams of the back of head, top of arms and legs are similar to Lenci dolls. Both use the punch-and-

296.

pull stitch. However, they are not as even as the Lenci stitch.
2. Earliest bodies were made of stockinette.
3. Bodies of the next dolls were made entirely of velvet.
4. Later dolls in the 1930s had velvet legs and arms and a cloth body.
5. Most dolls had a felt mask face.
6. There were no attached ears.
7. Some eyes were glass and some were painted, depending on the model.
8. Dolls have rounded mitt hands with stitching to indicate fingers; separate thumb.
9. The great majority of Chad Valley dolls have a cloth tag sewn to a part of the body. They were sewn on securely. Careful scrutiny can usually find indications of this tag.

SEE: *Illustration 298.*

Chad Stockinette Doll General Characteristics
1. Mask face covered with stockinette and oil painted.

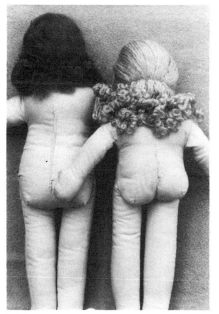

297.

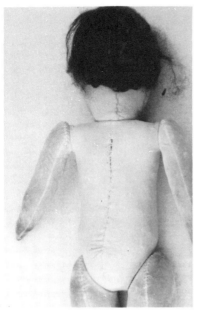

298.

2. Face consists of two pieces joined by heavy sewing thread.
3. Head and body stuffed with cotton.
4. Head and shoulder plate, arms and legs finished with waterproof paint.
5. Later dolls were made without elbow and knee joints.
6. Baby dolls had fatter bodies and heads than the child dolls.
7. In the 1920s the painted hair was "Dutch cut."
8. In the 1930s the painted hair had a side part.
9. Early dolls had sateen bodies; later dolls had heavy white cotton bodies.
10. Fingers indicated by careful stitching but thumb is separate.

MARKS: Chase trademark on thigh or under arm (wears off easily). "Chase Stockinet Doll//Made of Stockinet and cloth//stuffed with cot-ton//made by hand//Made by especially trained workers" (label sometimes sewn on doll)

Dean's Rag Book General Characteristics of A Doll
The illustration shows a large, early Dean's doll. Later dolls have some different characteristics.
1. Felt arms and head.
2. Dark pink cloth body and legs.
3. Painted face.
4. Eyes have white spot at upper left of eye; small brown eyelashes above and to side of eye. (This is not the same as the distinctive later eyes.)
5. Two-tone lips with painted thin lines at either side of mouth.
6. Large molded "bump" on chin.
7. Hole where ears should be; these anchor wig securely.
8. Machine-sewn lower head seam and hand-sewn upper head seam.
9. Hand-sewn upper arm and leg seams; machine-sewn upper body seam and hand-sewn lower body seam.
10. Unusual long, slender legs.
11. Entire body softly stuffed.
12. Middle three fingers indicated by stitching; thumb and small finger individually sewn.
13. Seam at ankle.

SEE: *Illustration 299.*

Deans Rag Book General Characteristics of Smaller, Later Dolls
These dolls do not have all of the above characteristics. They share:
1. The pink cloth body and legs.
2. Painted face.
3. Painted thin lines at either side of mouth.

4. Machine-sewn upper body seam and hand-sewn lower body seam.
5. Unusual long, slender legs.

They do not share:
1. The distinctive Dean's Rag Book painted eye (see *Illustration 66*).
2. Other characteristics vary with the type of doll.

Eros Dolls General Characteristics

Eros is a well-known maker of "tourist-type" Italian dolls. Many of the Eros dolls sold to collectors today are not as old as most of the dolls shown in this book. The older dolls are constructed entirely from cloth with pressed mask faces. The newer dolls have some plastic parts.

Body Characteristics of Eros Dolls:
1. Pink excelsior-filled body; small dolls may have a whitish body; back seam hand-sewn.
2. Most of the larger dolls have an extra piece of felt over the upper body.
3. One-piece smooth, pressed mask face and head; back seam hand-sewn but smoothed out neatly.
4. Painted right side-glancing eyes; white dot on left side of pupil.
5. Sewing machine seam in front and back of legs and arms; no ankle seam.
6. Larger dolls have cardboard in bottom of feet; the small dolls do not necessarily have this cardboard.
7. Metal hip pin that can be seen; arm mechanism cannot be seen.
8. Mitt hands with separate thumb; stitching indicates fingers.
9. Heavier brown eyebrows and thicker eyelashes than Magis; little or no eye shadow.

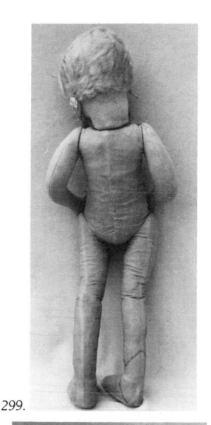

299.

300.

229

10. Only a slight indication of two-tone lips, if any.
11. Felt shoe with cardboard sole.
12. Costume material of cheaper quality but quite well designed and sewn.
13. For a comparison of Eros and Magis face and eyes, see page 153.

SEE: *Illustration 300.*

Fiore General Characteristics

1. Felt painted mask faces; back head seam hand-sewn with overcast white thread.
2. Rounded, bulging eyes with the "surprised" look in imitation of Lenci *Miniatures* and *Mascottes;* red dot in corner of each eye; heavy brownish-purple blusher above eye.
3. Glossy dark red oval mouth with only one color of lips.
4. Raised sculptured eyebrows.
5. Applied ears if hair does not cover head; single piece of felt which is sewn on to imitate shaped ear.
6. Dark pink cloth body.
7. Felt arms and legs.
8. Legs sewn on; no metal pins; leg seams in back only.
9. Mitt hand with flesh-colored thread seamed to indicate fingers.
10. Seam at ankle.
11. Felt shoes stitched around the sole for decorative effect.
12. Excellent quality provincial costumes.
13. Most dolls were marked "Made in Italy" on a ribbon tag which is sewn on the bottom of the shoe. This tag was not sewn on well and is often missing.
14. Came with paper wrist tag with "Fiore" printed on it.

15. Dolls sometimes came with accessories such as a basket or toy animal.

SEE: *Illustration 90,* page 79.

Gre-Poir Dolls General Characteristics
Dolls with cloth faces:

1. Jointed at neck, shoulders and hips.
2. Inside-out head seam at back of head; seam at each side of head.
3. Arms and legs have sewn top seams which are irregular.
4. Regular machine-stitch down the back of body.
5. Regular machine-stitch down the front of body to horizontal seam.
6. Unusual bulging lower front body construction with horizontal seam across the lower body.
7. Well-sculptured stiff, smooth mask face; no ears; small white dot is often on right side of lower lip.
8. One-stroke eyebrows which are a rather prominent feature.
9. Side-glancing eyes; large pupils; gray or gray-blue eye shadow above eyes (except on boy doll); gray or brown color at upper eye; thin but prominent painted eyelashes; white highlight on pupil.
10. Gre-Poir used hair eyelashes on some felt dolls and may have used them on some cloth dolls.
11. The mitt hands are so rounded there is only a slight indication of the little finger.
12. The legs are seamed in the front and back and have a seam at the ankle; the bottom of the sole has cardboard to make it stiff.
13. Legs are long and thin and gently pointed at knee; squarish, blunt toe line.

230

SEE: Illustration 301.
Dolls with felt faces:
1. Jointed at neck, shoulders and hips.
2. Cloth body with most of the above characteristics.
3. Felt arms and legs with most of the above characteristics.
4. Well-sculptured stiff felt face; no ears.
5. Dotted eyebrows.
6. Painted felt faces have less details than cloth faces.
7. Painted eyelashes above and below eye unless hair eyelashes are applied.

Felt Face:
1. Dotted eyebrows on most dolls. A few dolls have rather solid eyebrows.
2. Applied hair eyelashes on some

302.

dolls. Other dolls have painted eyelashes.
3. Eye liner around the eye.
4. Heart-shaped lips.
SEE: *Illustration 302. Betty Houghtailing Collection.*

Cloth Face:
1. Eyebrows are one painted line.
2. Thin, but prominent eyelashes.
3. Band of color at upper eye.
4. Very large pupil in eye.
5. Heart-shaped mouth.
SEE: *Illustration 96 (page 232). Diane Domroe Collection.*

Karavan General Characteristics
1. Felt-painted mask face over hard surface.
2. Side-glancing eyes.
3. Thin painted eyelashes above eyes; thin painted eyebrows.
4. Vertical mouth with two-tone lips.
5. Body and legs cut from one piece except for felt shoes which are sewn to body at ankle.
6. Arms sewn on at shoulders.

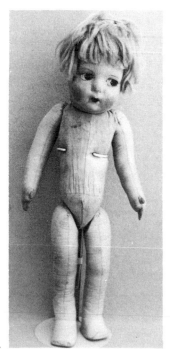

301.

96.

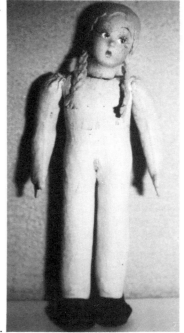

303.

7. Mitt hands with stitching indicating fingers.
SEE: *Illustration 303.*

Lenci Dolls General Characteristics

Some of the most collectible dolls of the 20th century are the lovely dolls from the House of Lenci. Here are some tips to help you identify them.

1. The Lenci dolls used a unique push-and-pull (zigzag) stitch on the back of the neck and the top of the arms and legs. This was widely imitated by their competitors. By studying the illustration in this guide, collectors can learn to identify the stitches more accurately.

2. Most Lenci dolls (except small Mascottes and Miniatures) have an applied ear made from two pieces of felt sewn together and then topstitched. The Norah Wellings and large Farnell (Alpha) dolls also had a similar ear, but their ear shapes are different.

3. The Lenci dolls are known for their two-tone lip color. The earlier dolls often have both the different colored lips and two dots on their lower lip (see *Illustration 305*). This characteristic was also imitated by competitors; however, the Lenci paint is quite distinctive.

4. The early bodies are usually made of felt but a few were cloth. The later bodies were cloth. Both hollow and stuffed bodies were used.

5. The underwear is usually either organdy or muslin. The organdy is often hemstitched (see *Illustration 304* which shows the Lenci "teddy"). The later muslin petticoats and pants are often

232

trimmed with felt. All are of excellent quality. Some Lenci dolls did not have petticoats; some later doll skirts were lined instead.

6. A few early dolls have a Lenci trademark nail (button) on some part of their body or clothing (see *Illustrations 136* and *142)*. The earliest nails had the Lenci name engraved in capital letters. There were also nails with the Lenci name engraved in script. This was discontinued a year or two after production started. More often the Lenci name was stamped on a foot. This mark has now usually worn off. Most Lenci dolls came with cloth or paper tags (see page 147).

7. Madame Lenci was a master of the sculptured face and the Lenci dolls have a rounder, softer, more artistic sculpture than the dolls of most other companies. However, the first dolls were not perfected and the collector who usually recognizes Lenci faces may pass them by (see *Illustration 305* to see the difference).

8. As the years passed, the Lenci company tried to make a smoother, more realistic cloth face which was more lifelike and competitive with the popular composition dolls (for the ultimate smooth-face Lenci doll see *Illustration 177)*. The author has also seen this smooth face in the *Lucia*-face series.

9. An unusual Lenci model has a jointed waist. The doll itself was tall and slim and often used for flappers, dancers and character dolls with elaborate costumes (see *Illustrations 194, 195* and *306)*.

10. The shoes on Lenci dolls are usually felt. However, there are well-cobbled leather shoes and boots on some dolls (see *Illustration 150)*.

11. There is a recognizable Lenci sock with a scallop (see *Illustration 304)*. A higher Lenci sock is also often found (see *Illustration 170)*.

12. Lenci used buttons that are a type of milk glass. Buttons with three or four holes were used on shoes.

13. Like many of the bisque dolls, the Lenci face mold was numbered. Even though the dolls do not have this number imprinted on them, a collector can memorize the faces just as they do the bisque faces. The list of Lenci dolls, starting on page 148, gives as many of those numbers as possible.

14. The variety of Lenci dolls over the years seems endless and new novelty dolls are being identified. Types include long-limbed boudoir dolls, regional, national, oriental, Indian, islander, personality, sports and holiday. The line included such novelties as animals, charms, fetishes, eggs and many others.

The search for the identity of a Lenci doll is easier as the collector studies the above characteristics. The colors are beautiful and the sculpture magnificent. At the end of the search, the collector can understand why these beautiful dolls have now become among the treasured art of the world.

Sewing Stitch:
The Lenci dolls used a unique push-and-pull (often called zigzag)

233

304.

stitch on the back of the neck and on the top of the arms and legs. This was widely imitated by their competitors. The comparisons in this book can help you identify the original.

This illustration is used because very few of the Lenci and Lenci-type dolls have this dart in the legs. Lenci did use this dart occasionally as the picture illustrates.

The socks on this doll are used on many of the Lenci dolls. They are knitted with a pointed top. They are well made and have not deteriorated as much as some of the socks and stockings on other types of felt dolls.

The doll wears the typical hemstitched teddy of the early Lenci dolls.

The model number of this doll is 450. The height is 13in (33cm). Other information about Lenci underwear can be found on page 232.
SEE: *Illustration 304.*

Face:
The faces of the early dolls did not have the same detailed sculpture as the later dolls. The doll on the left is an early #149V. The face is more round. She has an all-felt body as can be seen clearly in the picture. The mouth shape is also different from the later dolls. These early dolls are difficult to find.

The doll on the right is the #450. The face has a more sculptured look. This model has the raised eyebrows of a few of the Lenci models.

Another identification feature of Lenci dolls is the use of painted highlights (dots) on the bottom lips. These dots were not always used, especially on the dolls in the 1930s and 1940s.
SEE: *Illustration 305.*

Slim Body Doll with Jointed Waist:
This type of body has not generally been associated with the Lenci doll. However, it was used for unusual boudoir-type dolls with many types of clothes. Often it was used for provincial, nationality and flapper-type costumes (see *Illustration 194, 195* and *306).*

1. Special extra piece at neck which allows the head to move freely.
2. Unusual joints at shoulders and waist.
3. Seams at elbows.
4. Third and fourth fingers indicated by stitching.
5. Unusual pointed face.
6. Wide open, side-glancing eyes.
7. Various sizes.
8. It has most of the other characteristics of Lenci dolls.

This particular doll was dressed in a Russian cossack costume.
SEE: *Illustration 306. William Zito Collection.*

305.

Magis Dolls Small Dolls General Characteristics

1. White excelsior-filled body.
2. Painted left side-glancing eyes with white dot in right corner of pupil; the eyeballs are very rounded, and the paint is very glossy.
3. Mohair wigs on most dolls.
4. Eyebrows have a single painted line that is smaller than Eros.
5. Eyelashes have smaller and thinner paint strokes than Eros.
6. Eye shadow behind eyelashes.
7. Eyeballs are very rounded and bulging from the head.
8. An attempt is made to paint two-toned lips but they are not well defined; the color is more wine-colored than Eros or Lenci.
9. Mitt-shaped hands with separate thumb; stitching indicates fingers.
10. Pressed mask face with flesh-colored almost invisible stitching on the back seam; no ears; mask feels and looks more like felt than Eros.
11. Flesh-colored arms and legs.

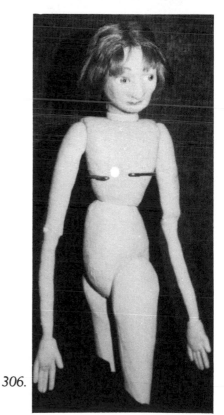

306.

235

12. Patch over mechanism on shoulder joint.
13. Metal pin joint at hips.
14. Front and back machine seams on legs and arms; no ankle seams.
15. Feet do not have cardboard in the sole.
16. Shoes most often are made of an embossed oilcloth type of material (see *Illustration 215*).

For comparison of Magis and Eros face and eyes, see page 247.

Magis Large Dolls General Characteristics — 14in (36cm)

The characteristics are the same with the following exceptions:
1. One-piece mask face is glued at the back rather than sewn; it looks like a hard welt.
2. Neck and arms sewn with a few large stitches to the body; white thread is used.
3. Pretty hands with attempt to make them look realistic; thumb separate; fingers indicated by stitching; sometimes there is nail polish which matches the lip color.
4. Pointed elbows and knees for more realism.

Magit Doll General Characteristics
1. Felt mask; no side seams on head; joined in back with horizontal hand-stitching.
2. Jointed at neck, shoulders and arms.
3. Cotton twill body and limbs stuffed with straw.
4. Rounded elbows.
5. Seam in back and front of arms.
6. Seam only in back of legs; ankles have unusual seam line which starts toward the back of the foot and rounds up toward the ankle and back down to the other side to the back of the foot.
7. A piece of heavy pressed paper (similar to cardboard) is sewn to the foot. This enables the doll to stand easily.
8. Mitt hands with nicely rounded fingers separated by a seam.
9. Machine seam down the middle of the front and back of body.
10. Hand-sewn overcast side seams on both sides of body. Hand-sewn overcast seams on arms and legs; does not look like Lenci stitching.
11. Wig is put on in unusual fashion. A pencil mark was made to show where the wig should be sewn.
12. Flat painted left side-glancing eyes. A little gray paint over and under the pupil; light gray blusher under and over the eyes. Flesh colored dot on left side of eye; lighter brown half moon

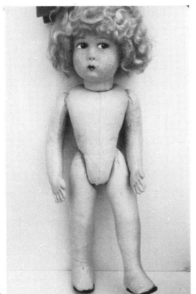

307.

308.

309.

shape under pupil. Nicely curved grayish eyebrows.

13. Very unusual mouth that is heart shaped with rounded lower lip and a tiny straight line on either side of mouth, two-tone lips with one tiny white dot in center of lower lip.

14. Stockings similar to Lenci.

15. Wig sewn on in strips.

SEE: *Illustration 307.*

Messina-Vat General Characteristics

1. All-felt body.

2. Pressed mask painted face.

3. Large white dot in upper right corner of eye; light brown dot in lower corner of eye.

4. Curved eyebrows low on forehead.

5. Lips have lighter red spot in middle.

6. Applied ears made of single piece of felt.

7. Unusual bump for chin.

8. Mohair wig put on in strips.

9. Leg seams in front and back; no seam in ankle.

10. Mitt hands with separate thumb.

11. Push-and-pull (zigzag) stitching which imitates Lenci.

12. Horizontal dart in lower body both in front and in back; crotch has push-and-pull seam.

MARKS: " *A* " on bottom of feet.

SEE: *Illustration 308.*

Illustration 309.

Perroti Doll General Characteristics

1. Dark felt for face, hands and legs. However, there is an attempt to make a variation in the darker skin tones, depending on the natives of the region depicted in the costuming.

2. Only a small attempt to joint each doll at the shoulders and hips.

3. Felt-sculptured mask face which is not as severely pressed as the later Lenci dolls. The felt feels like regular felt. The mask has side seams as well as a back seam

237

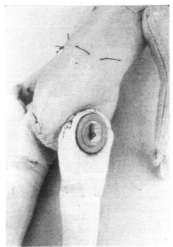

310.

311.

which is hand-sewn with white thread.
4. Very large black pupil of eye with curved line (often yellow) underneath. On the more expensive dolls there is some blue or brown eye shadow around the pupil. Each doll has eyelashes but they are different, depending on the type of face being painted.
5. Heart-shaped mouth. Sometimes the lower lip is a different color and sometimes it is not.
6. Bahai dolls have sewn-on legs with a seam at the hips and at the knee.
7. More expensive dolls have a metal hip pin which joins legs.
8. Most of the dolls have a rough hand-sewn seam on the upper arm.
9. Legs are seamed at the front and back.
10. Well-designed clothes using felt, organdy, rayon, velvet and cotton.
11. On the whole, the bodies do not seem to have the quality control found on the dolls made in the

United States and Europe, but time and money is spent on embroidery, applique and accessories.

SEE: *Illustration 310.*

Raynal General Characteristics
1. Seam on head is hand-stitched similar to Lenci.
2. Back of body is machine-stitched.
3. Silk mask face.
4. Unusually <u>wide</u> eyebrows either slanted <u>upward</u> or curved.
5. Two-tone lips with no highlights.
6. Squared-off mitt fingers with separate thumb.
7. Leg seam in front.

SEE: *Illustration 311. Jeanette Fink Collection.*

Vecchiotti (Italy)

Characteristics of 12in (31cm) doll:
1. No ears.
2. Face and head are made of felt which has been heavily pressed to make it look and feel smooth.

238

3. Sculptured and molded eyebrows.
4. Painted face with small feathery eyelashes above and to the sides of eyes.
5. Side-glancing eyes with faint white curved line under black pupil and white dot at inner end of line.
6. Two-tone small lips.
7. Thumb is stubbier than most other cloth dolls. If larger doll is holding something, the thumb and first finger may be made individually and the second, third and fourth fingers indicated only by stitching. Small dolls may have mitten-type hands with stubby thumb and fingers indicated only by stitching.
8. Seam in back of legs only; stocking material is used to cover white leg material.
9. Very fine thread-like mohair wig.
10. Felt shoes with cardboard sole joined to leg material at ankle.
11. "Made in Italy" tag may be sewn to bottom of foot.
12. Body and legs cut together out of white muslin.
13. Sturdy ribbon tag sewn into back seam of skirt.
14. Doll originally had a round gold tag with "Alberani//Vecchiotti//Millano" printed in embossed letters.
15. An additional tag gave the province or region of the costume.

Norah Wellings General Characteristics of Large Child Doll

Norah Wellings was greatly influenced by the Lenci dolls. In many ways she managed to come closer to the "flair" of Madame Lenci than most of the other cloth artists. There

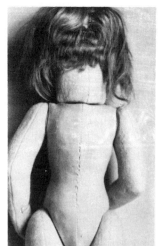

312.

was quality in the design and manufacture of her dolls.

Many of her body characteristics were similar to the Lenci dolls.

1. The push-and-pull (zigzag) stitching closely imitated Lenci. However, a comparison of *Illustrations 304* and *312* shows differences.
2. The felt is slightly rough.
3. The felt mask face is well-sculptured as are most of the Lenci dolls. It is also easily identifiable.
4. Beautiful painted side-glancing eyes with one white dot in upper left hand corner.
5. The eyebrows are small, pale and slightly dotted.
6. The mouth is small and heart-shaped with a tiny thin red line on each side.
7. The ears are double-stitched. This is again like Lenci although a careful examination of the ears shows that both are not exactly the same shape.
8. There are felt arms and legs and a cloth body.

9. The elbows and knees are sharply pointed.
10. The rather large hands have stitching indicating second and third fingers; very large first finger; thumb and small finger are not as much out of proportion.
11. There is a seam on the front and back of each leg and no ankle seam.

SEE: *Illustration 312.*

Smaller Novelty-type Dolls

Norah Wellings was a prolific designer of large and small dolls. Her small novelty-type dolls were very popular in many parts of the British Empire. Because of the variety, body characteristics can be very different. However, most of them have some common characteristics.

1. The cloth label is sewn securely somewhere on the body. If the label has been removed, usually the stitching marks can be detected. Labels have been found on many different parts of the body.
2. Stockinette was used for some of the faces with a pinkish cloth body, arms and legs.
3. Some small novelty dolls have felt faces with the unusual heart-shaped mouth with the fine red line on each side.
4. The face sculpture in some of the smaller character dolls is often among the best of all cloth dolls. Her ability to capture the looks of various ethnic groups, historical figures and storybook characters of the British Empire is extraordinary.
5. Some of the more inexpensive dolls did not have applied ears.
6. Many of the larger novelty and character dolls had double-stitched ears.
7. Glass eyes were used in some of her character dolls.
8. There is a tendency for Norah Wellings dolls to have slender, longer legs than some of the other English cloth dolls.
9. There was a variety in the types of hair (see page 247).
10. Many of these novelties used excellent quality velvet in their body construction or costuming.
11. There were many doll-related novelties, such as purses, in her large line.
12. Many companies imitated Norah Wellings. There are times when it is impossible to identify these dolls, such as sailors, unless there is a label (see Look-alikes, page 249).

Cloth Used in Doll Construction

Felt

The following companies are known to have used felt in making dolls or dolls' clothing in the 1920s-1930s. Other companies may also have used felt during the period.

1. Alexander (United States).
2. Allwin (United States).
3. Alma (Italy).
4. Alpha (Farnell).
5. Amberg (United States): Amfelt Art Dolls.
*6. Aux Trois Quartiers (France).
7. Averill (United States).
8. Bing (United States).
*9. Boccheciampe (France).
10. Borgfeldt (United States): *Playmate* dolls.

*11. Brogi (United States).
12. Carvaillo (France): *Venus* dolls.
*13. Cass, N.D. Company (United States).
14. Chad Valley (England).
*15. Charlier (France).
16. Crowley, Milna Co. (Austria).
*17. Clelia (France).
*18. Cramer, Eduard.
*19. Davis, Rees (United States): Mother Goose character dolls.
20. Dean's (England).
*21. Deptford Toy-Making Industry (England).
22. E.N.A.L.P. (Italy).
23. Eisen (United States).
24. Eros (Italy).
25. Farnell (Alpha) (England).
26. Fiore (Italy).
*27. Fleischmann & Bloedell (Germany and France): Cloth character dolls.
*28. Forster, Gustav (Germany).
*29. French Fashion Importing Co. (United States): Imported Poupées Ninon.
*30. Furga (Italy).
*31. Genevieve (France): French doll from Lafayette store.
32. Gerb's Poupées (France).
*33. Giotti (France): "Magati" trademark.
*34. Goldberger (United States): Eegee *Cigarette Girl* and other dolls.
*35. Grams, August (Germany).
*36. Greif Puppenkunst (Germany).
37. Gre-Poir (France and United States).
*38. Harmus, Jr., Carl (Germany).
39. Harwin (England).
*40. Haueisen, Richard (Germany).
*41. Hawksley & Company (England).
42. Hecht, Else (Germany).

*43. Hermann, Bernhard (Germany).
44. Holzer & Cie (Brazil).
45. Horsman & Aetna (United States).
46. Karavan (Italy).
*47. Koedever (Germany): Felt and plush toys.
*48. Kohler & Rosewald (Germany).
*49. Krauhs (Austria).
50. La Rosa Milano (Italy).
*51. Lazarski, Mme. Thabée (United States): Polish refugee dolls.
*52. Lenci (Italy).
53. Liberty (Holland): Distributed dolls marked "Lenci."
54. Magis (Italy).
55. Magit (Italy).
*56. Marcuse Day & Co. (England): *Emdee* line of felt and cloth character dolls.
*57. Marga (Hungary).
58. Messina-Vat (Italy).
59. Meyer & Lorang (United States).
60. Ninon (France).
*61. Ourine (France): Line called *Poupee Royale.*
*62. Pappe, Moritz (Germany).
63. Perotti (Brazil).
*64. Pfeiffer, Emil (Germany): Line of cloth dolls including *Hubsy.*
65. Poupées Nicette (France).
*66. Schelhorn, August (Germany): Novelty dolls.
*67. Schmey, Gustavust (Germany): Novelty dolls.
68. Steiff (Germany).
*69. Twinjoy Doll Co. (United States).
*70. Vogt, Anna (Germany): Jointed felt dolls.
71. Wellings, Norah (England).
*Companies not listed in the main section of this book.

Oilcloth Dolls or Oilcloth Used in the Doll Construction
*1. Asiatic Import Co. (United States): Fairy tale dolls.
*2. Brydone, Jack (Canada).
*3. Fleming Doll Co. (United States).
4. Horsman (United States).
5. Ideal (United States).
*6. Kat-A-Korner (United States).
7. Knickerbocker (United States).
8. Krueger (United States).
9. Live Long Toys (United States).
10. Magis (Italy).
*11. Oz Doll and Toy Company (United States).
*12. Rushton.
13. Sayco (Unites States): *Helen and Maria* dolls.
*Companies not listed in the main section of the book.

Stockinette Dolls
1. Alexander (United States): *Dionne Quintuplets.*
2. American Toy & Novelty Co. (United States).
*3. Bandeau Sales Co. (United States).
*4. Bonser Doll Company (United States).
5. Chad Valley (England): Early cloth dolls.
6. Chase (United States).
*7. Dressel, Cuno & Otto (Germany): *Heinerly* baby doll.
8. Farnell (Alpha) (England).
9. Kruse, Käthe (Germany): *Schlenkerchen.*
10. Rushton (United States): *Mawaphil.*
*11. Meaklin & Ridgway (United States): Represented English doll companies.
12. Nelke (United States).

*13. Plotnick (United States): Succeeded American Toy & Novelty Co.
14. Rushton (United States).
15. Ravca (France and United States).
16. W.P.A. Dolls (United States).
17. Wellings, Norah (England).
*Companies not listed in the main section of this book.

Velvet Used in Construction or Partial Construction of Doll
1. Alexander (United States).
*2. Allwin (England).
3. Chad Valley (England).
4. Dean's (England).
5. Farnell (Alpha) (England).
6. Knickerbocker (United States).
7. Mawaphil (United States).
8. Rushton (United States).
9. Wellings, Norah (England).
*Companies not listed in the main section of this book.

Country

Austria

*1. Baitz: Makers of German provincial and personality dolls.
2. Crowley.
3. Hauser (may have been connected with Emil Pfeiffer of Germany).
*4. Krauhs: Made felt dolls.
*Companies not listed in the main section of this book.

Brazil

1. Holzer & Cie.
2. Perotti.

England

*1. Art Toy Manufacturing Co.: *Bathing Jeff, Misska, Pierrot,* tea cosies.
*2. Austin Gray Ltd.: Art dolls, cabaret, *Beach Belle, Sailor, Saucy Joyce* with goo-goo eyes.
*3. Blande-Hawkes, Mabel: Fairies, *Father Christmas, Fluff, Baby Royal, Little Lady Anne, Toots, Hazel, Babs, My Dollie's Nana, Little Miss Vogue.*
*4. British Novelty Co.: Owned by Dean's Rag Book Co. Ltd.
*5. Burman, J. & A.J. (Zoo Soft Toy Company): Mascottes and plush toys.
6. Chad Valley.
7. Dean's.
*8. Donald, Ken: *Binkie Babs.*
9. Farnell (Alpha).
10. Harwin: Steiff look-alikes.
11. Liberty of London: Cloth soft-sculptured dolls.
*12. Meakin & Ridgway.
*13. Nowytske: Lenci-type doll including Ninon.
14. Wellings, Norah.

*Companies not listed in the main section of the book.

France

*1. Alart, Eugene and Ernst of Paris: Boudoir doll with Alart trademark on shoes.
*2. Boccheciampe of Paris: *Maguy* felt doll.
*3. Brogi: *Clélia* was trademark; felt and cotton.
*4. Brugeoise: Cloth dolls.
*5. Calvare: French art doll with chiffon face.
*6. Carvaillo: *Venus,* a Lenci look-alike.

*7. Charlier: Felt and silk dolls.
*8. Clarisee: Line of dolls sold at Louvre store; felt clothes.
*9. Copelia: Cloth art, art dolls, toy dolls; many exported.
*10. Duvall, Mlle.: Cloth dolls.
11. Eisen: Importer of French felt dolls.
*12. Gaume, Henriette: Cloth and wax art dolls.
13. Gerb's: Lenci look-alike cloth dolls.
*14. Giotti: *Magati,* or possibly *Magali,* as trademark; felt art dolls.
15. LPA Bennett Couturier: Cloth dolls; some had glass eyes.
16. La Poupées Nicette.
17. Lang, Emile: Cloth dolls with molded faces; some dressed as soldiers.
*18. Lauth-Sand, Mme. Aurore: Cloth dolls.
*19. Lazarski, Mme. Thabée: Operated a workshop where expensive dolls were made; sometimes used name *Mascotte.*
*20. Le Jouet Natura: Cloth dolls.
*21. Les Poupées Artistiques Francais: Member of Chambre Syndicale: ** Cloth boys, girls, clowns; dressed and undressed.
*22. Levallois: Made dolls, dolls heads, dolls face masks, etc.
*23. Magit: Art dolls; some had "M.A.P.I." mark.
24. Milobendzka, Madame Emilia: Designed for Blum-Lustig U.S.A.
25. Ninon: Lenci look-alikes.
*26. Ourine, G.: Cloth dolls called *Poupée Royale.*
*27. Oovre, Vera: Cloth dolls; one of her most famous was *Charlie Chaplin;* also made regional cos-

tumes with wooden shoes; black dolls; drummer boy wearing sabots.

*28. Perrimond, Gaston: Cloth art dolls called *La Poupée Nicette*; sometimes used "L.P.A." mark.

*29. Poulbot: Cloth dolls with silk faces that are needlesculp-tured; represented children of Paris.

*30. Poupées Consuela Fould: Art dolls with extreme styles of 1920s; expensive fabrics; fringe trimming; above-knee skirts.

*31. Printemps: Store that distributed dolls; *Martine* cloth dolls sold by them.

32. Ravca: Made stockinette-type dolls in France before coming to U.S.A.

33. Raynal: Cloth dolls.

34. S.F.B.J.

*35. Spaggari: Similar to Ravca.

*Companies not listed in the main section of the book.

**Chambre Syndicale des Fabricants de Jouets et Jeux et Engins Sportif, a French trade organization for the manufacture of toys.

Germany

1. Bing: Many cloth dolls including Käthe Kruse and Lenci look-alikes.

*2. Dressel, Cuno & Otto: Cloth doll with molded felt face; 1925-1926; *Heinerle*, stockinette baby doll; 1929-1930.

*3. Deuerlein, Joseph, Nachf.: Felt and leather dolls and toys.

*4. Eichhorn, Martin: Lenci look-alike; circa 1926.

*5. Gehren, Haneiseri: Steiff look-alikes; circa 1920.

*6. Grams, August: Made dressed and undressed felt dolls.

*7. Greif, Puppenkunst: Felt and plush art dolls; some had celluloid and bisque heads.

*8. Haueisen, Richard: Cloth and felt dolls; circa 1922.

*9. Heine & Schneider: Cardboard head covered with muslin; Käthe Kruse look-alike.

*10. Heinrich's Geschwister: Cloth art dolls; Lenci look-alike.

*11. Helk, Berthold: Cloth dolls and novelties.

*12. Henze & Steinhauser: Woolen dolls.

*13. Hermann, Bernard: Cloth boudoir dolls.

14. Kruse, Käthe: Cloth dolls.

15. Ludecke, Ilse: Some cloth dolls were Steiff look-alikes.

*16. Lyro-Puppen: Cloth dolls.

*17. Rogner, Hermann, Nachf: All-felt dolls.

18. Steiff, Margarete: Cloth doll with seam down middle of face.

*19. Thuringer Stoffpuppen-Fabrik: Many cloth dolls including *Harlequin* and *Santa Claus*.

*20. Weiersmuller, Willy: Cloth dolls including baby dolls.

*21. Zehner, Edmund: Cloth dolls; 1923-1926.

* Companies not listed in the main section of the book.

Italy

1. Alma.

2. Consuelo Originals.

*3. E.B.I.

4. E.N.A.P.L.

5. Eros.

6. Fiori.

7. Furga.

8. Karavan.

9. La Rosa.

10. Lenci.
11. Magis.
12. Magit of Torino.
*13. Marguerin.
14. Messina-Vat.
15. S.G.A.T.
16. Vecchiotti.
* Companies not listed in the main section of the book.

Spain

1. N.A.T.I.
2. T.A.F.

Spain After 1930s

*1. Klumpe.
*2. Roldan.
* Companies not listed in the main section of the book.

United States

1. Adler.
2. Alexander.
3. Altman, B.
4. Amberg.
5. American Art Dolls.
6. American Stuffed Novelty.
7. American Toy and Novelty.
*8. Anamay Doll Co.: Made cloth dolls.
9. Anita Novelty Doll Company.
*10. Atlantic Playthings Co.
*11. Aunt Jemima Mills Co.
12. Averill, Georgene.
13. Bloom, Charles and Braitling, Fred.
14. Blossom.
*15. Bonzer Products, Inc.
*16. Buzza Co.: Doll boxed with framed picture of doll and related poem.
17. Cayuga Felt.
18. Century Doll Company.

19. Chase.
*20. Chessler Doll Company: Inexpensive cloth dolls.
21. Cohen.
22. Community Craft.
*23. Cubeb.
24. Delevan.
25. Effanbee.
26. Etta.
27. European Doll Manufacturing.
*28. Flapper Novelty Doll Co.: Long-legged flapper dolls.
*29. Fleischmann, Katherine.
*30. Gerling Toy Co.
*31. Gre-Poir.
*32. Goldberger (Eegee).
33. Gund.
*34. Gutsel.
35. Hausman & Zatulove.
*36. Heizer, Dorothy.
37. Horsman.
*38. Ideal.
39. Irwin.
40. Kamkes (Kamkins).
*41. Kat-A-Korner Kompany: Oilcloth dolls; boudoir dolls; clowns.
42. Knickerbocker.
*43. Konroe Merchants.
*44. Libby Doll & Novelty Co.
45. Live Long Toys.
46. Meyer & Lorang.
*47. Mizpa Toy & Novelty Co.
48. Modern Toy.
49. Mollye'es.
50. Munzer, Alfred.
51. Mutual Novelty.
52. Nelke.
*53. Oakhurst Studios.
54. Pinky Winky.
55. Ross & Ross.
56. Royal Society.
*57. Ruffles Co.
58. Rushton.
*59. S. & H. Novelty.
60. S & L Manufacturing Co.

*61. Schoen & Yondorf Co. Inc. (Sayco).
*62. Silk Novelty.
*63. Smith, Ella: Handmade dolls made in Alabama.
64. Strobel & Wilken.
*65. Twinjoy: Two dolls in one.
*66. Unique Novelty Doll Co.: Boudoir dolls.
*67. Utley by Gertrude Rollinson.
68. Wolf.

* Companies not listed in the main section of this book.

Criers (Mechanical Sounds Inside Cloth Dolls)

1. Cohen, S. & Son.
2. Effanbee.
3. Etta.
4. Pinky Winky.

Ears

The applied ears are excellent identification features for cloth dolls. A large majority of cloth dolls have no applied ears.

I. Single Pieces of Felt: Each Company's Ear Shape is Unique
1. Alma: Felt folded to resemble an ear and stitched down.
2. Farnell (Alpha).
3. Fiore.
4. Lenci: On small *Mascotte* and *Miniature* type dolls.
5. Made in Denmark: Norah Wellings look-alike.
6. Messina-Vat: One piece of felt folded over and stitched on.
7. T.A.F.: One piece slightly gathered and stitched on doll.
8. Wellings, Norah: Small souvenir-type dolls; some small dolls have no ears.

II. Double Pieces of Felt Double Stitched
1. Chad Valley *Bambino*.
2. Farnell (Alpha): Only on the larger dolls.
3. Lenci: Most of the Lenci dolls have these ears except for *Mascottes* and *Miniatures*.
4. Wellings, Norah: Larger dolls.

III. Hole in Head for Fastening Wig
1. Dean's Rag Book A1 large doll.

Elastic Strung Bodies

1. Alma.   2. Altman.

Eyes

I. Small Lenci-type Dolls with Bulging Eyes
1. Fiore.
2. Lenci *Mascottes* and *Miniatures*.
3. Magis.
4. Vecchiotti.

II. Winkers
1. Farnell (Alpha).
2. Lenci.
3. N.A.T.I.

III. Real Eyelashes
1. Averill.
2. Blossom.
3. Etta.
4. Gre-Poir (some felt-faced dolls and possibly some cloth dolls).
5. Rushton (Mawaphil).

IV. Sculptured, Raised Eyebrows
1. Lenci: various model numbers.
2. Fiore: Eyebrows only slightly raised.

313.

V. Googlies
   1. Lenci glass-eyes.
   2. Lenci painted-eyes.
VI. Very Large Pupils in Eyes
   1. Gerb's.
VII. Glass Eyes
   1. Lenci.
   2. Chad Valley.
   3. I.P.A. Couturier.
VIII. Wide Diagonal Slanting Eyes
   1. Raynal.
IX. Bright Blue Eyes
   1. Etta

Comparison of Magis and Eros Eyes and Faces

Magis: (Doll on left) small rounded, painted bulging eyes; small eyelash lines; eye shadow on upper eye; pressed mask face that is not smooth.

Eros: (Doll on right) large flat painted eyes; larger paint strokes for eyelashes; longer, thicker eyebrows; very smooth pressed mask face.

SEE: *Illustration 313.*

Eyes

Eyelashes of Georgene Averill dolls: Some of the Averill dolls have regular eyelashes protruding from the doll's eyes.
SEE: *Illustration 314.*

Hair

I. Different Types of Hair on Norah Wellings Dolls
   1. Painted light brown hair.
   2. Mohair.
   3. Thread.

314.

4. Fur.
5. Human.
II. **Kinky Yarn Wig**
1. Averill.

Look-alikes

Averill and Mollye
1. Blossom (United States).
2. Community Craft (United States).
*3. D & D Dolls (United States).
4. Knickerbocker (United States).
5. Krueger (United States).
6. Rushton (United States).
7. Silk Novelty (United States).
* Companies not listed in the main section of the book.

Käthe Kruse
1. American Art Dolls *(Susie's Sister)*.
2. Bing (United States and Germany).
*3. Gerzon (Holland): Dolls had composition heads.
*4. Heine & Schneider (Germany): Dolls of pressed cardboard with cloth-covered muslin.
*5. Klotzer, Erich (Germany): Marked "E.K."
6. Lona Art Dolls: Some have celluloid heads.
7. Strobel & Wilken: Importing company in the United States with ties to Germany.
*8. Zwanger (Germany): Some dolls had composition heads.
* Companies not listed in the main section of the book.

Lenci
1. Alma (Italy).
2. Alpha Farnell (England).
3. Alexander (United States): Dickens characters.

4. Altman: Importer of dolls into United States.
5. American Stuffed Novelty (United States): *Trilby.*
6. Amfelt by Amberg (United States).
7. Averill (United States): Known also as Madame Hendren.
*8. Berlich, Ralph: Associated with Gre-Poir Dolls.
*9. Boccheciampe Maguy Dolls (France).
*10. Chad Valley (England).
11. Carvaillo (France): *Venus* dolls distributed by Bon Marche.
*12. Chantrain, E. (Belgium): Dolls called *Marvell.*
*13. Clarisse (France).
*14. Clelia (France): Felt or cloth dolls with diamond-shaped tag.
15. Consuelo Originals (Italy): Provincial dolls.
*16. Davis, Rees: *Lucille* doll.
17. Dean's (England): Some A1 dolls and *Posy* dolls.
18. Eros (Italy).
19. Fiori (Italy).
20. Gerb's Poupées (France).
*21. Giotti (France): Magat was trademark.
22. Gre-Poir (United States and France).
23. Hauser (Austria): Connected to Emil Pfeiffer of Germany.
*24. Heinrich Geschwester Art Dolls: Marked *Maya.*
25. Holzer & Cie (Brazil).
26. Karavan (Italy).
27. La Rosa (Italy).
*28. Liberty (Holland): Distributed Lenci dolls.
29. Magis (Italy).
30. Magit (Italy).
*31. Magit (France): Used M.A.P.I. for mark upon occasion.

*32. Marguerin (Italy).
33. Messina-Vat (Italy).
34. Meyer & Lorang (United States).
35. N.A.T.I. (Spain).
36. Ninon (French).
37. Perotti (Brazil).
38. Petterssen, Ronnaug (Norway).
*39. Pfeiffer, Emil (Germany): Some may have been made in Austria.
40. Poupée Nicette (France).
41. Raynal (France).
42. S.G.A.T. (Italy).
43. Silk Novelty (United States).
44. T.A.G. (Spain).
45. Vecchiotti (Italy).
46. Wellings, Norah (England).
* Companies not listed in the main section of this book.

Lenci Mascotte and Miniature
*1. Burman, J & A.J.
2. Eros (Italy).
3. Fiori (Italy).
4. Holzer & Cie (Brazil).
5. Karavan (Italy).
6. Magis (Italy).
7. N.A.T.I. (Spain).
8. Perotti (Brazil).
9. Poupées Nicette (France).
10. T.A.F. (Spain).
11. Vecchiotti (Italy).
* Companies not listed in the main section of the book.

Steiff
*1. Aux Trois Quartiers (store that sold Steiff look-alikes).
*2. Gehren, Haneiseri (Germany).
*3. Gutsel (United States).
4. Harwin & Company Ltd. (England).
5. Ludecke, Ilse (Germany).
*6. Polish Victims Relief Fund (Helen Paderwiski).
7. Unknown (see page 206).

* Companies not listed in the main section of the book.
Norah Wellings
1. Chad Valley.
2. Dean's.
3. Farnell (Alpha).
4. Lenci and other Italian and French cloth dolls.
5. Made in Denmark.

Types of Dolls

Animals
1. Alexander (United States).
2. Alma (Italy).
3. American Stuffed Novelty Co. (United States).
4. Averill (United States).
5. Chad Valley (England).
*6. Chessler (United States).
7. Dean's (England).
8. Effanbee (United States).
9. Hausman & Zatulove (United States).
10. Irwin & Co. (United States).
11. Knickerbocker (United States).
12. Lang, Emil (France).
13. Live Long Toys (United States).
14. Rushton (United States).
*15. Schoen & Yondorf (Sayco).
16. Steiff (Germany).
17. Wellings, Norah (England).
* Companies not listed in the main section of this book.

Aunt Jemima Dolls and Mammy Dolls
1. American Stuffed Novelty Co. (United States).
2. Bruckner (United States): *Topsy Turvy.*
3. Butler Bros. (United States).
*4. Davis Milling Co. (United States): Also known as Aunt Jemima Mills.
*5. Delevan, S.E. (United States).
*6. Toy Shop, New York (United States).
7. Wolf, Louis (United States and Germany).

* Companies not listed in the main section of this book.

Babics
1. Alexander (United States).
2. Averill (United States).
3. Chase (United States).
*4. Dressel, Cuno & Otto (Germany).
5. Etta (United States).
6. Gerber Products (United States).
7. Gre-Poir (United States and France).
8. Kruse, Käthe (Germany).
9. Lenci (Italy).
10. Pinky Winky (United States).
* Companies not listed in the main section of the book.

Boudoir Cloth Dolls (Bed Dolls)
The following makers of dolls are known to have made cloth long-legged boudoir or bed dolls. Many of these same manufacturers also made the same type of dolls with composition heads. Today collectors consider the dolls with cloth heads to be the most desirable and they are more expensive. However, there are exceptions to this rule.
1. *Adler:* Long-limbed dolls with a washable hand-printed, smiling face; spit curl on its forehead; often dressed in a clown suit.
*2. *Alart, Ernst:* Trademark pressed into sole of shoe; sculptured face; painted eyes, wig.
3. *American Stuffed Novelty: Collegiate* dolls; pressed cloth face; silk or mohair wig; long-limbed body.
*4. *American Wholesale Corporation:* Succeeded Baltimore Bargain House.
5. *Anita:* Made *French Head* flapper and boudoir dolls; some of their dolls had composition heads; also made pillows and novelties; one of the most prolific makers of this type of doll.
*6. *Arrow Doll Wig Co.:* Maker of boudoir dolls, among other dolls.
*7. *Austin Gray Ltd:* Cabaret dolls (England).
*8. *Baltimore Bargain House,* succeeded

by *American Wholesale Corporation:* Advertised flapper dolls among 150 company offerings in 1927; sold *Lucky Lindy,* one of the most famous of the male boudoir dolls; imported French novelties for their line.
*9. *Beaux Art Shade Co.:* Sold boudoir dolls with painted features in 1924 and perhaps other years.
*10. *Beers, Wm. P & Co.: Jazette* boudoir doll with conical hat.
11. *Bloom:* Beauty spot under painted eyes; very large eyelashes.
12. *Blossom:* Made exceptionally nice boudoir dolls with silk faces; some had applied real eyelashes.
13. *Blum Lustig:* Boudoir dolls by Mme. Milobendza.
*14. *Bon Marche:* Department store in Paris which sold boudoir and flapper dolls; often had dolls made to their specifications from various companies; one such doll wore a silk dress with a velvet hat and was named *Gladys.*
*15. *Butler Bros. Company:* American catalog company which sold a variety of boudoir dolls made to their specification.
*16. *Calvare:* French art doll with raffia-like hair.
*17. *Cowham, Hilda:* English doll artist; her designs were precursors of boudoir dolls; dolls had long legs and thin bodies.
18. *Eisen:* Imported Paris dolls.
*19. *Ekart, W.R.:* Made a *Pierrot* doll in black and orange.
*20. *England Art Toy Manufacturing Co.:* Pierrot.
21. *Etta:* All-woman company which made cloth art dolls.
22. *European Novelty:* Merged with *Anita Doll Company* and incorporated their boudoir line.
*23. *Flapper Novelty Co.:* Flapper college dolls; *Floppy Flo, Kiki, Mah Jong;* 1924.
*24. *Fleischman, Kitty:* Designed a line of

boudoir-type dolls including *Cabaret Girls* representing dancers in France, *Greenwich Village Artist, Cigarette Girl, Colonial Girls.*

*25. *Gerling:* Paris and New York.
*26. *Gerzon Co.:* Dutch company that advertised boudoir dolls in 1930.
*27. *Gibson, Charles E.* of New York: Patented a boudoir doll in 1922.
*28. *Goldberger (Eegee):* Maker of many types of dolls; advertised long-legged cigarette dolls with a felt head in 1925; patented two flappers in 1926; one in a short skirt; another with lounging pajamas.
*29. *Heho Art Dolls:* Paris sofa and auto dolls sold by Leo Weigert of Nürnberg, Germany.
*30. *Hollywood Imps:* Impish or flapper-type; aviator, aviatrix, football player, pajama girl; Dutch boy and girl; girl in swimsuit, and so forth.
*31. *Kat-a-Korner Kompany,* Nashville, Tennessee: In 1928 advertised they made a boudoir-type doll covered with cretonne that was over 36in (92cm).
*32. *Keney, Victor:* Keeneye boudoir doll; composition head.
*33. *King Tut Dolls:* Patented in 1926.
34. *Konroe Merchants:* Made cigarette girl that wore a pantsuit with striped cuffs which imitates the Lenci *Fadette.*
*35. *Lady Godwyn.*
*36. *Levallois.*
*37. *Leven, H. Josef* (Germany): Made *Flippant Flapper* in 1926.
*38. *Mizpah Toy and Novelty Co.:* Hair, clothes and shoes matched in color.
*39. *Morris, Claire of Los Angeles, California:* Made portrait boudoir and other art dolls.
*40. *Munich Art Dolls:* Advertised boudoir dolls in 1927-1928.
41. *Mutual Novelty:* Advertised boudoir dolls in 1927; made a cigarette doll. This doll may have been all-composition.
*42. *Paramount Doll Company* of New

York City: Advertised a flapper doll in 1926.
*43. *Petzgold, Erma (Munich Art Dolls):* Made boudoir dolls in 1927-1928.
44. *Pierrot and Pierette* (see separate list, page 252).
*45. *Pinner, Erma* (Berlin, Germany): Made early boudoir-type dolls using lovely brocades, laces, and so forth; these were later imitated in the workshops of the Paris couturiers.
*46. *Poiret, Paul* of Paris, France: Famous French couturier who is credited with dressing long-legged dolls to match the owner's costume in 1912. These were carried when the costume was worn.
*47. *Pollyana Doll Co.:* Dolls had long legs; bobbed silk hair; silk stockings.
*48. *Pompeian Art Works:* Made dolls for *Blum Lustig Toy Co. Inc.*
*49. *Sanlys, Inc.* (a French Shop): Advertised *Woops,* a medieval jester-type art doll.
*50. *Sterling Doll Co.:* Advertised boudoir dolls in 1930.
51. *T.A.F.* (Spain): Showed boudoir dolls in their 1934 catalog.
*52. *Unique Novelty Dolls:* Three styles of 32in (81cm) dolls.
*53. *Westwood, Ethel:* Made boudoir dolls; circa 1923-1927; dressed 36in (91cm) dolls in silks and satins; silver and gold cloth shoes; one style was a *Colonial Lady.*

* Companies not listed in the main section of the book.

Cigarette Dolls
1. Anita (United States).
*2. Bernard, Hermann.
*3. Cubeb (United States): Resembles Lenci *Fadette.*
*4. Fleischman, Katherine (United States).
*5. Gerzon (United States and France): *Apache.*
*6. Goldberger (Eegee) (United States).

251

7. Konroe Merchants (United States): Resembles Lenci *Fadette*.
8. Lenci (Italy): *Fadette*.
9. Mutual Novelty (United States).
10. Ravca (France).
11. Unknown: *Apache*-type boy in box with red cherries on it.
* Companies not listed in the main section of the book.

Cowboys, Cowgirls, Gauchos
1. Etta (United States).
2. Gre-Poir (United States and France).
3. Krueger (United States).
4. Lenci (Italy).
5. Perotti (Brazil).
6. T.A.F. (Spain).

Matadors
1. Lenci (Italy).
2. Perotti (Brazil).
3. T.A.F. (Spain).

Military Dolls
*1. Austin Gray Ltd. (England).
2. Chad Valley (England).
3. Dean's (England).
4. E.N.A.P.L. (Italy).
5. Farnell (Alpha) (England).
6. Harwin (England).
7. Kruse, Käthe (Germany).
8. Lang, Emil (France): Military models from several nations.
9. Lenci (Italy).
10. Nelke (United States).
11. Steiff (Germany).
*12. Twinzy (United States): Soldiers, sailors, aviators.
13. Wellings, Norah (England).
*14. Western Art Leather Co. (United States): Stuffed leather dolls.
* Companies not listed in the main section of the book.

Novelties-Bags Pocketbooks, Pillows, Clothes, Etc.
1. Anita Novelties (United States).
2. Dean's (England).
3. Eros (Italy).
4. Etta (United States).
5. European Novelty (United States).
6. Irwin (United States).
7. Lang, Emil (France).

8. Lenci (Italy).
9. Magis (Italy).
10. Messina-Vat (Italy).
11. Royal Society (United States).
12. S.F.B.J., (France).
13. Steiff (Germany).
14. T.A.F. (Spain).
*15. Unique Novelty (United States).
16. Wellings, Norah (England).
* Company not listed in the main section of this book.

Pierrot and Pierrette
1. Adler (United States): Long-legged doll with suit.
*2. All British Toy Company (England): Unbreakable *Pierrots*.
3. American Stuffed Novelty (United States).
*4. Art Toy Co. (England): *Misska* dolls dressed as *Pierrot*.
5. Blossom (United States): All-cloth *Pierrot* doll with silk face.
*6. Bon Marche (France): Catalog showed *Pierrot* with unbreakable head in 1923.
*7. British Doll Mfg. Co. (England): 1917.
8. Chad Valley (England): Stockinette *Pierrot* and *Pierrette;* 1920.
*9. Couturier Salons (France): Designers made cloth *Pierrot* dolls; Paul Poirot was one of the designers.
*10. Davis, Rees (United States): Made cloth *Pierrot* doll in 1922.
11. Dean's (England): Silk art *Pierrette* doll with flat face; 1928.
*12. East London (Federation of Suffragettes) Toy Factory (England): Molded cloth face; jointed at neck and shoulders; 1915.
*13. Ekart, W.R. (United States): Made *Pierrot* in orange and black suit.
14. Etta (United States): 1927.
*15. Gallais, P.J. & Cie (France): Produced *Pierrot* and *Pierette* in 1917-1925.
*16. Hansen, Laurie & Co. (England): Made a *Pierrot* and *Pierrette* in 1917.
*17. Lafayette Galeries (France): Sold *Pierrot* and *Pierrette* in 1927 dressed

in silk; trimmed with spangles and pompons.

18. Lenci (Italy): Felt *Pierrots* and *Pierrettes* in early 1920s.

*19. Louvre Store (France): Advertised a long-legged *Pierrot* in printed satin; 39½in (100cm); 1923.

*20. Marcuse, Day & Cie (England): Made a line of felt and cloth character dolls; *Pierrot* and *Pierrette* made in 1916.

21. Messina-Vat (Italy). Made *Pierrots* in 1924.

*22. Petzold, Dora (Germany): Made *Pierrots* in 1927-1928.

23. Steiff (Germany): Dressed felt dolls as *Pierrot*; 1924.

*24. Three Arts Toy Industry (England): Became Artistic Novelty Co.; made dolls of plush, velvet and felt; advertised a *Pierrot* in 1921.

*25. Twistum Toy Factory (United States): Made worsted *Pierrot* and *Pierrette* in 1919.

Many commercial dolls could be purchased and dressed at home with or without commercial patterns. Because the making of these cloth dolls was often a "cottage industry," it is difficult for the collector to determine if the doll is original to the company.

Women's magazines in the 1920s and early 1930s offered patterns for *Pierrot* and *Pierrette* dolls and costumes.

* Companies not listed in main section of this book.

Religious Dolls (United States)

1. Alexander.
2. Catholic nun dolls.
3. Methodist.
4. Moravian.
5. Presbyterian.

INDEX

Adler Favor & Novelty Co.; 7
Advertising; 67, 79, 186
Aerolite; 53
Alexander Doll Company; 8, 33-34
  Alice-in-Wonderland; 8, 10, 13
  Babbie; 13
  Baby; 13
  Black So-Lite Baby; 18
  Bobby-Q; 11, 14
  Bonny Bunny; 14
  Bunny Beau; 1
  Bunny Belle; 12, 14, 33
  Bunny Boy; 14
  David Copperfield; 10, 14, 34
  Dickens Series; 8
  Dionne Quintuplets; 8, 14
  Dottie Dumbunnie; 11, 15
  Eva Lovelace; 15
  Little Agnes; 15
  Little Dorrit; 15
  Little Emily; 16
  Little Nell; 16
  Little Red Riding Hood; 8, 16
  Little Shaver; 10-11, 16
  Little Women; 8, 9, 13, 15, 17
  Lively Cherub Baby; 16
  Lolly Lov-le-ler; 12
  March Hare; 17
  Oliver Twist; 10, 17
  Pip; 17
  Pitty Pat; 17
  Posey Pet; 12, 17
  Sir Lapin O'Hare; 18
  So-Lite Baby; 18
  Suzy-Q; 11, 14, 18
  Tiny Tim; 18
Al Doll; 38, 58, 60-61, 63-64
Alpha (see Farnell)
Alice in Wonderland (Series); 8, 10, 13,
  38, 54, 60-61, 65
Alma; 19-20, 37, 218, 225
  Russian Cossack Dancer; 19, 37
Altman, B & Company; 20, 21, 39,
  225
Amberg, Louis & Son; 22
American Art Dolls; 22
  Susie's Sister; 22
  Tootsie; 22
American Needlecraft, Inc.; 23
  Orphan Annie and Sandy; 23
American Stuffed Novelty Co.; 23-24
  Follies Girl; 24
  Flapper; 23
  Pierrot; 23
  Trilby; 23
  Yama Doll; 24
American Toy & Novelty Corp.; 25
  Priscilla; 25

Animals; 23, 48, 53, 62, 65, 68, 70,
  73, 75, 99, 136, 149, 150, 153
Anita Novelty Co.; 25, 74
  French Head Dolls; 25
Attwell, Mabel Lucie; 47
Aunt Jemima Dolls; 24, 68, 208, 216,
  249
Averill Mfg. Corp.; 26-31, 35, 36, 40,
  226
  Bescassine; 26, 31
  Chocolate Drop; 26
  Dolly Dingle; 26
  Egyptian Dolls; 26-27
  Miss America; 29, 36
  Nationality Dolls; 26, 30-31
  Nursery Rhyme Dolls; 29
  Patricia; 29, 30
  Peggy Ann; 26-27
  Raggedy Ann and Andy; 26, 28
  Snooks; 26-28
  Sweets; 26-28
  Wedding Party; 29, 35
  Wonder Dolls; 26
  Uncle Wiggly; 28, 40
Attwell, Mabel Lucie; 47
Aviator; 71
Babies; 18, 63-64, 72, 82, 108, 205,
  250
Bambina; 40, 47-48
Beddolls (see Boudoir Dolls)
Bescassine; 26, 31
Bessie Brooks; 55
Bing Corporation; 31-32
  Dutch Boy and Girl; 31
Black Dolls; 18, 26, 43-44, 51-52, 55,
  63, 66, 71, 75, 114, 118, 131, 150-153,
  158, 170, 212-213
Black So-Lite Baby; 18
Bloom, Chas. Inc.; 32
Blossom Doll Company; 32, 41
Blum-Lustig Toy Co.; 41
Bobby-Q; 11, 14
Bonny Bunny; 14
Bonzo; 40, 48
Boudoir Dolls; 24, 32, 41-43, 57, 62,
  64, 68, 70-74, 87, 104, 131, 140, 142,
  144-145, 151-152, 155-157, 183, 189,
  199, 202, 204, 211, 250
Brides and Bridal Parties; 29, 35
Brophy Doll Company; 26
Bruckner's Sons; 34, 43
  Dollypop; 43
  Pancake Baby; 44
  Tubby and Tubby-tot; 43
  Two-N-One; 44
Buds and Buddies; 68
Bull, John; 57
Bunny Beau; 13

Bunny Belle; 12, 14, 33
Bunny Boy; 14
Buttons, Effanbee; 70
Caresse; 53
Carina Series; 53
Carnival Dolls; 53
Cartoon Dolls; 23, 26, 44-45, 75,
  170-172, 179
Cayuga Products, Inc.; 45
Century Doll Co.; 45, 46
Chad Valley Co., Ltd.; 36, 40, 46-54,
  165, 226-227
  Aerolite Dolls; 53
  Bambina Series; 40, 47-48
  Black Boy; 52
  Bonzo; 48
  Caresse (La Petite); 53
  Carina Series; 53
  Carnival Dolls; 53
  Dopey (Snow White Series); 51-52
  Foot Guards; 49-50, 54, 226-227
  Golliwog; 53
  Jack Novelty Art Dolls; 53
  Jack O'Jingles; 53
  Little Red Riding Hood; 48-49
  Long John Silver; 36, 47
  Nationality Dolls; 54
  Nurse; 54
  Nursery Rhyme Dolls; 48-49, 55,
  165
  Policeman; 54
  Prince Edward; 50
  Princess Elizabeth; 49-51
  Princess Margaret Rose; 50
  Oriental Dolls; 53
  Royal Scout Mascot; 53
  Stockinette Dolls; 46-47
  Tango Tar Baby; 53
  Tinker Belle; 53
Chaplin, Charlie; 57, 62, 65
Chase Stockinette Doll; 54-55,
  227-228
  Alice in Wonderland Series; 54
  Bessie Brooks; 55
  Mammy Nurse; 55
  Pickaninnies; 55
  Silly Sally; 55
  Tommy Snooks; 55
  Tweedledee and Tweedledum; 55
  Washington, George; 55
Children of Today; 172
Cigarette Dolls; 25, 93, 104, 142-143,
  155, 183, 251
Chocolate Drop; 56
Clowns; 68, 102, 106, 115, 149, 171,
  204
Cohen & Son; 56
Commedia dello Art Characters; 42

Community Craft; 56
Consuela Originals; 6, 71
Corry, Grace; 46
Cot Cat; 61
Cowboys and Cowgirls; 73, 81, 88, 105, 114, 116, 152, 252, 229
Cowham, Hilda; 42, 62
Crowley, Milna & Co.; 57, 224
Dancing Dolls; 58-59, 63-64, 114-115, 155, 198
David Copperfield; 10, 14, 34
Dean's Rag Book Co. Ltd.; 38, 57-67, 64, 168, 228-229
A 1 Line; 38, 58, 60-61, 63-64
Advertising Dolls; 57, 67
Alice in Wonderland Series; 38, 60-61, 65
Brown, Erbie; 65
Boudoir Dolls; 64
Bull, John; 57
Cartoon Characters; 66, 68, 179
Celebrity Dolls; 57, 61-63, 65-67
Chaplin, Charlie; 57, 62, 65
Cherub Toddler Series; 64
Cosy Kids; 62
Cot Cat; 61
Cut Out Knockabout Dolls; 57
Dainty Dolls; 65
Dancing Dolls; 58-59, 64
Dinkie Dolls; 64
Evripoze; 63, 65
Felix the Cat; 65
Flower Doll Series; 63, 65
Flappers; 59, 64
Flower Doll Series; 63, 65
Frilly Dolls; 59, 64, 69, Back Cover
Girl Guide; 66
Golliwog; 63
Goo Goo Series; 62
Hay, Will; 67
Husheen Dolls; 65
Lillibet; 61, 66
Lane, Lupino; 67
Luvly Dolls; 64
Mickey Mouse; 62, 65, 67-68
Nationality Dolls; 66-67
Novelty Dolls; 64
Nursery Rhymes; 59, 62-63
Pauline Guilbert Dolls; 62
Peter Pan Series; 67
Pierrette and Pierrot; 64, 67
Playmate Series; 66
Playtime Series; 64
Policeman; 66
Posie Line; 63-64
Princess Dolls; 60, 64-65
Sam; 66
Scout Dolls; 66
Smart Set; 64
Sunshine Dolls; 64
Ta Ta Dolls; 63, 65

Travel Tots; 65
Trike Dolls; 54, 59, 64, 69, Back Cover
Tru-to-Life; 57, 59, 62-63
Delavan, S. E.; 68
Denmark Company; 69
Dickens Series; 8, 136, 152
Dionne Quintuplets; 8, 14
Dolly Dingle; 26
Dolly Jingles; 103
Dollypop; 43
Dottie Dumbunnie; 11, 15
Drayton, Grace; 26
EDMA (see European Doll Co.); 74
Egyptian Dolls; 26-27
E.N.A.P.L.; 69
Effanbee Doll Corporation; 70
Buttons, the Monk; 70
Eisen, Louis; 70
Apache; 70
Aviator; 70
Boudoir; 71
Gascon; 70
Jeanette; 71
Eros; 71, 229-230
Ethnic (see Nationality Dolls)
Etta Incorporated; 72, 73
European Doll Mfg. Co. Inc.; 74
Eva Lovelace; 15
Fangel, Maud Tousey; 26-27
Farnell, J.K. & Company (Alpha); 75-77
Cherub Dolls; 75
King Edward VIII; 75
King George VI; 75, 77
Fascist Boy; 21, 134, 150, 218
Felix the Cat; 65
Figi Wigi; 46
Fiore; 78-79
Flapper; 23-24, 32, 41, 57, 64, 154, 204, 229
Follies Dolls; 24
French Head Dolls; 25
Georgene Novelties, Inc.; 26, 28-30
Gerber Baby Products Co.; 79
Gerb's Poupees; 80
Golliwog; 53, 63
Gondolier; 72
Gre-Poir; 81-82, 168, 230-231
Gund; 82, 83
Harlequin; 151
Harry the Hawk; 215
Hauser; 84
Hausman & Zatulove; 84
Hecht, Else; 85
Hendren, Madame (see Averill)
Holzer & Cie; 85, 86
Horsman, E.I., & Aetna Doll Co.; 87
Ideal Toy and Novelty Company; 88, 97-98
Indian Dolls (American); 114-115, 118, 125-126, 151, 153

Irwin & Company Inc.; 99
Islander Dolls; 43, 75, 114, 212-213
"It" Dolls; 25
Josselyn; 99
Kamkins; 100, 101
Kampes, Louise R. Studio; 100, 101
Karavan; 101, 231
Kewpie; 102
Kidd, Miss Etta
Kimport Dolls; 78, 102
King Edward VIII; 75
King George VI; 75, 77
King Innovations; 102, 194
Knickerbocker Toy Co., Inc.; 102-104
Konroc Merchants; 104
Krueger, Richard; 104-197, 166
Krug; 78
Kruse, Kathe; 22, 107-110, 163
Ku-tee; 84
Kutie; 25
Kuzara's, Mme Portrait Dolls; 111
L.P.A. Bennett Couturier; 111
Lang, Emile; 113, 164, 197
La Rosa Company; 112
La Semaine De Suzette; 26, 30
Lenci De F. Scavini; 89-96, 113-160, 161-162, 164, 167, 232-234
Amor, Black Cupid; 153
Amore; 126
Bellhop; 114, 118, 120, 154
Candy Box; 153
Early Dolls; 96, 114-119
Fad-dette (Cigarette Doll); 93, 142-143, 149, 155
Fetishes; 92, 121, 148-150
Golfer, Plucci; 154
Harlequin; 151
Height Chart; 148-160
Liberty Dolls; 150-152
Lucia Face; 90, 95, 129, 130, 150
Madonna; 149
Mannequin; 146
Maria-Teresa; 153
Marks; 120, 138, 147-148
Marionettes; 151
Marotte; 149-150
Mascotte Dolls; 92, 122, 148-150
Miller Raquel; 156
Miniature Dolls; 90, 92, 122-125, 148-149, 164
Mozart; 150, 153
Mussolini's Facist Boy; 134, 150
Novelties; 120-122
Opium Pipe Smokers; 114, 117, 127, 150
Oriental Dolls; 89, 96, 114, 127, 132-133, 135, 143, 150-155, 159
Pan; 92, 121
Personality Dolls; 112, 129, 134, 150, 152-153, 156, 158, 160
Pickford, Mary; 153
Pierrot; 154-155

255

Pocketbooks; 94, 122, 150, 153
Pompadour, Madame; 129, 152, 156
Puppets; 149-150
Rapunzel; 150
RolyPoly; 125, 149
Rope Jumper Dolls; 91, 114, 129, 150-151
Smooth-faced Dolls; 94, 130, 136
Sports Dolls; 115, 119, 139, 140-141, 150, 152, 154
Swivel-jointed waist dolls; 155
Temple, Shirley; 158
Valentino, Rudolph; 145, 158
Winker Dolls; 115, 118, 127, 150
Liberty of London; 160, 166
Beefeater; 160
Coronation and Royalty; 160, 169-170
Historical Figures; 160
Lillibet; 61, 66
Little Agnes; 15
Little Dorrit; 15
Little Emily; 16
Little Lulu; 26
Little Nell; 16
Little Red Riding Hood; 8, 16, 48, 49, 68
Little Shaver; 10-11, 16
Little Women; 8, 9, 13, 15, 17
Live Long Toys; 170-172
Lively Cherub Baby; 16
Lolly Lov-le-ler; 12
Long John Silver; 36, 47
Lupino Lane; 67
Ludecke, Ilse; 172-174
Magis; 174-176, 235-236, 174
Magit; 176, 218, 236-237
Mannequin (see Boudoir dolls)
March Hare; 17
Mary Had a Little Lamb; 29-30, 88
Matador; 188, 204, 229, 252
Mawaphil Dolls; 196
Messina-Vat; 176-178, 219, 237
Methodist Dolls; 54, 178
Meyer & Lorang; 179
Mickey Mouse; 62, 65, 67-68, 104
Military (Soldiers, Sailors); 49-50, 54, 57, 62, 75-77, 107, 113, 122-125, 134, 150, 160, 164, 213-216
Milobendzka, Madame Emilia; 41
Minnehaha; 26
Miss America; 29, 36
Missionary Dolls; 178
Meyer & Lorang; 179
Modern Toy Co., Inc.; 179
Mollye; 100, 179-181, 226
Moravian Dolls; 182
Munich Art Dolls; 42
Mutual Novelty Corp.; 183
N.A.T.I.; 184-185, 223
Nationality Dolls (Ethnic); 19-21,

26, 30-31, 37, 42, 54, 56, 66-69, 71-72, 75-81, 85-86, 101-102, 111, 113-160, 169-170, 174-176, 180-181, 184-191, 194, 196, 201-204, 209-216, 221-222
Nelke Corporation; 186
Ninon; 187
Novelty Dolls; 54, 73-74, 90, 99, 114, 120-122, 148, 187-188, 196-197, 198, 202-204, 212, 252
Nurse; 54
Nursery Rhymes Dolls; 29-30, 48-49, 52-53, 55, 57, 59, 62-63, 69, 88, 138, 153, 155-156, 158-159, 160, 165, 171, 196
O'Neill, Rose; 102
Oliver Twist; 10, 17
Orphan Annie and Sandy; 23, 44, 171
Oriental Dolls; 53, 56, 89, 96, 127, 132, 143, 150-153, 155, 159
Patricia; 29-30
Peggy Ann; 27
Perotti, João; 88-190, 220-221, 237-238
Personalities; 25, 57, 61-63, 66-67, 99, 100, 158
Peter Pan; 53, 67
Petterssen, Ronnaug; 190-191
Pharaoh; 26
Pierrette and Pierrot; 23, 46, 53, 67, 72, 74, 114, 117, 151, 153-155, 191, 195
Pinky Winky Products; 192
Pip; 17
Pirate; 36, 47, 73, 94, 222, 229
Pitty Pet; 17
Pocketbooks and Bags; 73-74, 94, 122, 150-154, 187-188
Poir (see Gre-Poir)
Poirot, Paul; 42
Policeman; 54, 66, 120, 123, 186, 213
Popeye; 45, 66, 68
Posy Pet; 12, 17
Poupees Nicette; 192
Presbyterian Dolls; 193
Prince Edward; 50
Princess Elizabeth; 49-50, 160, 170
Princess Margaret Rose; 50-51
Priscilla, Priscilla and John; 25, 99
Pryor, Roger; 5
Queen Elizabeth; 212
Queen Mary; 160-169
Raggedy Ann and Andy; 26, 28, 179-180
Rauser, Katherine; 68
Ravca; 194
Raynal, Les Poupees; 194, 238
Rockwell, Grace Corry; 45
Royal Society; 168, 195-196
Royalty; 49-50, 75, 77, 160, 169-170, 196, 212
Rushton Company; 196-197

Russian Cossack Dancer; 19-20, 37, 199
S.F.B.J.; 197
S & H Novelty Co.; 198
Sailors (see Military dolls)
Sayco (Schoen and Yondorf); 198
Scarecrow; 88
Scootles; 106
Sheik; 206
Silk Novelty Dolls; 198-199
Silly Sally; 55
Sir Lapin O'Hare; 18
Ski Dolls; 71, 122, 140
Sluggo; 26
Snow White and *Dwarfs*; 51-53, 97-98, 102-103, 105, 166
Snooks; 26-28
Snooks, Tommy; 55
So-Lite Baby; 18
Soldiers (see Military Dolls)
Steiff; 199
Stockinette Dolls; 46-47, 52
Storybook Dolls; 88
Strobel & Wilken Co. Inc.; 200
Susie's Sister; 22
Sweets; 26-28
Suzy-Q; 11, 14, 18
T.A.F.; 200-204, 222
Temple, Shirley; 158
Tiny Tim; 18
Tinker Belle; 53
Tootsie; 22
Topsy-Turvy; 34, 44, 198
Trike Doll; Back Cover
Trilby; 23-24
Tubby and *Tubby-tot*; 43
Tutankhamen; 26
Tweedledee and *Tweedledum*; 55
Uncle Sam; 100
Uncle Wiggly; 28, 40
Unique Novelty Dolls; 204
Unknown; 205-206
U-Shab-ti; 26
Valentino, Rudolph; 112, 145, 158, 206
Vecchiotti, A. Alberani; 206-207, 238-239
Venus; 207
WPA; 4, 207-209
Wedding Party; 29, 35
Wellings, Norah; 210-217, 220, 222, 239-240
Welsch Specialty Dolls; 32
Winker; 77, 115, 118, 127, 150, 160, 166, 169-170, 185, 205, 223
Wonder Dolls; 26
Wolf Doll; 216
Yama Doll; 24